First World War
and Army of Occupation
War Diary
France, Belgium and Germany

8 DIVISION
Headquarters, Branches and Services
Royal Army Ordnance Corps
Deputy Assistant Director Ordnance Services
and Royal Army Veterinary Corps
Assistant Director Veterinary Services
13 December 1914 - 30 April 1919

WO95/1692

The Naval & Military Press Ltd
www.nmarchive.com
Published in association with The National Archives

Published by

The Naval & Military Press Ltd

Unit 10 Ridgewood Industrial Park,

Uckfield, East Sussex,

TN22 5QE England

Tel: +44 (0) 1825 749494

www.naval-military-press.com

www.nmarchive.com

This diary has been reprinted in facsimile from the original. Any imperfections are inevitably reproduced and the quality may fall short of modern type and cartographic standards.

© **Crown Copyright**
Images reproduced by permission of The National Archives, London, England, 2015.

Contents

Document type	Place/Title	Date From	Date To
Heading	8th Division D.A.D.O.S. May 1915-Jun 1919		
Miscellaneous	May 1915 June 1919		
Heading	8th Division DADOS. 8th Division 10.5.15-30.6.15		
Heading	Confidential War Diary of D.A.D.O.S. 8th Division (Major E.M. DeSmidt) From 12-5-15 To 30-6-15		
War Diary	Sailly	12/05/1915	30/06/1915
Heading	8th Division DADOS. 8th Division Vol II		
Heading	Confidential War Diary of D.A.D.O.S. 8th Division (Major E.m Desmidt) A.A.W. From 1-7-15 To 31-7-15		
War Diary	Sailly	01/07/1915	31/07/1915
Heading	8th Division DADOS. 8th Division Vol.III August.15		
Miscellaneous	Aug1-11.		
Heading	Confidential War Diary Of D.A.D.O.S. 8th Division From 1st August 1915 To 31st August 1915 (Volume 4)		
War Diary	Sailly	12/08/1915	31/08/1915
Heading	8th Division DADOS. 8th Division Vol. IV Sept. 15		
Heading	Confidential War Diary of D.A.D.O.S. 8th Division From 1st September 1915 To 30th September 1915		
War Diary	Sailly	01/09/1915	30/09/1915
Heading	D.A.D.O.S. 8th Div Oct-15 Vol V		
Heading	Confidential War Diary of D.A.D.O.S. 8th Division From 1st October 1915 To 31st October 1915		
War Diary	Sailly	01/10/1915	31/10/1915
Heading	Confidential War Diary D.A.D.O.S. 8th Division From 1st November 1915 To 30th November 1915 (Volume VI)		
War Diary	Sailly	01/11/1915	24/11/1915
War Diary	Steenbecque	25/11/1915	30/11/1915
Heading	D.A.D.O.S. 8th Div Dec Vol.VII		
Heading	Confidential War Diary D.A.D.O.S. 8th Division From 1st December 1915 To 31st December 1915 (Volume 8)		
War Diary	Steenbecque	01/12/1915	31/12/1915
Heading	D.A.D.O.S. 8th Div Jan Vol.VIII		
Heading	Confidential War Diary of D.A.D.O.S. 8th Div From 1st Jan 1916 To 31st Jan 1916 (Volume.9)		
War Diary	Sailly	30/01/1916	31/01/1916
War Diary	Sailly	15/01/1916	29/01/1916
War Diary	Steenbecque	01/01/1916	12/01/1916
War Diary	Sailly	13/01/1916	14/01/1916
Heading	Confidential War Diary of D.A.D.O.S. 8th Divn From 1st Feb 1916 To 29th Feb 1916 (Volume.9.)		
War Diary	Sailly	01/02/1916	29/02/1916
Heading	Confidential War Diary of D.A.D.O.S. 8th Divn From 1st March 1916 To 31st March1916 (Volume10)		
War Diary	Sailly Sur La Lys	01/03/1916	27/03/1916
War Diary	Flesselles	28/03/1916	31/03/1916
Heading	Confidential War Diary of D.A.D.O.S. 8th Divn From 1st April 1916 To 30th April 1916 (Volume 11)		
War Diary	Flesselles	01/04/1916	03/04/1916
War Diary	Henencourt	04/04/1916	30/04/1916

Heading	Confidential War Diary of D.A.D.O.S. 8th Div From 1st May 1916 To 31st May 1916 (Volume 13)		
War Diary	Henencourt	01/05/1916	31/05/1916
Heading	Confidential War Diary of D.A.D.O.S. 8th Div From 1st July1916 To 31st July 1916 (Volume 15)		
War Diary	Henencourt	01/07/1916	01/07/1916
War Diary	Belloy	02/07/1916	03/07/1916
War Diary	Cavillon	04/07/1916	06/07/1916
War Diary	Brvay	07/07/1916	14/07/1916
War Diary	Bethune	15/07/1916	29/07/1916
War Diary	La Bourse	30/07/1916	31/07/1916
Heading	Confidential War Diary of D.A.D.O.S. 8th Div From 1st August 1916 To 31st August 1916 (Volume 16)		
War Diary	Labourse	01/08/1916	31/08/1916
Heading	Confidential War Diary of D.A.D.O.S. 8th Division From 1st September 1916 To 30th September 1916 (Volume 17)		
War Diary	Labourse	01/09/1916	30/09/1916
Heading	Confidential War Diary of D.A.D.O.S. 8th Div From 1st Oct 1916 To 31st Oct 1916 (Volume 18)		
War Diary	Labourse	01/10/1916	13/10/1916
War Diary	Hallencourt	14/10/1916	15/10/1916
War Diary	Treux	16/10/1916	19/10/1916
War Diary	Carnoy	20/10/1916	31/10/1916
Heading	Confidential War Diary of D.A.D.O.S. 8th Div From 1st Nov 1916 To 30th Nov 1916 (Volume 19)		
War Diary	Carnoy	01/11/1916	17/11/1916
War Diary	Treux	18/11/1916	18/11/1916
War Diary	Belloy	19/11/1916	30/11/1916
Heading	Confidential War Diary D.A.D.O.S. 8th Division From 1st Dec1916 To 31st Dec1916 (Volume 20)		
War Diary	Belloy St Leonard	01/12/1916	31/12/1916
Heading	Confidential War Diary of D.A.D.O.S. 8th Div From1st January 1917 To 31st January 1917 (Volume 21)		
War Diary	Bray	01/01/1917	10/01/1917
War Diary	Belloy St Leonard	11/01/1917	22/01/1917
War Diary	Chipilly	23/01/1917	26/01/1917
War Diary	Bray	27/01/1917	31/01/1917
Heading	Confidential War Diary of D.A.D.O.S. 8th Div From 1st Feb 1917 To 28th Feb 1917 (Volume 22)		
War Diary	Bray	01/02/1917	10/02/1917
War Diary	Chipilly	11/02/1917	25/02/1917
War Diary	Suzanne	26/02/1917	28/02/1917
Heading	Confidential War Diary of D.A.D.O.S. 8th Div From 1st Mar 1917 To 31st Mar1917 (Vol 23)		
War Diary	Suzanne	01/03/1917	07/03/1917
War Diary	Bray	08/03/1917	21/03/1917
War Diary	Suzanne	22/03/1917	26/03/1917
War Diary	Curlu	27/03/1917	31/03/1917
Heading	Confidential War Diary of D.A.D.O.S. 8th Div From 1st April 1917 To 30th April 1917 (Vol 24)		
War Diary	Curlv	01/04/1917	09/04/1917
War Diary	Moislains	10/04/1917	22/04/1917
War Diary	Nurlu	23/04/1917	30/04/1917
Heading	Confidential War Diary of D.A.D.O.S. 8th Div From May 1917 To 31st May 1917 (Vol 25)		

War Diary	Nurlu	01/05/1917	29/05/1917
War Diary	Corbie	30/05/1917	31/05/1917
Heading	Confidential War Diary of D.A.D.O.S. 8th Div From 1st June 1917 To 30th June 1917 (Vol 26)		
War Diary	Merris	01/06/1917	10/06/1917
War Diary	Caestre	11/06/1917	12/06/1917
War Diary	Ovderdom (winnipee Camp)	13/06/1917	16/06/1917
War Diary	Ovderdom	17/06/1917	30/06/1917
Heading	Confidential War Diary of D.A.D.O.S. 8th Div From 1st July 1917 To 31st July 1917 (Volume 27)		
War Diary	Busse Boom	01/07/1917	09/07/1917
War Diary	Bomy	10/07/1917	18/07/1917
War Diary	Busse Boom	19/07/1917	31/07/1917
Heading	War Diary of D.a.d.e.s 8th Div. Form 1st Aug 1917 To 31st Aug 1917 (Vol 28)		
War Diary	Busse Boom	01/08/1917	19/08/1917
War Diary	Caestre	20/08/1917	26/08/1917
War Diary	De Seule	27/08/1917	31/08/1917
Heading	Confidential War Diary of D.A.D.O.S. 8th Division From 1st September 1917 To 30th September 1917 (Vol 29)		
War Diary	De Seule	01/09/1917	29/09/1917
Heading	War Diary Oct 17-31st 1917 D.A.D.O.S. 8th Div No. 30		
War Diary	Le Seule	01/10/1917	26/10/1917
Heading	War Diary Nov 1 To 30th 1917 No. 31 D.A.D.O.S. VIII Division		
War Diary	De Seule	03/11/1917	13/11/1917
War Diary	Poperinghe	14/11/1917	30/11/1917
Heading	War Diary Dec 1-Dec 31st 1917 No. 32		
War Diary	Vlamertinghe	01/12/1917	02/12/1917
War Diary	Wizernes	05/12/1917	26/12/1917
War Diary	Vlamertinghe	27/12/1917	31/12/1917
Heading	War Diary Jany 1-Jany 31-1918 No.33 D.A.D.O.S. VIII DIV		
War Diary	Vlamertinghe	01/01/1918	09/01/1918
War Diary	Steenvoorde	18/01/1918	31/01/1918
Heading	War Diary Feby 1-Feby 28-1918 No. 34		
War Diary	Steenvoorde	01/02/1918	10/02/1918
War Diary	Vlamertinghe	11/02/1918	28/02/1918
Heading	War Diary March 1-31 1918 No. 35		
War Diary	Vlamertinghe	05/03/1918	05/03/1918
War Diary	Abeele	05/03/1918	10/03/1918
War Diary	Wizernes	13/03/1918	13/03/1918
War Diary	Harbonieres	22/03/1918	22/03/1918
War Diary	Domart	24/03/1918	24/03/1918
War Diary	Famechon	28/03/1918	28/03/1918
War Diary	Field	31/03/1918	31/03/1918
Heading	War Diary April 1-30 1918 No. 36		
War Diary	Cottenchy	01/04/1918	01/04/1918
War Diary	Cavillon	03/04/1918	11/04/1918
War Diary	Hangest	12/04/1918	16/04/1918
War Diary	Hangest	16/04/1918	19/04/1918
War Diary	Camon	20/04/1918	25/04/1918
Heading	War Diary May 1-31 1918 No. 37		
War Diary	Camon	01/05/1918	01/05/1918

War Diary	Huppy	03/05/1918	03/05/1918
War Diary	Chery Chartreuve	04/05/1918	11/05/1918
War Diary	Ventelay	12/05/1918	27/05/1918
War Diary	Montigny	27/05/1918	28/05/1918
War Diary	Lhery	28/05/1918	28/05/1918
War Diary	B. de Rarrey	29/05/1918	29/05/1918
War Diary	Mar Oevilly	30/05/1918	30/05/1918
War Diary	Villers Aux Bois	31/05/1918	31/05/1918
Heading	War Diary June 1-30 1918 No. 38		
War Diary	Villers Aux Bois	01/06/1918	01/06/1918
War Diary	Bergeres-Les-Vertus	03/06/1918	05/06/1918
War Diary	Pleurs	10/06/1918	10/06/1918
War Diary	Sezanne	13/06/1918	13/06/1918
War Diary	Huppy	14/06/1918	19/06/1918
War Diary	Priville-Escarbotin	22/06/1918	22/06/1918
War Diary	Friville	23/06/1918	30/06/1918
Heading	War Diary July 1-31-1918 No. 39 DADOS 8th Div		
War Diary	Friville	01/07/1918	19/07/1918
War Diary	Mont St Eloy	20/07/1918	27/07/1918
Heading	War Diary August 1-31st 1918 No. 40		
War Diary	Mt St Eloy	03/08/1918	23/08/1918
Miscellaneous	D.A.G. Base	30/09/1918	30/09/1918
Heading	War Diary September 1-30 1918 No. 41		
War Diary	Mont St Eloy	01/09/1918	30/09/1918
Miscellaneous	D.A.G. 3rd Echelon	01/11/1918	01/11/1918
Heading	War Diary October 1-31 1918 No. 42		
War Diary	Mont St Eloy	01/10/1918	01/10/1918
War Diary	Victory Camp 518.8 G.3.6	03/10/1918	09/10/1918
War Diary	Stirling Camp 518-g-13.b.	14/10/1918	14/10/1918
War Diary	Laurent Blancy	15/10/1918	18/10/1918
War Diary	Planque	19/10/1918	19/10/1918
War Diary	Raches	20/10/1918	20/10/1918
War Diary	Cattelet	21/10/1918	24/10/1918
War Diary	Marchlennes	27/10/1918	31/10/1918
Heading	War Diary November 1-30 1918 No 43		
War Diary	Marchiennes	03/11/1918	08/11/1918
War Diary	Onnaing	10/11/1918	10/11/1918
War Diary	Thulin	12/11/1918	12/11/1918
War Diary	Tertre	13/11/1918	15/11/1918
War Diary	Tournai	16/11/1918	30/11/1918
Heading	War Diary December 1-31 1918 No. 44		
War Diary	Tournai	01/12/1918	16/12/1918
War Diary	Enghien	17/12/1918	31/12/1918
Miscellaneous	8th Div.	01/02/1919	01/02/1919
Heading	War Diary January 1-31 1919 No. 45 D.A.D.O.S. 8th Div.		
War Diary	Enghien	01/01/1919	31/01/1919
Heading	War Diary Feby 1-28 1919 No. 48 D.A.D.O.S. 8th Div		
War Diary	Enghien	01/02/1919	15/02/1919
War Diary	ATH	16/02/1919	27/02/1919
Heading	War Diary March 1-31 1919 No.47		
War Diary	ATH	01/03/1919	31/03/1919
Heading	War Diary No. 48 April 1-30 1919 D.A.D.O.S. 8th Div.		
War Diary	ATH	03/04/1919	16/04/1919
Heading	War Diary May 1-31 1919 No.49 D.A.D.O.S. 8th Div		

War Diary	ATH	02/05/1919	30/05/1919
Heading	War Diary June 1-30 1919 No. 50 D.A.D.O.S. 8th Div		
War Diary	ATH	01/06/1919	28/06/1919
Heading	8th Division A.D.V.S. DEC 1914-APL 1919		
Miscellaneous	A.D.V.S Subject.		
Heading	A.D.V.S. 8th Division Vol. 1 13-28-12-14		
War Diary	Lagorgue	13/12/1914	28/12/1914
Heading	ADVS. 8th Division Vol. II		
Heading	Confidential War Diary of Major P.J. Harris A.D.V.S. 8th Division From 1-1-15 To 31-1-15.		
War Diary	La Gorgue	01/01/1915	31/01/1915
Heading	Confidential War Diary of Major P.J. Harris A.D.V.S. 8th Division From 1-2-15 To 28-2-15 Vol III		
War Diary	Lagorgue	01/02/1915	27/02/1915
Heading	Confidential War Diary of Major P.J. Harries A.D.V.S. 8th Division From 1-3-15 To 31-3-15. Vol. IV		
War Diary	Lagorgue	01/03/1915	27/03/1915
War Diary	Sailly	28/03/1915	31/03/1915
Heading	Confidential War Diary From 1-4-15 To 30-4-15 Major P.J. Harris A.D.V.S. 8th Division Vol V		
War Diary	Sailly	01/04/1915	30/04/1915
Heading	Confidential War Diary Of Major P.J. Harris A.D.V.S. 8th Division From 1-5-15 To F31-5-15 Vol VI		
War Diary	Sailly	01/05/1915	31/05/1915
Heading	8th Division Confidential War Diary of Major P.J. Harris A.D.V.S. 8th Division From 1 June To 30 June Vol VII		
War Diary	Sailly	01/06/1915	29/06/1915
Heading	Confidential War Diary of Major P.J. Harries A.D.V.S. 8th Division From 1st July To 31st July Vol. VIII		
War Diary	Sailly	05/07/1915	31/07/1915
Heading	8th Division Confidential War Diary of Major P.J. Harris A.D.V.S. 8th Division From 1st Aug 15 To 31 Aug 15 Vol IX		
War Diary	Sailly	01/08/1915	31/08/1915
Heading	8th Division Confidential War Diary of Major P.J. Harris A.D.V.S. 8th Division From 1-9-15 To 30.9.15 Vol X		
War Diary	Sailly	01/09/1915	30/09/1915
Heading	8th Division Confidential War Diary of Major P.J. Harris A.D.V.S. 8th Division From 1-10-15 To 31-10-15 Vol XI		
War Diary	Sailly	01/10/1915	31/10/1915
Heading	Confidential War Diary of Major P.J Harris A.D.V.S. 8th Division From 1-11-15 To 30-11-15 Vol XII		
War Diary	Sailly	01/11/1915	24/11/1915
War Diary	Blaringham	24/11/1915	30/11/1915
Heading	Confidential War Diary of Major. P.J. Harris A.D.V.S. 8th Division From 1st December 1915 To 31st December 1915 Vol XIII		
War Diary	Blaringhem	01/12/1915	31/12/1915
Heading	Confidential War Diary of Major P.J Harris A.D.V.S. 8th Division Vol XIV From 1-1-16 To 31-1-16		
War Diary	Blaringhem	01/01/1916	12/01/1916
War Diary	Sailly	13/01/1916	31/01/1916

Heading	Confidential War Diary of Major P.J. Harris A.D.V.S. 8th Division From 1.2.16. To 29.2.16 Vol 15		
War Diary	Sailly	01/02/1916	29/02/1916
Heading	Confidential War Diary of Major P.J. Harris A.D.V.S.8th Division From 1-3-16 To 31.3.16 Vol XVI		
War Diary	Sailly	01/03/1916	28/03/1916
War Diary	Flesselles	29/03/1916	31/03/1916
Heading	Confidential War Diary of Major P.J. Harris A.D.V.S. 8th Division From 1-4-16 To 30-4-16		
War Diary	Flesselles	01/04/1916	04/04/1916
War Diary	Henecourt	05/04/1916	30/04/1916
Heading	Confidential War Diary of Major P.J. Harris A.D.V.S. 8th Division From1-5-16 To 31-5-16		
War Diary	Henencourt	01/05/1916	31/05/1916
Heading	Confidential War Diary Major P.J. Harris A.D.V.S. 8th Division From 1-6-16 To 30-6-16		
War Diary	Henencourt	01/06/1916	30/06/1916
Heading	Confidential War Diary of Major P.J. Harris A.D.V.S. 8th Division From 1st July 1916 To 31st July 1916		
War Diary	Henencourt	01/07/1916	02/07/1916
War Diary	Belloy	03/07/1916	03/07/1916
War Diary	Cavillon	04/07/1916	06/07/1916
War Diary	Bruay	07/07/1916	14/07/1916
War Diary	Bethune	15/07/1916	22/07/1916
War Diary	La Bourse	22/07/1916	31/07/1916
Heading	Confidential War Diary of Major P.J. Harris A.D.V.S. 8th Division From 1-8-16 To 31-8-16		
War Diary	La Bourse	01/08/1916	31/08/1916
Heading	Confidential War Diary of Major P.J. Harris A.D.V.S. 8th Div From 1-9-16 To 30-9-16		
War Diary	La Bourse	01/09/1916	19/09/1916
War Diary	Lillers	20/09/1916	29/09/1916
War Diary	Labourse	30/09/1916	30/09/1916
Heading	Confidential War Diary of Major P.J. Harris A.D.V.S. 8th Div From 1 Oct 1916 To 31st Oct 1916		
War Diary	Labourse	01/10/1916	12/10/1916
War Diary	Bethune	13/10/1916	13/10/1916
War Diary	Pont Remy	14/10/1916	14/10/1916
War Diary	Hallencourt	15/10/1916	16/10/1916
War Diary	Ailly-Sur Somme	17/10/1916	17/10/1916
War Diary	Ailly	18/10/1916	20/10/1916
War Diary	Minden Post	21/10/1916	30/10/1916
War Diary	Ptreux	31/10/1916	07/11/1916
War Diary	Montauban	08/11/1916	18/11/1916
War Diary	Treux	19/11/1916	20/11/1916
War Diary	Belloy St Leonard	21/11/1916	21/11/1916
War Diary	Belloy	22/11/1916	30/11/1916
War Diary	Bray-Sur Somme	01/01/1917	11/01/1917
War Diary	Belloy	12/01/1917	23/01/1917
War Diary	Chirilly	24/01/1917	28/01/1917
War Diary	Bray	29/01/1917	12/02/1917
War Diary	Corbie	13/02/1917	21/02/1917
War Diary	Suzanne	22/02/1917	08/03/1917
War Diary	Bray	09/03/1917	27/03/1917
War Diary	Curlu	28/03/1917	10/04/1917

War Diary	Moislains	11/04/1917	04/05/1917
War Diary	Nurlu	05/05/1917	30/05/1917
War Diary	Heilly	31/05/1917	31/05/1917
War Diary	Nurlu	13/05/1917	27/05/1917
War Diary	Heilly	01/06/1917	01/06/1917
War Diary	Merris	02/06/1917	11/06/1917
War Diary	Caestre	12/06/1917	13/06/1917
War Diary	Winnipeg Camp	14/06/1917	19/06/1917
War Diary	Scottish Lines	20/06/1917	30/06/1917
War Diary	Busse Boom (Scottish Lines)	01/07/1917	10/07/1917
War Diary	Bomy	11/07/1917	21/07/1917
War Diary	Busse Boom	22/07/1917	19/08/1917
War Diary	Caestre	20/08/1917	27/08/1917
War Diary	Steenwerck	28/08/1917	14/11/1917
War Diary	Watou	15/11/1917	18/11/1917
War Diary	Mersey Camp	19/11/1917	01/12/1917
War Diary	Vlamertinghe	01/12/1917	03/12/1917
War Diary	Wizernes	04/12/1917	27/12/1917
War Diary	Mersey Camp	28/12/1917	31/12/1917
War Diary	Mersey Camp Vlamertinghe	01/01/1918	19/01/1918
War Diary	Steenvoorde	20/01/1918	11/02/1918
War Diary	Mersey Camp	12/02/1918	28/02/1918
War Diary	Mersey Camp Vlamertinghe	01/03/1918	08/03/1918
War Diary	Abeele	09/03/1918	13/03/1918
War Diary	Wizernes	14/03/1918	22/03/1918
War Diary	Chaulnes	23/03/1918	23/03/1918
War Diary	Foucaucourt	24/03/1918	26/03/1918
War Diary	Domart	27/03/1918	28/03/1918
War Diary	Jumel	29/03/1918	30/03/1918
War Diary	Sains-en-Amienois	31/03/1918	03/04/1918
War Diary	Cavillon	04/04/1918	12/04/1918
War Diary	Bertangle	13/04/1918	20/04/1918
War Diary	Camon	21/04/1918	03/05/1918
War Diary	Chery Chartreuve	04/05/1918	13/05/1918
War Diary	Roucy	14/05/1918	27/05/1918
War Diary	Chatillon	28/05/1918	28/05/1918
War Diary	Oeilly	29/05/1918	29/05/1918
War Diary	St. Martinse	30/05/1918	30/05/1918
War Diary	Villers	31/05/1918	31/05/1918
War Diary	Villers-Aux-Bois	01/06/1918	03/06/1918
War Diary	Bergers	04/06/1918	10/06/1918
War Diary	Pleurs	11/06/1918	13/06/1918
War Diary	Huppy	14/06/1918	23/06/1918
War Diary	Friville	24/06/1918	20/07/1918
War Diary	Villers-Au Bois	21/07/1918	23/07/1918
War Diary	Chateau D'Acq	24/07/1918	03/10/1918
War Diary	Ecurie	04/10/1918	14/10/1918
War Diary	Athies	15/10/1918	18/10/1918
War Diary	Flers	19/10/1918	20/10/1918
War Diary	Cattelet	21/10/1918	22/10/1918
War Diary	Marchiennes	23/10/1918	10/11/1918
War Diary	Stamand	11/11/1918	12/11/1918
War Diary	Tertre	13/11/1918	16/11/1918
War Diary	Tournai	17/11/1918	17/12/1918
War Diary	Enghien	18/12/1918	03/03/1919
War Diary	ATH	04/03/1919	31/03/1919

War Diary   Ath Belgium   01/04/1919 30/04/1919

8TH DIVISION

D. A. D. O. S.
MAY 1915 – JUN 1919

Index..................

DADOS

SUBJECT.

No.	Contents.	Date.
	May 1918 / June 1919	

8th Division

121/6073

DADOS. 8th Division

I 10.6.15 - 30.6.15

WAR DIARY
or
INTELLIGENCE SUMMARY.

(Erase heading not required.)

Army Form C. 2118.

Hour, Date, Place	Summary of Events and Information	Remarks and references to Appendices
	Confidential

War Diary of
D.A.D.O.S. 8th Division
(Major E.M. De-Schmid)
From 10-5-15 to 30-6-15 | |

Instructions regarding War Diaries and Intelligence Summaries are contained in F.S. Regs., Part II. and the Staff Manual respectively. Title pages will be prepared in manuscript.

WAR DIARY
or
INTELLIGENCE SUMMARY

Army Form C. 2118.

Hour, Date, Place	Summary of Events and Information	Remarks and references to Appendices
12th May 1915. Sailly	Visited railhead - Divnl H.Q. of London Terr. Bat. machine guns. 22º Cuirassiers interviewed - Sent away for smoke helmets & respirators -	
13th —	Visited railhead - 8 machine guns arrived for Staff Rifles. 12th Brigade, F. Lines & ministers — the 7th Divs. & Ancestor both lost 1	
14th —	Sub Cmd? - Bailey hill in transit to town exhibits. Esbrouck — H.H. (Jobs) 10/1 machine guns. Visited railhead:	
15th —	Visited railhead. O.O.F. 4.7 arrived for 1st R.B.	

Army Form C. 2118.

WAR DIARY
or
INTELLIGENCE SUMMARY

(Erase heading not required.)

Instructions regarding War Diaries and Intelligence Summaries are contained in F. S. Regs., Part II. and the Staff Manual respectively. Title pages will be prepared in manuscript.

Hour, Date, Place	Summary of Events and Information	Remarks and references to Appendices
16th May Sailly	Visited Workshop. 5 machine guns assist for 2 R. Berks & 2 Devons.	Lut
17th	Visited workshops. Had sample M.G. carrier made	On arrival in resp'd advance Two men carrying a pole with attachment support the gun. Lut
18th	— do — Box discs asked for & local sample made found satisfactory —	Lut
19th	— do — 13th London Rgt. Left to join S.H.Q. Troops —	Lut
20th	— do — One A.F. 4.7" assist for 1. W. Rdrs R.F.A.	Lut
21st	— do — machine guns for 1 "City of London" arrived.	Lut

WAR DIARY
or
INTELLIGENCE SUMMARY

(Erase heading not required.)

Army Form C. 2118.

Instructions regarding War Diaries and Intelligence Summaries are contained in F.S. Regs, Part II. and the Staff Manual respectively. Title pages will be prepared in manuscript.

Hour, Date, Place	Summary of Events and Information	Remarks and references to Appendices
22 May 1915	Fairhead - Bought made of galvanised iron tank for storing water in trenches	With a view of kg + 60 found into factory. [a]
23"	—	
24"	Received 7 trench magnifying sights microscope - also 3 machine guns /n Vickers Sub Denmark + 7 spare - 4.7" carriers for 112 n B.C. -	[a]
25"	—	[a]
26" 1.27	ordinary routine -	[a]
28"	Arrangements made for disposing trucks + respirators - 2 machine guns lent to 2 East Riflles + 2 Northant super tech -	[a]

1247 W 3299 200,000 (E) 8/14 J.B.C. & A. Forms/C. 2118/11.

Army Form C. 2118.

WAR DIARY
or
INTELLIGENCE SUMMARY

(Erase heading not required.)

Instructions regarding War Diaries and Intelligence Summaries are contained in F. S. Regs., Part II. and the Staff Manual respectively. Title pages will be prepared in manuscript.

Hour, Date, Place	Summary of Events and Information	Remarks and references to Appendices
29 May Sally	Visited railhead	
30 "	do — 4.7 gun arrived for 112th B.H. Bty. but was reassigned to 2nd Division	
31 "	— Sgt. Beck arrived for training	
1 June	— 3"6" R.H.A. left the division — Handcart wanted for use in trenches. Improvised breech	
2 "	— 6" howitzer Battery left	
3 "	— "	
4 to 6"	— Received final supply of rockets for repair of smoke helmets	Cases anth. field ambulances
7 to 15"	To England on leave — Nothing unusual occurred during absence	

Army Form C. 2118.

WAR DIARY
or
INTELLIGENCE SUMMARY

(Erase heading not required.)

Instructions regarding War Diaries and Intelligence
Summaries are contained in F. S. Regs., Part II.
and the Staff Manual respectively. Title pages
will be prepared in manuscript.

Hour, Date, Place		Summary of Events and Information	Remarks and references to Appendices
14th June	Maricod Mavibead	Lt. Col. Wallace left for England (leave)	Col
15th	"	—	Col
16th	"	1st Mal Roving R.J.A & 25th Fokkers Contay R.E. left the division	Col
17th & 21st	"	—	Col
22nd	"	8th Lth See Joined up & formed a composite regiment with J. L. Res.	Col
23rd	"	A section of the 33rd B.A.C R.F.A Joined.	Col
24th	"	57th B.A.C R.F.A with section of Brigade & the Ammu Colum Joined up.	Col

1247 W 3299—200,000 (E) 8/14 J.B.C. & A. Forms/C. 2118/11.

Army Form C. 2113.

WAR DIARY
or
INTELLIGENCE SUMMARY

(Erase heading not required.)

Instructions regarding War Diaries and Intelligence Summaries are contained in F. S. Regs., Part II. and the Staff Manual respectively. Title pages will be prepared in manuscript.

Hour, Date, Place	Summary of Events and Information	Remarks and references to Appendices
25th June 15 Sailly	Visited trenches — Ordinary routine.	
26th "	"	
27th "	Cond? Harland left for 1st Army H.Q.?	Ord
	Ordnance refilling point closed for a fortnight —	Not account to have a refilling point as presented one road of ration road of enemy fire.
28th "	" — Moved refilling point	Ord
		About 1½ hours work & the long loads.
29th 1.30	" — Ordinary routine.	Ord.

13/6/49

St. Division

JADOS 8th Division

Vol II

Army Form C. 2118.

WAR DIARY
INTELLIGENCE SUMMARY.
(Erase heading not required.)

Instructions regarding War Diaries and Intelligence Summaries are contained in F.S. Regs., Part II. and the Staff Manual respectively. Title pages will be prepared in manuscript.

Hour, Date, Place	Summary of Events and Information	Remarks and references to Appendices
	Confidential War Diary of: D.A.D. of 8th Division (Major E. M. de Smidt) A.D. From:- 1-7-15 To:- 31-7-15	

Army Form C. 2118.

WAR DIARY
or
INTELLIGENCE SUMMARY

(Erase heading not required.)

Instructions regarding War Diaries and Intelligence Summaries are contained in F. S. Regs., Part II. and the Staff Manual respectively. Title pages will be prepared in manuscript.

Hour, Date, Place	Summary of Events and Information	Remarks and references to Appendices
July 1915. Sailly	Visited Vaillant also H.Qrs 2 Army & Fifth central + ordinary routine duties	(a)
2	- do -	(a)
3, 4, 5	- do -	
6	- do - Flies very bad; units demand crushers	purchased locally.
	Field Ambulances now & returned bolts	(a) Repeats to III Corps who pounded 20 in all.
7	- do - Conference at H.Q.C.? III Corps -	
8, 9, 10, 11, 12	- do - Nothing unusual - Ordinary routine duties.	(a)
13	- do - Received 10 rifles with magnifying sights & 3 telescopes for distribution.	(a)
14	- do - Sg. Long joined for instruction. Conference at Holland III Corps H.Q.	(a)

Army Form C. 2118.

WAR DIARY
or
INTELLIGENCE SUMMARY

(Erase heading not required.)

Instructions regarding War Diaries and Intelligence Summaries are contained in F. S. Regs., Part II. and the Staff Manual respectively. Title pages will be prepared in manuscript.

Hour, Date, Place	Summary of Events and Information	Remarks and references to Appendices
15th July. Sa. Hq.	Visited Railhead — Routine duties —	(a)
16 —	do — 4 bomb throwers received —	Arms issued to French + workshops are trying steel arms as has
17 —	— do —	
18 —	— do — Railhead changed from Steinwerck to La Forgue — Accommodation improved —	(a)
19 —	— do — 15 Vermorel sprayers issued from III Corps	
20 —	— do —	
21 —	— do — Conference III Corps A.D.C. 19th Inf. Brigade	(a)
22 —	— do — Visited O.O. 19 & Inf. Bn. also 1st Army A.O.D. Offrs. for railhead arrived —	(a)
23 —	— do — Visited O.O. 19 2.B. + III Corps Travelling Workshops —	(a)

1247 W 3299 200,000 (E) 8/14 J.B.C.&A. Forms/C. 2118/11.

Army Form C. 2118.

WAR DIARY
or
INTELLIGENCE SUMMARY
(Erase heading not required.)

Instructions regarding War Diaries and Intelligence Summaries are contained in F. S. Regs., Part II. and the Staff Manual respectively. Title pages will be prepared in manuscript.

Hour, Date, Place	Summary of Events and Information	Remarks and references to Appendices
24th July 1915. Sailly.	Visited railhead - AD/S 1st Army came - Routine duties	A1
25th "	- do - Complaints received as to repair of smoke helmets carried out by 25th Field Ambulance	Arrangements to carry out work. A1
26th July	Railhead transferred temporarily to Thiennes -	1st Division detraining at La Gorgue.
27 "	- do - Routine duties	
28th	- do - Conference III Corps HQ Bailleul	A1
29th	Visited railhead transferred back to La Gorgue - also 19th Inf. Brigade.	A1
30th	Visited railhead - Sub conductor arrived in relief of U/MCO Dickinson I.O.D with 19th Inf. Brigade - Routine duties.	
31st	- do - Conference at 1st H.Q. Routine duties	A1

121/6754

8th Division

ORDRS. 8th Division

August 15

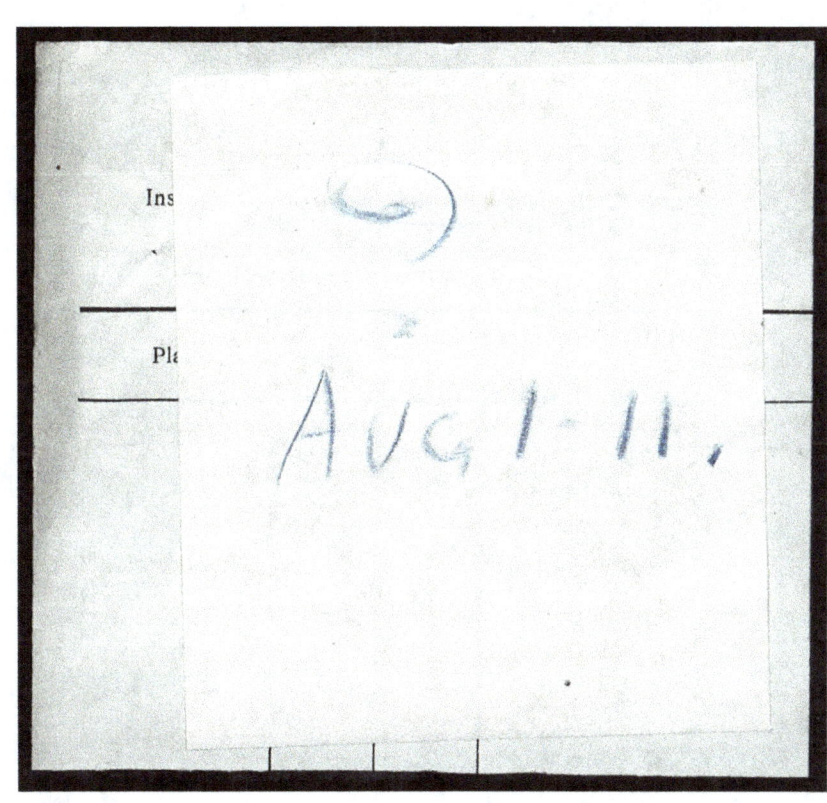

Army Form. C. 2118

WAR DIARY
or
INTELLIGENCE SUMMARY
(Erase heading not required.)

Confidential

War Diary
of
Canadian 1st Division

From 1st August 1915 to 31st August 1915

(Volume 4)

A.D'S OFFICE AT THE BASE — 6 SEP 1915 — A.O.C. SECTION

Army Form C. 2118.

WAR DIARY
or
INTELLIGENCE SUMMARY

(Erase heading not required.)

Instructions regarding War Diaries and Intelligence Summaries are contained in F. S. Regs., Part II. and the Staff Manual respectively. Title pages will be prepared in manuscript.

Hour, Date, Place	Summary of Events and Information	Remarks and references to Appendices
12th August 1915 SAILLY	Capt. E SIGRIST. D.C.H.O. assumed the duties of D.A.D.V.S	EJ
13th " "	Depreciated routine duties	EJ
14th " "	Visited Railhead - Routine duties	EJ
15th " "	Routine duties	EJ
16th " "	Sick - Engagement - (2 x S) Lake Pattern Knuckle helmets received	EJ
17th " "	Visited Railhead - Routine duties 19th Infantry Brigade transferred to 2nd Divn.	EJ
18th " "	A.D.C. Attachment. 19th Infy Bde. left for new division	EJ
19th " "	1 machine gun received for 2nd R Berks Regt to replace unserviceable	EJ
20th " "	1 machine gun received for 1st Middlesex Regt Case unserviceable	EJ

Army Form C. 2118.

WAR DIARY
or
INTELLIGENCE SUMMARY
(Erase heading not required)

Instructions regarding War Diaries and Intelligence Summaries are contained in F. S. Regs., Part II. and the Staff Manual respectively. Title pages will be prepared in manuscript.

Hour, Date, Place	Summary of Events and Information	Remarks and references to Appendices
21st August 1915. SAILLY	Visited Rollard - Routine duties	EJ
22nd "	11 Thacker Machine Gun received for 8th Middlesex Regt - 1st supply in dissention of amalgamation with 7th Middlesex Regt	EJ
23rd "	Regimental routine	EJ
24th "	Ordinary routine	EJ
25th "	Visited Rollard - Attended conference at Corps Headquarters	EJ
26th "	Routine duties	EJ
27th "	do — Attended conference at Divisional Headquarters	EJ
28th "	Routine duties	EJ

Army Form. C. 2118

WAR DIARY
or
INTELLIGENCE SUMMARY

(Erase heading not required.)

Instructions regarding War Diaries and Intelligence Summaries are contained in F. S. Regs., Part II. and the Staff Manual respectively. Title Pages will be prepared in manuscript.

Place	Date	Hour	Summary of Events and Information	Remarks and references to Appendices
SHILLY	29/5	8pm	Visited Railhead - Routine duties. EJ	
— " —	30/5	8pm	Routine duties. EJ	
— " —	31/5	8pm	Routine duties - Attended Divisional Headquarters conference EJ	

Signed Capt.
D.A.D.O.S. 7th Division

8th Division

D.A.D.O.S. 8th Division.
Vol IV
Sept. 15

Army Form. C. 2118

WAR DIARY
or
INTELLIGENCE SUMMARY
(Erase heading not required.)

Confidential

War Diary
of
D.A.D.O.S. 5th Division

from 1st September 1915
to 30th September 1915

(Volume 5)

Army Form. C. 2118

WAR DIARY
or
INTELLIGENCE SUMMARY

(Erase heading not required.)

Instructions regarding War Diaries and Intelligence Summaries are contained in F. S. Regs., Part II. and the Staff Manual respectively. Title Pages will be prepared in manuscript.

Place	Date	Hour	Summary of Events and Information	Remarks and references to Appendices
SAILLY	1.9.15	7.45pm	Inspected Divisional Ordnance Workshops - 11 carpenters, 1 tailor, 1 shoemaker, + 2 Estimators furnished by Infantry brigades. Attended Conference at Corps Headquarters.	A/
— " —	2.9.15	9.10pm	Under instructions of C.R.A. 23rd Bn. fitted out an aero-used Bomb with improved fuze, lighter, formed for detonation purposes. The machine gun received for Blinked Loopholes	B/
— " —	3.9.15	4 pm	Enemies carried forms of trek shelling to change of arcs + aims for demonstration purposes. Attended conference at Divisional Headquarters.	C/
— " —	4.9.15	7.40 pm	Departmental Routine	D/
— " —	5.9.15	7.45 pm	— do —	E/
— " —	6.9.15	4.30pm	— do —	E/

Army Form. C. 2118

WAR DIARY
of
INTELLIGENCE SUMMARY
(Erase heading not required.)

Instructions regarding War Diaries and Intelligence Summaries are contained in F. S. Regs., Part II. and the Staff Manual respectively. Title Pages will be prepared in manuscript.

Place	Date	Hour	Summary of Events and Information	Remarks and references to Appendices
SAILLY	7.9.15	7 pm	Routine duties. Conference Divisional Headquarters	D
— " —	8.9.15	7.30 pm	— do — — " — III Corps	D
— " —	9.9.15	4.45 pm	— do — One machine gun received for 10th Hampshire Territorials	D
— " —	10.9.15	8.10 pm	— do — Conference Divisional Headquarters	D
— " —	11.9.15	7.30 pm	— do — Visited III Corps workshop	D
— " —	12.9.15	4.50 pm	— do — Visited Railhead	D
— " —	13.9.15	4.55 pm	— do —	D
— " —	14.9.15	7.40 pm	— do — Conference Divisional Headquarters	D
— " —	15.9.15	7.35 pm	— do — — " — III Corps	D

Army Form. C. 2118

WAR DIARY
OF
INTELLIGENCE SUMMARY
(Erase heading not required.)

Instructions regarding War Diaries and Intelligence Summaries are contained in F. S. Regs., Part II. and the Staff Manual respectively. Title Pages will be prepared in manuscript.

Place	Date	Hour	Summary of Events and Information	Remarks and references to Appendices
SAILLY	16.9.15	5.15 pm	Routine duties - Relieved by D.A.D.S. 12th Army	
"	17.9.15	8.30 pm	"	
"	18.9.15	4.00 pm	Conference Divisional Headquarters	
"	19.9.15	5.10 pm	Visited Orchard 65th Trench Mortar Battery from Trench Mortar School formed division	
"	20.9.15	6.0 pm	"	
"	21.9.15	7.0 pm	Conference Divisional Headquarters	
"	22.9.15	5.0 pm	"	
"	23.9.15	8.15 pm	Corps Headquarters	
"	24.9.15	7.30 pm	"	
"	25.9.15	7.15 pm	Conference Divisional Headquarters	
"	26.9.15	4.45 pm	One Vickers machine gun received to replace one received from Armagh by shell fire. (for 2/5 Lanc. Regt.)	

WAR DIARY
INTELLIGENCE SUMMARY

Army Form. C. 2118

(Erase heading not required.)

Instructions regarding War Diaries and Intelligence Summaries are contained in F. S. Regs., Part II. and the Staff Manual respectively. Title Pages will be prepared in manuscript.

Place	Date	Hour	Summary of Events and Information	Remarks and references to Appendices
SAILLY	27.9.15	10.0 pm	Routine duties	
— " —	28.9.15	6.0 pm	Conference preceeded Headquarters there. Vickers machine guns received for 2/Lincoln Regt. & one for 2/Rifle Bde. to replace maxims lost in action 25th inst.	gl
— " —	29.9.15	5.0 pm	J and K Batteries Stokes 4" mortars from French Mortar School ST. VENANT joined 7th Division	gl
— " —	30.9.15	5.45 pm	Special conference preceeded Headquarters. Subject winter accommodation	gl

Signed Major
D.A.A.G. 8th Division

12/7466

bro

J. DADDS ста Dis.

Dec 15

Vol II

Army Form. C. 2118

WAR DIARY
or
INTELLIGENCE SUMMARY

(Erase heading not required.)

Instructions regarding War Diaries and Intelligence Summaries are contained in F. S. Regs., Part II. and the Staff Manual respectively. Title Pages will be prepared in manuscript.

Confidential

War Diary
of
D.A. & Q.M.G. 8th Division
from 1st October 1915 to 31st October 1915

(Volume 6)

Place	Date	Hour	Summary of Events and Information	Remarks and references to Appendices

Army Form. C. 2118

WAR DIARY
INTELLIGENCE SUMMARY
(Erase heading not required.)

Instructions regarding War Diaries and Intelligence Summaries are contained in F. S. Regs., Part II. and the Staff Manual respectively. Title Pages will be prepared in manuscript.

Place	Date	Hour	Summary of Events and Information	Remarks and references to Appendices
SAILLY	1.10.15	7.30pm	Routine duties - Conference concerning arrangement Headquarters	GJ
"	2.10.15	5.0pm	"	GJ
"	3.10.15	6.0pm	" Two Vickers machine guns issued to 1st London Regt	GJ
"	4.10.15	7.10pm	"	GJ
"	5.10.15	7.30pm	" Divisional Headquarters Conference	GJ
"	6.10.15	4.0pm	" Corps Conference	GJ
"	7.10.15	7.45pm	" Divisional Headquarters Conference	GJ
"	8.10.15	5.30pm	"	GJ
"	9.10.15	7.30pm	"	GJ
"	10.10.15	7.0pm	" Visited trenches	GJ
"	11.10.15	7.0pm	"	GJ
"	12.10.15	7.30pm	" Conference concerning Headquarters. Divisional entrance workshops visited by Corps Commander	GJ
"	13.10.15	7.0pm	" Conference Corps Headquarters	GJ

Army Form. C. 2118

WAR DIARY
or
INTELLIGENCE SUMMARY
(Erase heading not required.)

Instructions regarding War Diaries and Intelligence Summaries are contained in F. S. Regs., Part II. and the Staff Manual respectively. Title Pages will be prepared in manuscript.

Place	Date	Hour	Summary of Events and Information	Remarks and references to Appendices
SAILLY	14.10.15	9.0 pm	Regimental Routine	J
"	15.10.15	7.30 pm	Conference Divisional Headquarters	J
"	16.10.15	7.15 pm	" " "	J
"	17.10.15	6.45 pm	63rd French Mortar Battery joined - from 20th Division	J
"	18.10.15	6.30 am	Major E. SIGRIST, DAAG 7th Division proceeding on short visit 26th cmdt. duty in the interim being performed by Capt. F. FANE. APM 7th Division	J
"	19.10.15	5 pm	Conference Divisional Headquarters	ff
"	20.10.15	5.15 pm	Conference Corps Headquarters	ff
"	21.10.15	4.30 pm	Daily Routine	ff
"	22.10.15	6 pm	" - Conference Divisional Headquarters	ff
"	23.10.15	4.3 pm	Daily Routine	ff

Army Form. C. 2118

WAR DIARY
INTELLIGENCE SUMMARY
(Erase heading not required.)

Place	Date	Hour	Summary of Events and Information	Remarks and references to Appendices
Sailly	24.10.15	3 pm	Daily Routine	J.J.
"	25.10.15	3 pm	"	J.J.
"	26.10.15	6 pm	"	J.J.
"	27.10.15	9.15 pm	Conference Divisional Headquarters	
"	—	—	Conference Corps Headquarters Major E. SIGIST temporary duty from Corps	E.J.
"	28.10.15	9.15 pm	Departmental Routine	E.J.
"	29.10.15	4.30 pm	Conference Divisional Headquarters	E.J.
"	30.10.15	5.0 pm	" Visit of by D.A.A.G 1st Army	E.J.
"	31.10.15	7.30 pm	Departmental Routine	E.J.

B. Wyndham Taylor
Major S. Division

Army Form. C. 2118

WAR DIARY
INTELLIGENCE SUMMARY
(Erase heading not required.)

Instructions regarding War Diaries and Intelligence Summaries are contained in F. S. Regs., Part II. and the Staff Manual respectively. Title Pages will be prepared in manuscript.

Place	Date	Hour	Summary of Events and Information	Remarks and references to Appendices

Confidential

War Diary
of
2nd/5th Division

from 1st November 1915 to 30th November 1915

(Volume VI)

D/
7071

Army Form. C. 2118

WAR DIARY
or
INTELLIGENCE SUMMARY

(Erase heading not required.)

Instructions regarding War Diaries and Intelligence Summaries are contained in F. S. Regs., Part II. and the Staff Manual respectively. Title Pages will be prepared in manuscript.

Place	Date	Hour	Summary of Events and Information	Remarks and references to Appendices
SAILLY	1/1/15	9.15 pm	Departmental Routine	EJ
"	2/1/15	4.30 pm	do — Conference Divisional Headquarters	EJ
"	3/1/15	9.30 pm	do — do - Corps	EJ
"	4/1/15	4.45 pm	do — Visited III Corps S.O.M.	EJ
"	5/1/15	5.15 pm	do — Conference Divisional Headquarters	EJ
"	6/1/15	4.30 pm	do — For W. Supply of 10% Establishment	EJ
"	7/1/15	7.30 pm	do — Telescopes received for Infty. Battns	EJ
"	8/1/15	7.45 pm	do —	EJ

Army Form. C. 2118

WAR DIARY
or
INTELLIGENCE SUMMARY
(Erase heading not required.)

Instructions regarding War Diaries and Intelligence Summaries are contained in F. S. Regs., Part II. and the Staff Manual respectively. Title Pages will be prepared in manuscript.

Place	Date	Hour	Summary of Events and Information	Remarks and references to Appendices
SAILLY	9/11/15	4.30 pm	Daily Routine - Conference Divisional Headquarters	J.L.
— " —	10/11/15	8.30 pm	— " — — do — Corps Headquarters	J.L.
— " —	11/11/15	9.0 pm	— " —	J.L.
— " —	12/11/15	8.15 pm	— " — Conference Divisional Headquarters	J.L.
— " —	13/11/15	9.30 pm	— " —	J.L.
— " —	14/11/15	6.30 pm	— " —	J.L.
— " —	15/11/15	9.0 pm	— " — Visited G.O.C. 4th Corps	J.L.
— " —	16/11/15	5.30 pm	— " — Conference Divisional Headquarters	J.L.
— " —	17/11/15	7.30 pm	— " — — do — Corps	J.L.
— " —	18/11/15	7.15 pm	— " — 181st Brigade relieved by G.O.C. Guards Division in III Corps area	J.L.

Army Form. C. 2118

WAR DIARY
INTELLIGENCE SUMMARY
(Erase heading not required.)

Instructions regarding War Diaries and Intelligence Summaries are contained in F. S. Regs., Part II. and the Staff Manual respectively. Title Pages will be prepared in manuscript.

Place	Date	Hour	Summary of Events and Information	Remarks and references to Appendices
SAILLY	19/11/15	7.45 pm	Departmental Orders - Visited Railhead Experience Divisional Headquarters	E.J.
-"-	20/11/15	7.30 pm	Despatched 370 tents complete with boards & floors & 11 tent shelters with floor boards to STEENBECQUE in preparation for 5th Division camp forming there. 1 N.C.O. & 1 private A.D.C. left in charge.	E.J.
-"-	21/11/15	9.15 pm	Visited Railhead. Despatched 200 more tents with tent bottoms to STEENBECQUE - in further part.	E.J.
-"-	22/11/15	7.30 pm	Visited Railhead. Despatched 95 tents with tent bottoms to STEENBECQUE in further part.	E.J.
-"-	23/11/15	9.15 pm	Visited Railhead.	E.J.

Army Form. C. 2118

WAR DIARY
or
INTELLIGENCE SUMMARY

(Erase heading not required.)

Place	Date	Hour	Summary of Events and Information	Remarks and references to Appendices
SAILLY	24/7/15	7.30 p.m.	Departmental orders. Visited Railhead. Divisional Headquarters removed to BLARINGHEM	BP
STEEMBECQUE	25/7/15	9.30 p.m.	"	BP
—	26/7/15	9.30 p.m.	D.A.D.O.S. and advance refilling point removed to STEENBECQUE.	BP
—	27/7/15	9.30 p.m.	Divisional workshops removed to STEENBECQUE. 161st and 190th Companies R.E. removed to 20th Division.	BP
—	28/7/15	9.30 p.m.	Visited D.Q.M.G. III Corps	BP
—	29/7/15	5.15 p.m.	Railhead removed to STEENBECQUE from LA GORGUE. Visited Railhead	BP
—	30/7/15	5.45 p.m.	"	BP

D.A.D.D.K.D 8th Dec

Army Form C. 2118.

WAR DIARY
or
INTELLIGENCE SUMMARY.
(Erase heading not required.)

Confidential

War Diary
of
D.A.Q.M.G. 5th Division

From 1st December 1915
to
31st December 1915.

(Volume 8)

WAR DIARY
INTELLIGENCE SUMMARY
(Erase heading not required.)

Army Form. C. 2118

Instructions regarding War Diaries and Intelligence Summaries are contained in F. S. Regs., Part II. and the Staff Manual respectively. Title Pages will be prepared in manuscript.

Place	Date	Hour	Summary of Events and Information	Remarks and references to Appendices
STEENBECQUE	1 12/15	9.30 p.m.	Departmental Routine – Visited Divisional Headquarters	
"	2 12/15	8.30 p.m.	"	
"	3 12/15	10.30 p.m.	"	
"	4 12/15	5.45 p.m.	Visited Divisional Headquarters and	
"	5 12/15	11.15 p.m.	D.H.Q. 1st Army	
"	6 12/15	10.30 p.m.	Visited Divisional Headquarters	
"	7 12/15	9.30 p.m.	"	
"	8 12/15	10.15 p.m.	"	
"	9 12/15	11.0 p.m.	"	
"	10 12/15	9.30 p.m.	"	
"	11 12/15	9.30 p.m.	Visited Divisional Headquarters	

Army Form. C. 2118

WAR DIARY
or
INTELLIGENCE SUMMARY
(Erase heading not required.)

Instructions regarding War Diaries and Intelligence Summaries are contained in F. S. Regs., Part II. and the Staff Manual respectively. Title Pages will be prepared in manuscript.

Place	Date	Hour	Summary of Events and Information	Remarks and references to Appendices
STEENBECQUE	12/12/15	9.15 pm	Regimental Routine	
"	13/12/15	9.30 pm	"	
"	14/12/15	9.15 pm	"	
"	15/12/15	9.30 pm	"	
"	16/12/15	4.20 pm	Visited Divisional Headquarters and incidents	
"	17/12/15	6.30 pm	"	
"	18/12/15	4.15 pm	"	
"	19/12/15	6.30 pm	"	
"	20/12/15	5.0 pm	Visited Divisional Headquarters	
"	21/12/15	9.15 pm	"	

Army Form C. 2118.

WAR DIARY
INTELLIGENCE SUMMARY.
(Erase heading not required.)

Instructions regarding War Diaries and Intelligence Summaries are contained in F. S. Regs., Part II. and the Staff Manual respectively. Title pages will be prepared in manuscript.

Place	Date	Hour	Summary of Events and Information		Remarks and references to Appendices
STEENBECQUE	22/12/15	4.30 pm	Departmental duties.	Visited Divisional Headquarters	
"	23/12/15	4.2 pm	Do	Do	
"	24/12/15	9.15 pm	—	Do	
"	25/12/15	7.30 pm	Do	Do	
"	26/12/15	6.50 pm	Do	Do — also Packham	
"	27/12/15	6.20 pm	Do	Do	
"	28/12/15	4.0 pm	—	Do — Visited Hqrs III Corps	
"	29/12/15	7.0 pm	Do	Do — Visited Hqrs III Corps	
"	30/12/15	6.15 pm	Do	Do — Visited Hqrs 1st Army	
"	31/12/15	7.30 pm	Do	Do — Visited ADMS III Corps	

E. Wyner Major
DADMS 5th Divn

D. and O.S. & D.ii
Jan
Vol VIII

Army Form C. 2118.

WAR DIARY
INTELLIGENCE SUMMARY.
(Erase heading not required.)

Confidential

War Diary of D.A.D.O.S. 8th Division

From 1st January 1916 to 31st January 1916.

(Volume 9)

R. Long Lieut Col
for D.A.D.O.S. 8th Div.

WAR DIARY
or
INTELLIGENCE SUMMARY.

Army Form C. 2118.

Place	Date	Hour	Summary of Events and Information	Remarks and references to Appendices
SAILLY	30/1/16	7.15pm	Departmental Routine. Conference III Corps Cavalry Divl. Hd.Qrs.	H.S.
	31/1/16	9am	— do — Conference Divisional Head Quarters	H.S.

Recent hard roed for D.A.D.O.S. & men.

Army Form C. 2118.

WAR DIARY
INTELLIGENCE SUMMARY.
(Erase heading not required.)

Instructions regarding War Diaries and Intelligence Summaries are contained in F. S. Regs., Part II. and the Staff Manual respectively. Title pages will be prepared in manuscript.

Place	Date	Hour	Summary of Events and Information	Remarks and references to Appendices
SAILLY	15/6	7.30 pm	Departmental Routine. Visited Divisional Headquarters	DJ
— " —	16/6	7.20 pm	Do — Do —	DJ
— " —	17/6	7.30 pm	Do — also CRA 1st Army	DJ
— " —	18/6	7.45 pm	Do — also G.O.C. III Corps	DJ
— " —	19/6	7.15 pm	Do — Visited Divisional Headquarters	DJ
— " —	20/6	9.20 pm	Do — Do —	DJ
— " —	21/6	7.10 pm	Do — Do —	DJ
— " —	22/6	7.30 pm	Do — Do —	DJ
— " —	23/6	7.45 pm	Do — Do — + Inspected III Corps	DJ
— " —	24/6	9.30 pm	Do — Inspected Divisional Headquarters	DJ
— " —	25/6	12.20 am	Proceeded on leave ended 3rd February 1916. Only on the interim	DJ
			kept performed by Lieut. K. GREIG. A.D.C.	
— " —	26/6	7 pm	Departmental Routine. Visited Divisional Headquarters	KG
— " —	27/6	7.30 pm	do	KG
— " —	28/6	7 pm	Conference Divisional Headquarters	KG
— " —	29/6	7 pm	do Divisional Headquarters	KG

Army Form C. 2118.

WAR DIARY
or
INTELLIGENCE SUMMARY.
(Erase heading not required.)

Instructions regarding War Diaries and Intelligence Summaries are contained in F. S. Regs., Part II. and the Staff Manual respectively. Title pages will be prepared in manuscript.

Place	Date	Hour	Summary of Events and Information	Remarks and references to Appendices
STEENBECQUE	1/7/16	7.30 pm	Departmental Duties. Visited Divisional Headquarters	E.J.
— " —	2/7/16	6.30 pm	Do	Do	E.J.
— " —	3/7/16	7.30 pm	Do	Do	E.J.
— " —	4/7/16	7.0 pm	Do	Do	E.J.
— " —	5/7/16	7.0 pm	Do	Do	E.J.
— " —	6/7/16	9.15 pm	Do	Do	E.J.
— " —	7/7/16	7.30 pm	Do	Do	E.J.
— " —	8/7/16	6.25 pm	Do	Do	E.J.
— " —	9/7/16	4.0 pm	Do	Do	E.J.
— " —	10/7/16	8.15 pm	Do	Do	E.J.
— " —	11/7/16	9.0 pm	Do	Do	E.J.
— " —	12/7/16	7.20 pm	Do —	Officer & Repelling point removed to S.P.C.S.T (Shet 36) Railhead changed	E.J.
SAILLY	13/7/16	7.30 pm	—	to BAC ST MAUR from STEENBECQUE Visited Divisional Headquarters	E.J.
— " —	14/7/16	7.20 pm	Do —	Visited Divisional Headquarters, S.O.M. III Corps, & Railhead.	E.J.

Army Form C. 2118.

WAR DIARY
or
INTELLIGENCE SUMMARY.
(Erase heading not required.)

Confidential.

War Diary of D.A.D.O.S. 8th Divn.

from 1st Feb 1916. to 29th Feb. 1916.

C^olonel to ADV J.

R. Stacey Lieut A.D.O.S.
DADOS 8th Divn

Army Form C. 2118.

WAR DIARY
~~INTELLIGENCE SUMMARY.~~
(Erase heading not required.)

Instructions regarding War Diaries and Intelligence Summaries are contained in F. S. Regs., Part II. and the Staff Manual respectively. Title pages will be prepared in manuscript.

Place	Date	Hour	Summary of Events and Information	Remarks and references to Appendices
SAILLY	1/2/16	7.30a	Divisional Routine	Visited Divisional Head Qrs	R.Q
—	2/2/16	6.7pm	— do —	— do —	R.Q
—	3/2/16	1.15pm / 9.20	— do —	— do —	R.Q
—	4/2/16	12.30 pm	Major E. SIGRIST, D.A.D.O.S. resumed duty from leave		El
—	5/2/16		Major E. SIGRIST, D.A.D.O.S. left division. Lieut K.C.GREIG, A.O.D. takes over duties	hq 7pm H⁺ Army for duty.	El
—	6/2/16	7.30am	Divisional Routine	Conference III Corps. Visited Divl Head Qrs	R.Q
—	7/2/16	7pm	— do —	Visited Divisional Head Qrs (Conference)	R.Q
—	8/2/16	6.30pm	— do —	Visited Divisional Head Qrs	R.Q
—	9/2/16	"	— do —	— do —	R.Q
—	10/2/16	7pm	— do —	— do —	R.Q
—	11/2/16	7.15pm	— do —	Divisional H.Q. Conference	R.Q
—	12/2/16	"	— do —	Visited Divisional Head Qrs	R.Q
—	13/2/16	7pm	— do —	— do —	R.Q
—	14/2/16	7.30 "	— do —	Divisional H.Q. Conference	R.Q
—	15/2/16	"	Lieut K.C.GREIG, DADOS proceeded on leave until 22/2/16 Duties in interim performed by Major A.V.BOYD, R.A.		R.Q

Army Form C. 2118.

WAR DIARY
or
INTELLIGENCE SUMMARY.
(Erase heading not required.)

Place	Date	Hour	Summary of Events and Information	Remarks and references to Appendices
SAILLY	15/9/16		Divisional Routine	App
"	16/9/16		do	App
"	17/9/16		do	App
"	18/9/16		do	App
"	19/9/16		do	App
"	20/9/16		do	App
"	21/9/16		do	App
"	22/9/16		do	App
"	23/9/16	6.30pm	LIEUT K.C. GREIG rejoined duties	App
"	24/9/16	10am	do. Rachine returned to LA GORGUE	App
"	25/9/16		do	App
"	26/9/16	7.30pm	DUC SHAS m Coupee, Rachine returned to BAO ST MAUR	App
"	27/9/16		Crates Divisional Routine Quarters Rachine returned to LA GORGUE	App
"	28/9/16		ADOS III Corps Conference Crates DUC SHAS 2pm	App
"	29/9/16	7pm	DUC SHAS 2pm Coupee	App
"	30/9/16	"	do	App

Army Form C. 2118.

WAR DIARY
or
INTELLIGENCE SUMMARY.
(Erase heading not required.)

Confidential

War Diary of D.A.D.O.S. 8th Division

from 1st March 1916 to 31st March 1916

Volume D 10

Kethey Capt. A.O.D.
D.A.D. O.S. 8th Div.

Army Form C. 2118.

WAR DIARY
or
INTELLIGENCE SUMMARY.
(Erase heading not required.)

Instructions regarding War Diaries and Intelligence Summaries are contained in F. S. Regs., Part II. and the Staff Manual respectively. Title pages will be prepared in manuscript.

Place	Date	Hour	Summary of Events and Information	Remarks and references to Appendices
SAILLY S.L. LYS	1/3/16	6.30 pm	Regimental Routine. Traced Divisional Headquarters	ADS
"	2/3/16	7 pm	do	ADS
"	3/3/16	6.30 pm	Divl H.Q. Conference / Lieut D. Cansdale. A O D joined Division for instruction	ADS
"	4/3/16	7.15 pm	do Traced Divisional Headquarters	ADS
"	5/3/16	"	do — III Corps Conference (ADOS)	ADS
"	6/3/16	6.30 pm	Traced Roads. Divl HQ Confce	ADS
"	7/3/16	"	Traced Divl Head Quarters	ADS
"	8/3/16	7 pm	do	ADS
"	9/3/16	"	do	ADS
"	10/3/16	"	Traced Roads. Divl Head Quarters Confce	ADS
"	11/3/16	6.30 —	Traced Divl Head Quarters	ADS
"	12/3/16	7 pm	do — III Corps Conference (ADOS)	ADS
"	13/3/16	"	Divl HQ Conference Confce	ADS
"	14/3/16	"	Traced Divl Head Qrs	ADS
"	15/3/16	"	do — Lieut D. Cansdale left Divn to proceed to 34th Divn	ADS

Army Form C. 2118.

WAR DIARY
or
INTELLIGENCE SUMMARY.
(Erase heading not required.)

Instructions regarding War Diaries and Intelligence Summaries are contained in F. S. Regs., Part II. and the Staff Manual respectively. Title pages will be prepared in manuscript.

Place	Date	Hour	Summary of Events and Information	Remarks and references to Appendices
SAILLY SUR LA LYS	10/3/16	6.45 PM	Divisional Routine. Visited Divl Headquarters	KCG
"	17/3/16	"	do	KCG
"	13/3/16	7pm	do. Divl Headquarters	KCG
"	19/3/16	6.45pm	do. Visited Divl Headquarters	KCG
"	20/3/16	"	Conference III Corps. Visited Divl Headquarters	KCG
"	21/3/16	"	Divl Headqrs. Conference Visited Rawlins	KCG
"	22/3/16	7pm	Visited Divl Headquarters	KCG
"	23/3/16	6.40pm	do	KCG
"	24/3/16	"	Divl Head Quarters Conference Visited Rawlins	KCG
"	25/3/16	"	Visited Divisional Headquarters	KCG
"	26/3/16	7pm	do Visited Rawlins	KCG
"	27/3/16	"	do do	KCG
FIESSELLES	28/3/16	"	Division moved to FIESSELLES. Visited Rawlins	KCG
"	29/3/16	6pm	Divisional Routine. Visited Rawlins & Divl HQ	KCG
"	30/3/16	"	do do	KCG
"	3/3/16	"	do do	KCG

Richard Capn A.D.C.
Base 8 D...

Army Form C. 2118.

WAR DIARY
or
INTELLIGENCE SUMMARY.
(Erase heading not required.)

Confidential

War Diary of D.A.D.O.S. 8th Divn

From 1st April 1916 to 30th April 1916.

(Volume 11)

Vol XII

N. Roberts Captn A.O.D
D.A.D.O.S
8th Divn

Army Form C. 2118.

WAR DIARY
or
INTELLIGENCE SUMMARY.
(Erase heading not required.)

Instructions regarding War Diaries and Intelligence Summaries are contained in F. S. Regs., Part II. and the Staff Manual respectively. Title pages will be prepared in manuscript.

Place	Date	Hour	Summary of Events and Information	Remarks and references to Appendices
FLESSELLES	1/4/16	7pm	Visited Rawheas (LONGPRE) + Divl HdQuartrs	Rep
"	2/4/16	"	do + Divisional Routine	Rep
"	3/4/16	"	Visited Divisional HdQuartrs — do —	Rep
HENENCOURT	4/4/16	6pm	Division moved to HENENCOURT	Rep
"	5/4/16	7pm	Divisional Routine Visited Divl HdQuartrs	Rep
"	6/4/16	"	Rawheas moves to MERICOURT — do — Divl Routine	Rep
"	7/4/16	"	Divisional Routine Visited Divl HdQuartrs + Rawheas	Rep
"	8/4/16	6pm	— do — — do —	Rep
"	9/4/16	6.30pm	— do — — do —	Rep
"	10/4/16	"	— do — — do — + Rawlinson	Rep
"	11/4/16	7pm	— do — — do — + DDOS 4th Army	Rep
"	12/4/16	"	— do — — do — + Rawlinson	Rep
"	13/4/16	6.30	— do — — do — + ADOS III Corps	Rep
"	14/4/16	7pm	— do — do	Rep
"	15/4/16	"	— do — — do —	Rep
"	16/4/16	6pm	— do — — do — + Rawheas	Rep

Army Form C. 2118.

WAR DIARY
or
INTELLIGENCE SUMMARY.
(Erase heading not required.)

Instructions regarding War Diaries and Intelligence Summaries are contained in F. S. Regs., Part II. and the Staff Manual respectively. Title pages will be prepared in manuscript.

Place	Date	Hour	Summary of Events and Information	Remarks and references to Appendices
HENENCOURT	17/4/16	7 pm	Divisional Routine Trains Part Head Quarters (Failed)	[sig]
"	18/4/16	7 pm	do do	[sig]
"	19/4/16	6.30 pm	do do 4 Trenches	[sig]
"	20/4/16	"	do do	[sig]
"	21/4/16	"	do do	[sig]
"	22/4/16	"	do do	[sig]
"	23/4/16	"	do Trenches & A.D.O.S VII Corps	[sig]
"	24/4/16	6.30 pm	do do	[sig]
"	25/4/16	"	do do & Trenches	[sig]
"	26/4/16	"	do do	[sig]
"	27/4/16	"	do do	[sig]
"	28/4/16	"	do do	[sig]
"	29/4/16	"	do do	[sig]
"	30/4/16	"	do do — Visit of Inspection by D.O.S	[sig] Capt. D.A.D.O.S 8th Divn

Army Form C. 2118.

WAR DIARY
or
INTELLIGENCE SUMMARY.
(Erase heading not required.)

Vol 17

Confidential

War Diary of D.A.D.O.S. 8th Divn
From 1st May 1916. To 31st May 1916
(Appendices — 3)

R.A. Kirby Capt A.O.D.
D.A.D.O.S. 8th Divn

Army Form C. 2118.

WAR DIARY
or
INTELLIGENCE SUMMARY.
(Erase heading not required.)

Instructions regarding War Diaries and Intelligence Summaries are contained in F. S. Regs., Part II. and the Staff Manual respectively. Title pages will be prepared in manuscript.

Place	Date	Hour	Summary of Events and Information	Remarks and references to Appendices
HENENCOURT	1/5/16	6pm	Draft Routine Orders 2122 & Tailored	KG
"	2/5/16	7pm	"	KG
"	3/5/16	"	"	KG
"	4/5/16	"	"	KG
"	5/5/16	7.30	" & Tailored	KG
"	6/5/16	"	"	KG
"	7/5/16	7pm	ADOS III Corps Confce & Tailored	KG
"	8/5/16	"	"	KG
"	9/5/16	"	"	KG
"	10/5/16	"	" & Tailored	KG
"	11/5/16	6.30pm	"	KG
"	12/5/16	"	"	KG
"	13/5/16	7pm	ADOS III Corps Confce & Tailored	KG
"	14/5/16	"	"	KG
"	15/5/16	"	" & Tailored	KG
"	16/5/16	"	"	KG

Army Form C. 2118.

WAR DIARY
or
INTELLIGENCE SUMMARY.
(Erase heading not required.)

Instructions regarding War Diaries and Intelligence Summaries are contained in F. S. Regs., Part II. and the Staff Manual respectively. Title pages will be prepared in manuscript.

Place	Date	Hour	Summary of Events and Information	Remarks and references to Appendices
HEMENCOURT	17/5/16	7pm	Divisional Routine	K9
"	18/5/16	"	"	K9
"	19/5/16	"	" + Hawthorn	K9
"	20/5/16	6/30pm	" + ADOS III Corps	K9
"	21/5/16	7pm	"	K9
"	22/5/16	"	Capt KCGREIG proceeded on leave. Duties performed during absence by 2nd Lieut H.E.ELLIS 11 Sherwood Foresters	K9
"	23/5/16	"	Divisional Routine	418.
"	24/5/16	"	"	418.
"	25/5/16	"	"	1118.
"	26/5/16	"	"	1118.
"	27/5/16	"	"	1118.
"	28/5/16	"	"	418.
"	29/5/16	"	"	1118. 3/14
"	30/5/16	"	"	3/14
"	31/5/16	"	"	1118.

K.C.Greig Capt
ADOS 8th Division
1/6/16

Army Form C. 2118.

WK 19

WAR DIARY
or
INTELLIGENCE SUMMARY
(Erase heading not required.)

Instructions regarding War Diaries and Intelligence Summaries are contained in F. S. Regs., Part II. and the Staff Manual respectively. Title pages will be prepared in manuscript.

Hour, Date, Place	Summary of Events and Information	Remarks and references to Appendices
	Confidential	
	War Diary of D.A.D.O.S. 8th Divn from 1st July 1916 to 31st July 1916 (Volume 15)	D.A.D.O.S. 8th Divn 1st July 1916 to 31st July 1916
	[signature] Major D.A.D.O.S. 8th Divn	
	1/8/16	

1247 W 3299 200,000 (E) 8/14 J.B.C. & A. Forms/C. 2118/11.

Army Form C. 2118.

WAR DIARY
or
INTELLIGENCE SUMMARY.
(Erase heading not required.)

Instructions regarding War Diaries and Intelligence Summaries are contained in F.S. Regs., Part II. and the Staff Manual respectively. Title pages will be prepared in manuscript.

Place	Date	Hour	Summary of Events and Information	Remarks and references to Appendices
HEMENCOURT	1/7/16	7.30	Divisional Routine. Divl Headquarters Railhead	KOR
BELLOY	2/7/16	"	Divisional HQuarters moved to BELLOY S/SOMME Railhead VIGNACOURT	KOR
"	3/7/16	7 p	Divisional Routine. Divl HQuarters & Railhead	KOR
CAPILLON	4/7/16	7.30	Divl HQrs moved to CAPILLON. Railhead Do	KOR
"	5/7/16	"	Divisional Routine. Divl Railhead & Headquarters	KOR
"	6/7/16	7 p	do Divl Headquarters	KOR
BRAY	7/7/16	6.30	Divl Headqrs moved to BRAY. Railhead LILLERS	KOR
"	8/7/16	7.30	Divl Divl Headqrs & Railhead + APOS I Corps	KOR
"	9/7/16	7 p	Divisional Routine & Divl Headquarters	KOR
"	10/7/16	"	do	KOR
"	11/7/16	7.30	do	KOR
"	12/7/16	"	do & Railhead	KOR
"	13/7/16	"	do	KOR
"	14/7/16	6.30	do	KOR
BETHUNE	15/7/16	6.30	Divl Head Quarters moved to BETHUNE Railhead LILLERS	KOR
"	16/7/16	7 p	Divisional Routine. Divl HeadQuarters Railhead BETHUNE	KOR

WAR DIARY
or
INTELLIGENCE SUMMARY.
(Erase heading not required.)

Army Form C. 2118.

Instructions regarding War Diaries and Intelligence Summaries are contained in F.S. Regs., Part II. and the Staff Manual respectively. Title pages will be prepared in manuscript.

Place	Date	Hour	Summary of Events and Information	Remarks and references to Appendices
BETHUNE	17/7/16	7p	Divisional Routine Orders Div Headquarters	KS
"	18/7/16		do do	KS
"	19/7/16		do do 1 Reinforcement	KS
"	20/7/16		do do	KS
"	21/7/16		do do	KS
"	22/7/16		do Div Headquarters moves to SAILLY LA BOURSE	KS
"	23/7/16		do Div Headquarters	KS
"	24/7/16		do do 4 Reinforcements	KS
"	25/7/16		do Reinfd removes to NOEUX LES MINES Div Headquarters	KS
"	26/7/16		do do Div Headquarters	KS
"	27/7/16		do do	KS
"	28/7/16		do do 4 Reinforcements	KS
"	29/7/16		do do	KS
LA BOURSE	30/7/16		do Ordnance Depot moves to LA BOURSE Div Headquarters	KS
"	31/7/16		do Div Headquarters	KS

H. Stephens Capt
DADOS
2nd Division

1/8/16.

Army Form C. 2118.

WAR DIARY
or
INTELLIGENCE SUMMARY
(Erase heading not required.)

Instructions regarding War Diaries and Intelligence Summaries are contained in F. S. Regs., Part II. and the Staff Manual respectively. Title pages will be prepared in manuscript.

Hour, Date, Place	Summary of Events and Information	Remarks and references to Appendices
	Confidential	
	War Diary of D.A.D.O.S. P. to Div from 1st August 1916 to 31st August 1916 (Volume 16)	
	1/9/16.	

Army Form C. 2118.

WAR DIARY
or
INTELLIGENCE SUMMARY

(Erase heading not required.)

Instructions regarding War Diaries and Intelligence Summaries are contained in F. S. Regs., Part II. and the Staff Manual respectively. Title pages will be prepared in manuscript.

Hour, Date, Place	Summary of Events and Information	Remarks and references to Appendices
LA BOURSE 1/8/16 7p	Divisional Routine Orders Nos. in (DRO)	
2/8/16	do	
3/8/16	do	
4/8/16	do	
5/8/16	do	do	Stackhead
6/8/16	do	do	
7/8/16	do	do	HQ DD 1 Corps
8/8/16	do	do	Stackhead
9/8/16	do	do	
10/8/16	do	do	
11/8/16	do	do	
12/8/16	do	do	
13/8/16	do	do	
14/8/16	do	do	
15/8/16	do	do	ADOS 1st Corps
16/8/16	do	do	HQ DD 1st Army
17/8/16	do		
18/8/16	do		

Army Form C. 2118.

WAR DIARY
or
INTELLIGENCE SUMMARY

(Erase heading not required.)

Instructions regarding War Diaries and Intelligence Summaries are contained in F. S. Regs., Part II. and the Staff Manual respectively. Title pages will be prepared in manuscript.

Hour, Date, Place	Summary of Events and Information	Remarks and references to Appendices
LA BOURSE 19/8/16	Divisional Mounted Troops Divl HeadQuarters	
20/8/16	do do	
21/8/16	do do	
22/8/16	do do	
23/8/16	do do Staff Work	
24/8/16	do do	
25/8/16	do do	
26/8/16	do do	
27/8/16	do do	
28/8/16	do do	
29/8/16	do do	
30/8/16	do do	
31/8/16	do do	
31/8/16		Kenning Capt D.A.D.O.S 2nd Divn

Army Form C. 2118.

WAR DIARY
or
INTELLIGENCE SUMMARY

(Erase heading not required.)

Summary of Events and Information	Remarks and references to Appendices
Confidential	
War Diary of DADOS to Divn from 1st September 1916 to 30th Sept 1916. (Volume 4)	

Signed
DADOS
8th Divn

DADOS Form C 21

Army Form C. 2118.

WAR DIARY
or
INTELLIGENCE SUMMARY

(Erase heading not required.)

Instructions regarding War Diaries and Intelligence Summaries are contained in F. S. Regs., Part II. and the Staff Manual respectively. Title pages will be prepared in manuscript.

Hour, Date, Place	Summary of Events and Information	Remarks and references to Appendices
LABOURSE 1/9/16 7²⁄₅	Divisional Routine Orders Daily Road for	[signature]
2/9/16 "	do do do (MOEUVRES MINES)	[signature]
3/9/16 "	do do	[signature]
4/9/16 "	do do	[signature]
5/9/16 "	do do	[signature]
6/9/16 "	do do ADOS 1ˢᵗ Corps	[signature]
7/9/16 "	do do	[signature]
8/9/16 "	do do	[signature]
9/9/16 "	do do	[signature]
10/9/16 "	do do ADOS 1ˢᵗ Corps	[signature]
11/9/16 "	do do	[signature]
12/9/16 "	do do	[signature]
13/9/16 "	do do	[signature]
14/9/16 "	do do Fauchere	[signature]
15/9/16 "	do do	[signature]
16/9/16 "	do do	[signature]
17/9/16 "	do do	[signature]
18/9/16 "	do do	[signature]
19/9/16 "	do do	[signature]
20/9/16 "	do do	[signature]

Army Form C. 2118.

WAR DIARY
or
INTELLIGENCE SUMMARY
(Erase heading not required.)

Instructions regarding War Diaries and Intelligence Summaries are contained in F.S. Regs., Part II. and the Staff Manual respectively. Title pages will be prepared in manuscript.

Hour, Date, Place	Summary of Events and Information	Remarks and references to Appendices
LABOURSE 21/9/16 7PM	Divisional Honhous Charges ARAOTH (Dul)	
22/9/16 "	do do & Railhead	
23/9/16 "	do do	
24/9/16 "	do do	
25/9/16 "	do do & ADOS 1st Corps	
26/9/16 "	do do	
27/9/16 "	do do	
28/9/16 "	do do & ADOS 1st Corps	
29/9/16 "	do do	
30/9/16 "	do	

1/10/16.

Lt Col
DADOS
2nd Div

Army Form C. 2118.

Vol 22

WAR DIARY
or
INTELLIGENCE SUMMARY

(Erase heading not required.)

Instructions regarding War Diaries and Intelligence Summaries are contained in F. S. Regs., Part II. and the Staff Manual respectively. Title pages will be prepared in manuscript.

Hour, Date, Place	Summary of Events and Information	Remarks and references to Appendices
	Confidential	
	War Diary of DADOS 8th Divn From 1st Oct to 31st Oct 19.	
	(Volume 8)	
	[signed] Capt. DADOS 8th Divn	

Army Form C. 2118.

WAR DIARY
or
INTELLIGENCE SUMMARY
(Erase heading not required.)

Instructions regarding War Diaries and Intelligence Summaries are contained in F.S. Regs., Part II. and the Staff Manual respectively. Title pages will be prepared in manuscript.

Hour, Date, Place			Summary of Events and Information	Remarks and references to Appendices
LA BOURSE	1/10/16	7pm	Divisional Routine Orders Duke HQ 2/c.	KR
	2/10/16	7pm	do & ADOS 1st Corps	KR
	3/10/16	do	do	KR
	4/10/16	do	do 46 Railhead	KR
	5/10/16	do	do	KR
	6/10/16	do	do & ADOS 1st Corps	KR
	7/10/16	"	do	KR
	8/10/16	"	do	KR
	9/10/16	"	do (Railhead)	KR
	10/10/16	7.30	do & ADOS 1st Corps	KR
	11/10/16	7.90	do	KR
	12/10/16	7.30	do	KR
	13/10/16	8.0	do & Railhead	KR
HALLENCOURT	14/10/16		Division move to HALLENCOURT RAILHEAD HANGEST	KR
	15/10/16		" under orders to move Orders ADOS XIV Corps	KR
TREUX	16/10/16		" move to TREUX Railhead EDGE HILL	KR
	17/10/16		Division under orders to move Orders Railhead	KR
	18/10/16		do	KR
	19/10/16		do	KR

Army Form C. 2118.

WAR DIARY
or
INTELLIGENCE SUMMARY
(Erase heading not required.)

Instructions regarding War Diaries and Intelligence Summaries are contained in F.S. Regs., Part II. and the Staff Manual respectively. Title pages will be prepared in manuscript.

Hour, Date, Place			Summary of Events and Information	Remarks and references to Appendices
CARNOY	20/10/16	7.30	Division moved to CARNOY PLATEAU.	KS
"	21/10/16	7.30	Divisional Routine	KS
"	22/10/16	7 pm	do	KS
"	23/10/16	7 pm	do	KS
"	24/10/16	8 pm	do & Bairshead & Div. H.Q. ADOS XIV Corps	KS
"	25/10/16	do	do & Bairshead	KS
"	26/10/16	7 pm	do & ADOS XIV Corps	KS
"	27/10/16	"	do & Bairshead	KS
"	28/10/16	"	do	KS
"	29/10/16	"	do	KS
"	30/10/16	"	do Div. H.Q. moved to	KS
"	31/10/16	"	Bairshead to EDGE HILL	KS

31/10/16

R. Young Capt.
DADOS
p. too

Army Form C. 2118.

WAR DIARY
or
INTELLIGENCE SUMMARY
(Erase heading not required.)

Instructions regarding War Diaries and Intelligence Summaries are contained in F. S. Regs., Part II. and the Staff Manual respectively. Title pages will be prepared in manuscript.

Hour, Date, Place	Summary of Events and Information	Remarks and references to Appendices
	Confidential War Diary of DADOS 8th Divn from 1st Nov 1916 to 30th Nov 1916 (Volume 19) H. Keating Capt DADOS 8th Divn	Vol 23

Army Form C. 2118.

WAR DIARY
or
INTELLIGENCE SUMMARY
(Erase heading not required.)

Instructions regarding War Diaries and Intelligence Summaries are contained in F. S. Regs., Part II. and the Staff Manual respectively. Title pages will be prepared in manuscript.

Hour, Date, Place			Summary of Events and Information	Remarks and references to Appendices
CARNOY	1/11/16	8.30 pm	Divisional Routine Orders Dud 31.10.16 at TRIEUX Packed EDGE HILL	[signature]
"	2/11/16	"	do	[signature]
"	3/11/16	7 pm	Orders Div of 2.11.16 at Packhed	[signature]
"	4/11/16	7.30	do	[signature]
"	5/11/16	do	do	[signature]
"	6/11/16	do	do → ADOS XIV Corps	[signature]
"	7/11/16	7.30	do → Packhed	[signature]
"	8/11/16	7 pm	do	[signature]
"	9/11/16	do	do Rd Tp of MONTAUBAN Packhed PLATEAU	[signature]
"	10/11/16	do	do	[signature]
"	11/11/16	8 am	do → Packhed	[signature]
"	12/11/16	do	do	[signature]
"	13/11/16	do	do → ADOS XIV Corps	[signature]
"	14/11/16	do	do	[signature]
"	15/11/16	do	do	[signature]
"	16/11/16	7.30 pm	do	[signature]

Army Form C. 2118.

WAR DIARY
or
INTELLIGENCE SUMMARY

(Erase heading not required.)

Instructions regarding War Diaries and Intelligence Summaries are contained in F. S. Regs., Part II. and the Staff Manual respectively. Title pages will be prepared in manuscript.

Hour, Date, Place	Summary of Events and Information	Remarks and references to Appendices
TREUX 18/11/6 8 p.m.	Division moved to TREUX further EDGEHIVE	KS
BELLOY 19/11/6	" " BELLOY ST LEONARD further	KS
" 20/11/6 8.30	Division at Rothure Reserve Divn. 4th Army	KS
" 24/11/6 8 p.m.	do	KS
" 27/11/6 do	do y AROS XV Corps	KS
" 25/11/6 9.30 p.m.	do y Gaukland	KS
" 24/11/6 do	do	KS
" 25/11/6 do	do	KS
" 26/11/6 do	do Gaukland	KS
" 27/11/16 7 p.m.	do do	KS
" 28/11/16 8 p.m.	do	KS
" 29/11/16 do	do	KS
" 30/11/16 do	do	KS

Nesbury Capt.
DAA & QMG
2nd Divn

Army Form C. 2118.

DADOS Vol 24

WAR DIARY
or
INTELLIGENCE SUMMARY

(Erase heading not required.)

Instructions regarding War Diaries and Intelligence Summaries are contained in F. S. Regs., Part II. and the Staff Manual respectively. Title pages will be prepared in manuscript.

Hour, Date, Place	Summary of Events and Information	Remarks and references to Appendices
	Confidential War Diary of D.A.D.O.S. 8th Division from 1st Dec 1916 to 31st Dec 1916 (Volume 20) [signature] Capt DADOS 8th Divn 14/1/7	

Army Form C. 2118.

WAR DIARY
or
INTELLIGENCE SUMMARY
(Erase heading not required.)

Instructions regarding War Diaries and Intelligence Summaries are contained in F.S. Regs., Part II. and the Staff Manual respectively. Title pages will be prepared in manuscript.

Hour, Date, Place	Summary of Events and Information	Remarks and references to Appendices
BELLOY ST LEONARD 1/11/16 7pm	Divisional Routine Orders Dist Spead Quarters	HQ
2/11/16 "	do	HQ
3/11/16 8pm	do	HQ
4/11/16 7pm	do ADOS XV Corps	HQ
5/11/16 do	do —Parkes	HQ
6/11/16 do	do	HQ
7/11/16 7.30pm	Capt K.G. GREIG DADOS proceeded on 10 days leave to England	HQ
	Duties undertaken by Revd F Henderson CLELAND, Scottish Rifles	
8/11/16 to 16th Dec	Divisional Routine Orders on	HQ
7/11/16 7pm	do Capt K.C.G. GREIG returned from leave	HQ
8/11/16 "	do and took over from Revd F. Parker	HQ
9/11/16 do	do T.O.M	HQ
10/11/16 7.30	do	HQ
21/11/16 do	do	HQ
22/11/16 do	do	HQ
23/11/16 do	do	HQ
24/11/16 do	do +Parker	HQ
25/11/16 do	do	HQ
26/11/16 do	do	HQ
1/12/16 do	do	HQ
2/12/16 do	do	HQ
8/12/16 do	do	HQ
9/12/16 do	do +Parker	HQ
10/12/16 do	do	HQ
11/12/16 do	do	HQ
12/12/16 do	do	HQ

Army Form C. 2118.

WAR DIARY
or
INTELLIGENCE SUMMARY
(Erase heading not required.)

Vol 25

Instructions regarding War Diaries and Intelligence Summaries are contained in F. S. Regs., Part II. and the Staff Manual respectively. Title pages will be prepared in manuscript.

Hour, Date, Place	Summary of Events and Information	Remarks and references to Appendices
	Confidential	
	War Diary of DADOS 8th Divn from 1st January 1917 to 31st January 1917 (Volume 2)	
	R Young Colonel DADOS 8th Divn	

Army Form C. 2118.

WAR DIARY
or
INTELLIGENCE SUMMARY

(Erase heading not required.)

Instructions regarding War Diaries and Intelligence Summaries are contained in F.S. Regs., Part II. and the Staff Manual respectively. Title pages will be prepared in manuscript.

Hour, Date, Place	Summary of Events and Information	Remarks and references to Appendices
BRAY 1/1/17	Division at BRAY. Railhead BRAY. Trains ADOS XIV Corps	MS
2/1/17	Divisional Reserve. Trains Div MT & Railhead	MS
3/1/17	do	ASS
4/1/17	do	AM
5/1/17	do — & ADOS XV Corps	MS
6/1/17	do	MS
7/1/17	do	ASS
8/1/17	do	MSS
9/1/17	do	MOS
10/1/17	do — to Railhead	PS
BELLOY ST LEONARD 11/1/17	Division moves to BELLOY ST LEONARD. Railhead HANGEST. Divisional Reserve. Trains Divisional Res. Dp & Railhead	MS
12/1/17	do & Railhead	NS
13/1/17	do	MS
14/1/17	do	ASS
15/1/17	do	AOS
16/1/17	do	MSS
17/1/17	do	MS
18/1/17	do	KSS
19/1/17	do	NSS
		ASS

1247 W 8299 200,000 (E) 8/14 J.B.C. & A. Forms/C. 2118/11.

Army Form C. 2118.

WAR DIARY
or
INTELLIGENCE SUMMARY

(Erase heading not required.)

Instructions regarding War Diaries and Intelligence
Summaries are contained in F. S. Regs., Part II.
and the Staff Manual respectively. Title pages
will be prepared in manuscript.

Hour, Date, Place	Summary of Events and Information	Remarks and references to Appendices
BELLOY ST LEONARD		
20/1/17	Personnel Routine Works Donnevral ReasDr.	
21/1/17	do	
22/1/17	do + Gawkers	
23/1/17	do	
CHIPILLY		
24/1/17	Divan move to CHIPILLY Relieved DELHR. onto DADOS 4 Army	
25/1/17	Personnel Routine Works Divonal keet Gawfire	
26/1/17	do do + works by DADOS	
27/1/17	do	
BRAY		
28/1/17	Divan move to BRAY. Routines BRAY	
29/1/17	Divonal Routine Ordered Routines + DADS XV Corps	
30/1/17	do	
31/1/17	do	

RSpring Capt
DADOS
8th Divn

1/4/17

Army Form C. 2118.

No. M 26

WAR DIARY
or
INTELLIGENCE SUMMARY

(Erase heading not required.)

Confidential

War Diary of DADOS 8th Divn
from 1st Feb 1917 to 28th Feb 1917
(Volume 22)

R Strongh Capt
DADOS
8th Divn

Army Form C. 2118.

WAR DIARY
or
INTELLIGENCE SUMMARY
(Erase heading not required.)

Instructions regarding War Diaries and Intelligence Summaries are contained in F. S. Regs., Part II. and the Staff Manual respectively. Title pages will be prepared in manuscript.

Hour, Date, Place		Summary of Events and Information	Remarks and references to Appendices
BRAY	1/7/17	Divl. Rowhrs. Charges Railhead	[sig]
"	2/7/17	do	[sig]
"	3/7/17	do Marker Railhead	[sig]
"	4/7/17	do	[sig]
"	5/7/17	do	[sig]
"	6/7/17	do visits ADOS XV Corps & Divisional H.Q.	[sig]
"	7/7/17	do Visits Div. Ip. Dn.	[sig]
"	8/7/17	do do	[sig]
"	9/7/17	do do	[sig]
"	10/7/17	do do + Railhead	[sig]
CHIPILLY	11/7/17	Domicile at CORDIE. Railhead BELAIR. Visits H.Q.	[sig]
"	12/7/17	Divisional Routine Visits Div. Sup. Dn.	[sig]
"	13/7/17	do	[sig]
"	14/7/17	do + ADOS XV Corps.	[sig]
"	15/7/17	do + Railhead	[sig]
"	16/7/17	do	[sig]
"	17/7/17	do	[sig]
"	18/7/17	do Gave lunches at Railhead as no Office allowed	[sig]
"	19/7/17	do	[sig]
"	20/7/17	do	[sig]

Army Form C. 2118.

WAR DIARY
or
INTELLIGENCE SUMMARY

(Erase heading not required.)

Instructions regarding War Diaries and Intelligence Summaries are contained in F. S. Regs., Part II. and the Staff Manual respectively. Title pages will be prepared in manuscript.

Hour, Date, Place			Summary of Events and Information	Remarks and references to Appendices
CHIPILLY	2/4/17	7pm	Divisional Routine. Viartes Div HQ Moves dumps at Radbed.	RCg
"	22/4/17	"	do Div HQ moves to CURLU.	RCg
"	23/4/17	"	do Reserved to respond morning view of evacuation of store Railhead BRAY.	RCg
"	24/4/17	"	do Viartes Railhead moves Div RQr.	RCg
"	25/4/17	"	do	RCg
"	26/4/17	"	do	RCg
SUZANNE	27/4/17	"	Move to SUZANNE. Ammn Base to continue moves moves Div RQr	RCg
"	28/4/17	"	Divisional Routine.	RCg
"	29/4/17	"	do	RCg

2/3/17.

Stephen Cope
DAPOS
8 Div

Army Form C. 2118.

WAR DIARY
or
INTELLIGENCE SUMMARY
(Erase heading not required.)

Confidential

War Diary of R.A.D.O.S. 2nd Army
from 1st March 1917 to 31st March 1917

(Vol 23)

Acting Capt
DADOS
2nd Army

Army Form C. 2118.

WAR DIARY
or
INTELLIGENCE SUMMARY

(Erase heading not required.)

Instructions regarding War Diaries and Intelligence Summaries are contained in F. S. Regs., Part II. and the Staff Manual respectively. Title pages will be prepared in manuscript.

Hour, Date, Place		Summary of Events and Information	Remarks and references to Appendices
SUZANNE	1/3/17	Divisional Routine. Divisional Schedules	[initials]
	2/3/17	do. Visits DG HQrs	[initials]
	3/3/17	do.	[initials]
	4/3/17	do. + Fairhead	[initials]
	5/3/17	do.	[initials]
	6/3/17	do. + ADOS XV Corps	[initials]
	7/3/17	do. + Fairhead	[initials]
	8/3/17	do.	[initials]
BRAY	9/3/17	Moved to BRAY. Div HQ to MARTINPAS.	[initials]
	10/3/17	Divisional Routine. Visited RE Offr	[initials]
	11/3/17	do.	[initials]
	12/3/17	do. + Fairhead	[initials]
	13/3/17	do.	[initials]
	14/3/17	do.	[initials]
	15/3/17	do. + ADOS XV Corps	[initials]
	16/3/17	do. + Fairhead	[initials]
	17/3/17	do.	[initials]
	18/3/17	do. + Fairhead	[initials]
	19/3/17	do.	[initials]
	20/3/17	do. + Fairhead	[initials]

Army Form C. 2118.

WAR DIARY
or
INTELLIGENCE SUMMARY
(Erase heading not required.)

Instructions regarding War Diaries and Intelligence Summaries are contained in F. S. Regs., Part II. and the Staff Manual respectively. Title pages will be prepared in manuscript.

Hour, Date, Place	Summary of Events and Information	Remarks and references to Appendices
BRAY 21/2/17 7pm	Divisional Routine orders	Roy
SUZANNE 22/2/17	Move to Camp 2a (SUZANNE)	Roy
23/2/17	Divisional Routine	Roy
24/2/17	do. & ADOS XI Corps	Roy
25/2/17	do.	Roy
26/2/17	do. & Aeroplane	Roy
27/2/17	do.	Roy
28/2/17	do.	Roy
CURLU 1/3/17	Move to CURLU (Camp 76).	Roy
2/3/17	Routine	Roy
3/3/17	do. & Aeroplane	Roy
4/3/17	do.	Roy
5/3/17	do. & ADOS XI Corps	Roy

11/4/17

Manning Capn
D.A.D.O.S
33 Div

Army Form C. 2118.

WAR DIARY
or
INTELLIGENCE SUMMARY

(Erase heading not required.)

Confidential

War Diary of D.2 Division Dep
from 1st March 1917 to 30 April 1917

(inclusive)

K Spring Capt
Dep: O.C.
2nd Div

1917

Army Form C. 2118.

WAR DIARY
or
INTELLIGENCE SUMMARY

(Erase heading not required.)

Instructions regarding War Diaries and Intelligence Summaries are contained in F. S. Regs., Part II. and the Staff Manual respectively. Title pages will be prepared in manuscript.

Hour, Date, Place	Summary of Events and Information	Remarks and references to Appendices
CURLU 1/4/17 10am	Divisional Routine. Orders Div HQ & ADOS & V Corps.	
2/4/17	do. Lieut M.T. SMITH AOD joined for instruction	
3/4/17	do. Orders DW HQ & Bucked (BRAY)	
4/4/17	do.	
5/4/17	do.	
6/4/17	do. + ADOS II Corps	
7/4/17	do.	
8/4/17	do.	
9/4/17	do.	
MOISLAINS 10/4/17	Div. moves to MOISLAINS. Orders Div HQrs.	
11/4/17	Orders Div HQrs.	
12/4/17	do.	
13/4/17	do.	
14/4/17	do. + Roisel	
15/4/17	do. + ADOS IV Corps	
16/4/17	CAPT K.C. GREIG proceeded to leave. Lieut M.T. SMITH A.O.D.	
17/4/17	do. Visited Divl HQ and A.D.O.S. XV Corps	A.8.
18/4/17	do. ditto	A.8.

Army Form C. 2118.

WAR DIARY
or
INTELLIGENCE SUMMARY

(Erase heading not required.)

Instructions regarding War Diaries and Intelligence Summaries are contained in F. S. Regs., Part II. and the Staff Manual respectively. Title pages will be prepared in manuscript.

Hour, Date, Place	Summary of Events and Information	Remarks and references to Appendices
MOISLAINS. 19/4/17	Battalion Rested and visited by H.Q.	A.9.
20/3/17	Ditto	A.9.
21/4/17	Ditto	A.9.
22/4/17	Ditto. Battalion moved to GUIZON C H.Q.	
MURLU 23/4/17	Ditto. moved to MURLU	A.9.
24/4/17	Ditto	A.9.
25/4/17	Ditto	A.9.
26/4/17	Ditto and Ranknest at P.30.5	A.9.
27/4/17	Ditto	A.9.
28/4/17	Ditto Captain Going returned from leave and returned to duties	A.9.
29/4/17	Do works carried	
30/4/17	do	
	1/5/17	

[signature]

Army Form C. 2118.

WAR DIARY
or
INTELLIGENCE SUMMARY.
(Erase heading not required.)

Vol 29

Instructions regarding War Diaries and Intelligence Summaries are contained in F. S. Regs., Part II. and the Staff Manual respectively. Title pages will be prepared in manuscript.

Place	Date	Hour	Summary of Events and Information	Remarks and references to Appendices
			Confidential	
			War Diary of D.A.D.O.S. 8th Division from 1st May 1917 to 31st May 1917 (App 25)	
	1917		R Seymour Cox D.A.D.O.S. 8th Divn	

Army Form C. 2118

WAR DIARY
or
INTELLIGENCE SUMMARY

(Erase heading not required.)

Instructions regarding War Diaries and Intelligence Summaries are contained in F. S. Regs., Part II. and the Staff Manual respectively. Title pages will be prepared in manuscript.

Hour, Date, Place	Summary of Events and Information	Remarks and references to Appendices
NIEPPE 1/5/17	Depot Routine	
2/5/17	do	
3/5/17	do	
4/5/17	do	
5/5/17	do	
6/5/17	do	Nieppe B.H. Finished (Painted GREEN)
7/5/17	do	do Garage Pump
8/5/17	do	do
9/5/17	do	do
10/5/17	do	do ADOS XI Corps
11/5/17	do	do inspected
12/5/17	do	do
13/5/17	do	do
14/5/17	do	do ADOS XI Corps
15/5/17	do	do inspected
16/5/17	do	do
17/5/17	do	do ADOS XI Corps
18/5/17	do	do
19/5/17	do	do
20/5/17	do	do Finished
21/5/17	do	do
22/5/17	do	do ADOS XI Corps
23/5/17	do	do

Army Form C. 2118.

WAR DIARY
or
INTELLIGENCE SUMMARY.
(Erase heading not required.)

Instructions regarding War Diaries and Intelligence Summaries are contained in F. S. Regs., Part II. and the Staff Manual respectively. Title pages will be prepared in manuscript.

Place	Date	Hour	Summary of Events and Information	Remarks and references to Appendices
NURLU	23/5/17	7am	Depot Bathue moved to HQ	
"	24/5/17	"	Do & Bakehouse YADOS II Corps.	
"	25/5/17	"	Do	
"	26/5/17	"	Do	
"	27/5/17	"	Do attached	
"	28/5/17	"	Do	
"	29/5/17	"	Do	
CORBIE	30/5/17	"	Moved to CORBIE	
"	31/5/17	"	Arrived Div HQ	

R Stirling Capt
DADOS
8 to Divn

Army Form C. 2118.

WAR DIARY
or
INTELLIGENCE SUMMARY.

(Erase heading not required.)

DA 575

Confidential

War Diary of DADOS 8th Divn
from 1st June 1917 to 30th June 1917
(No. 26)

1/7/17

[signature] Col.
DADOS
8th Divn

Army Form C. 2118.

WAR DIARY
or
INTELLIGENCE SUMMARY.
(Erase heading not required.)

Instructions regarding War Diaries and Intelligence Summaries are contained in F. S. Regs., Part II. and the Staff Manual respectively. Title pages will be prepared in manuscript.

Place	Date	Hour	Summary of Events and Information	Remarks and references to Appendices
METEREN	1/6/17	8pm	Division moved to METEREN Road head CAESTRE	
"	2/6/17	10am	Departmental Routine. Visited Railhead & ADOS XIV Corps & DADVS HQ	
"	3/6/17		do	
"	4/6/17		do	& Railhead
"	5/6/17		do	
"	6/6/17		Visited ADOS XIV Corps & 70M	
"	7/6/17		"	
"	8/6/17		Visited Div ADsc & Railhead	
"	9/6/17		do	
"	10/6/17		do	
"	11/6/17		do & Railhead	
CAESTRE	12/6/17		Division moved to CAESTRE	
"	13/6/17		Dept Routine. Visited Div ADsc	
OUDERDOM (WINNIPEG CAMP)	13/6/17		Division moved to WINNIPEG CAMP Railhead RENINGHELST	
"	14/6/17		Dept Routine. Visited ADOS II Corps & Railhead	
"	15/6/17		Visited Div ADsc	
"	16/6/17		do	

Army Form C. 2118.

WAR DIARY
or
INTELLIGENCE SUMMARY.
(Erase heading not required.)

Instructions regarding War Diaries and Intelligence Summaries are contained in F. S. Regs., Part II. and the Staff Manual respectively. Title pages will be prepared in manuscript.

Place	Date	Hour	Summary of Events and Information	Remarks and references to Appendices
OUDERDOM	17/5/17	—	Departmental Routine. Orders No. 2,000.	
do	18/5/17		do	do ADOS II Corps
"	19/5/17		do	do 9 Stationary
"	20/5/17		do	do 9 "
"	21/5/17		do	do 9 "
"	22/5/17		do	do 9 Stationary
"	23/5/17		do	do "
"	24/5/17		do	do "
"	25/5/17		do	do ADOS II Corps
"	26/5/17		do	do 9 Stationary
"	27/5/17		do	do 9 "
"	28/5/17		do	do
"	29/5/17		do	do 9 Stationary
"	30/5/17		do	

R. Whiting Capt
ADOS
II Corps

Army Form C. 2118.

WAR DIARY
or
INTELLIGENCE SUMMARY.
(Erase heading not required.)

Vol 31

Confidential

War Diary of DADOS 8th Division
from 1st July 1917 to 31st July 1917
(The Curry)

HSmyth Col
DADOS
8th Division

1/8/17

Army Form C. 2118.

WAR DIARY
or
INTELLIGENCE SUMMARY.
(Erase heading not required.)

Place	Date	Hour	Summary of Events and Information	Remarks and references to Appendices
BUSSEBOOM	1/7/17	—	Departmental Routine. Arranged DAC ADOS & Parking	
"	2/7/17		do. do & ADOS II Corps	
"	3/7/17		do do	
"	4/7/17		do do	
"	5/7/17		do & Parking	
"	6/7/17		do do	
"	7/7/17		do & ADOS II Corps	
"	8/7/17		do	
"	9/7/17		do	
BOM?	10/7/17		Division moved to BOMY area	
"	11/7/17		Depot Routine	
"	12/7/17		do	
"	13/7/17		do & forward area for Artillery	
"	14/7/17		do	
"	15/7/17		do & Parking (ALLERTS)	
"	16/7/17		do & forward area	
"	17/7/17		do	
"	18/7/17		do & Parking	
"	19/7/17		do & Parking	

Army Form C. 2118.

WAR DIARY
or
INTELLIGENCE SUMMARY.
(Erase heading not required.)

Instructions regarding War Diaries and Intelligence Summaries are contained in F. S. Regs., Part II. and the Staff Manual respectively. Title pages will be prepared in manuscript.

Place	Date	Hour	Summary of Events and Information	Remarks and references to Appendices
BOMY	17/7/17		Depot Routine. Charles Dir R.E.	
	18/7/17		do do attached	
BUSSEBOOM	19/7/17		Division entrained to BUSSEBOOM attached RENINGHELST	
	20/7/17		Depot Routine. Div H.Q. & ADOS & 5th Army.	
	21/7/17		do do & ADOS II Corps.	
	22/7/17		do do	
	23/7/17		do do attached	
	24/7/17		do do attached	
	25/7/17		do do & ADOS II Corps (Conference)	
	26/7/17		do do	
	27/7/17		do do	
	28/7/17		do do attached	
	29/7/17		do do	
	30/7/17		do do	
	31/7/17		do do	

R. Ching Capt RAD
D.A.D.O.S. 8th Division
31/7/17

Army Form C. 2118.

WAR DIARY
or
INTELLIGENCE SUMMARY.
(Erase heading not required.)

Confidential

War Diary of ADMS 8th Divn
from 1st Aug 1917 to 31st Aug 1917
(Vol 28)

Returning Colt
DADOS
8th Divn

Army Form C. 2118.

WAR DIARY
or
INTELLIGENCE SUMMARY.
(Erase heading not required.)

Instructions regarding War Diaries and Intelligence Summaries are contained in F. S. Regs., Part II. and the Staff Manual respectively. Title pages will be prepared in manuscript.

Place	Date	Hour	Summary of Events and Information	Remarks and references to Appendices
BUSSEBOOM	1/8/17	7pm	Departmental Routine. Visits ADOS II Corps & Div. H.Q.	[initials]
"	2/8/17		do. Visits Div. H.Qrs.	[initials]
"	3/8/17		do. do.	[initials]
"	4/8/17		do. do. & Railhead	[initials]
"	5 "		do. do.	[initials]
"	6 "		do. do.	[initials]
"	7 "		do. do. & ADOS II Corps.	[initials]
"	8 "		do. do. & Railhead	[initials]
"	9 "		do. do.	[initials]
"	10 "		do. do.	[initials]
"	11 "		do. do. & Railhead	[initials]
"	12 "		do. do.	[initials]
"	13 "		do. do. ADOS II Corps.	[initials]
"	14 "		do. do.	[initials]
"	15 "		do. do.	[initials]
"	16 "		do. do.	[initials]

Army Form C. 2118.

WAR DIARY
or
INTELLIGENCE SUMMARY.

(Erase heading not required.)

Instructions regarding War Diaries and Intelligence Summaries are contained in F. S. Regs., Part II. and the Staff Manual respectively. Title pages will be prepared in manuscript.

Place	Date	Hour	Summary of Events and Information	Remarks and references to Appendices
BUSSEBOOM	Aug 17	7pm	Departure Route Marches Du HQ Rouhead	[sig]
	18		do	[sig]
	19		do of HDOS II Corps	[sig]
CAESTRE	20		Move to CAESTRE Rouhead CAESTRE	[sig]
	21		Regimental Tactical Marches ADC & 2nd ANZA Corps of Dir H Qrs	[sig]
	22		Marches Dir H Q & Rouhead	[sig]
	23		N.W. & HDCS Conference	[sig]
	24		do	[sig]
	25		do	[sig]
	26		do	[sig]
DE SEULE	27		Move to DE SEULE at STEENWERCK Rouhead STEENWERCK	[sig]
	28		Departmental Routine	[sig]
	29		do Capt K C GREIG A.O.D. departed on Leave. Duties undertaken by Lieut. from R.H. READ. Rifle Regt & on Duw Secret of Supply	[sig]
	30		do	[sig]
	31		do Third day without stores from Base	[sig]

Army Form C. 2118.

WAR DIARY
or
INTELLIGENCE SUMMARY.
(Erase heading not required.)

Vol 33

Confidential

War Diary of D.A.D.G.S., 8th Division
from 1st September 1917 to 30th September, 1917
(N° 29)

4/10/17

A.D. Tennant
Captain
D.A.D.O.S 8th

Army Form C. 2118.

WAR DIARY
or
INTELLIGENCE SUMMARY.
(Erase heading not required.)

Instructions regarding War Diaries and Intelligence Summaries are contained in F.S. Regs., Part II. and the Staff Manual respectively. Title pages will be prepared in manuscript.

Place	Date	Hour	Summary of Events and Information	Remarks and references to Appendices
De Seule	1/9/17		Departmental Routine	Maj ? for SoMFO
"	2/9/17		"	Maj ? for DADOS
"	3/9/17		"	Maj ? for SoMFO
"	4/9/17		Called on I.O.M.	Maj ? for DADOS
"	5/9/17		Called on Staff Capt 24th & 23rd Brigades	Maj ? for DADOS
"	6/9/17			15
"	7/9/17			15
"	8/9/17			15
"	9/9/17		Capt R.C. GREIG returns from leave	Do
"	10/9/17		Visited DAD	15
"	11/9/17		Do & ADOS XIII Corps & DDOS 2nd Army	15
"	12/9/17		Do Visited 2 DDOS	15
"	13/9/17		Do	15
"	14/9/17		Do aGardens	15
"	15/9/17		Do	15
"	16/9/17		Do	15

Army Form C. 2118.

WAR DIARY
or
INTELLIGENCE SUMMARY.
(Erase heading not required.)

Instructions regarding War Diaries and Intelligence Summaries are contained in F. S. Regs., Part II. and the Staff Manual respectively. Title pages will be prepared in manuscript.

Place	Date	Hour	Summary of Events and Information	Remarks and references to Appendices
DE SEULE	1/9/17		Departmental Routine Duties Fires N gun	
"	10/9/17		do	
"	11/9/17		do	
"	16/9/17		do	
"	20/9/17		do	
"	22/9/17		do	
"	23/9/17		do	
"	24/9/17		do	
"	25/9/17		do	
"	26/9/17		do Capt K C GREIR Handed over duties to Capt A D TENNANT & proceeded to take up duties of DADOS 58 Divn	
"	?		Took over duties of DADOS 8th Divn on transfer from 58th Divn. Authority F.M. 981 of 13.9.17	
"	27/9/17		visited VIII Corps, IInd Army, V ARMY + D.H.Q.	
"	28/9/17		visited Base.	

A D Tennant Capt
29/9/17 DADOS 8th Divn

Army Form C. 2118.

WAR DIARY
or
INTELLIGENCE SUMMARY.
(Erase heading not required.)

WAR DIARY.

Oct 1st – 31st, 1917

D.A.D.O.S. 8th Div.

No. 30

Army Form C. 2118.

WAR DIARY
or
INTELLIGENCE SUMMARY.
(Erase heading not required.)

Instructions regarding War Diaries and Intelligence Summaries are contained in F. S. Regs., Part II. and the Staff Manual respectively. Title pages will be prepared in manuscript.

Place	Date	Hour	Summary of Events and Information	Remarks and references to Appendices
LE SEULE	1/12		Called at D.H.Q. Fourth day NO stores received.	
"	2/12		30 tons stores received – Capt Robinson retd from leave	
"	3/12		Called on A.D.O.S. VIII Corps – D.H.Q.	
"	18/12		4 days without stores. 30 to 35 tons received to day	
"	20/12		visited Base. is delay in receiving stores.	
"	26/12		Capt Parson (WC) AOD reported for temporary instruction as per authority Ord. Comms. North wire N/611 of 24/12	

A D Dennant Capt
DADOS 8th Divn

1/1/17

Army Form C. 2118.

DA4758 8

JM35

WAR DIARY
or
INTELLIGENCE SUMMARY.
(Erase heading not required.)

WAR DIARY

Nov 1 to 30th 1917

No. 31

A Beaumont Capt.
DADOS.

VIII Division

Army Form C. 2118.

WAR DIARY
or
INTELLIGENCE SUMMARY.
(Erase heading not required.)

Instructions regarding War Diaries and Intelligence Summaries are contained in F. S. Regs., Part II. and the Staff Manual respectively. Title pages will be prepared in manuscript.

Place	Date	Hour	Summary of Events and Information	Remarks and references to Appendices
Dr Seule	3/1/17		Capt Brown A.D.P. returned to Base on completion of period of instruction. Visited Base.	
"	4/1/17		Visited G.H.Q.	
"	10/1/17		Visited 1st Can Div & 3rd Can Div re taking over.	
"	12/1/17		Visited 1st Can Div & Mingo & Kilo on site at Blaringhe as a Dressing Station	
"	13/1/17		O/C Section left for Poperinghe accompanied by a/sm Larson to take over 4 posts at Kaslins to replace those handed over to 3rd Australians.	
Poperinghe	14/1/17		Removed to Revd D Mitchell Poperinghe & Lieut Con Robertson to Ypres.	
"	16/1/17		Gen Robertson finished clearing Stores from Dr Seule & valid H.Q. Corps.	
"	17/1/17		Visited Mondelghe where a/m Larson is to take over from 3rd Can Div.	
"	23/1/17		O'Dav instructed to note on the Mondelghe huts also as Poperinghe for Gas Reserve there. Made preliminary arrangements with Town Major.	
			Received orders to move to 24th Bgde had worn on us clothing on demands & they came out of the line. One Bath. Cases for clothing (Showers) on a wire r/Bgde.	
	24/1/17		Came out of line same day as were received. Received Notes HQ & had interview with O.C.	

Army Form C. 2118.

WAR DIARY
or
INTELLIGENCE SUMMARY.
(Erase heading not required.)

Instructions regarding War Diaries and Intelligence Summaries are contained in F. S. Regs., Part II. and the Staff Manual respectively. Title pages will be prepared in manuscript.

Place	Date	Hour	Summary of Events and Information	Remarks and references to Appendices
POPERINGHE	25/7		Visited G & Q	
	26/7		Attended conference at VIII Corps re Gun ahead. Saw Town Major re billets for new D.A.D. Heard rumour to say 49th Div had moved & him that rumour was untrue.	
	27/7		Wrote DADOS 49th Div re Gun return. Advised by Q to be ready to move on 2nd Proxo.	
	29/7		Moved office to Vlamertinghe. Q says place was fixed, but found I had not been done.	
	30/7		Visited new area. Arranged to move on 2nd & 3rd. No phone in yet.	

A Desmond Cpl
DADOS 8th Divn

3/7
12/7

WAR DIARY
or
INTELLIGENCE SUMMARY.

WAR DIARY

Dec 1 – Dec 31ˢᵗ 1917

No 32

A.O. Seward (?) Col
D A D O S
VIII DIVN

Army Form C. 2118.

WAR DIARY
or
INTELLIGENCE SUMMARY.
(Erase heading not required.)

Instructions regarding War Diaries and Intelligence Summaries are contained in F. S. Regs., Part II. and the Staff Manual respectively. Title pages will be prepared in manuscript.

Place	Date	Hour	Summary of Events and Information	Remarks and references to Appendices
Wisernes	13/7/17		No Stores in Dispersal	
"	2/8/17		Moved Office to Wisernes & Dunstores	
VIZERNES	5/8		Cleaning & preparing dismantled Ford Stores to R.A.	
"	8/8/17		Arranged with Capt. Salvage for Revolvers (70) Bandoliers, Petrol tins. Had Co. Lt. 1st service 2nd Lot	
"	12		Issued 23, 24, 25 M.G. Co. has Coy from 31/c —	
"	14		Issued 218 M.G. Co. has Coy at 5 o/c —	
"	26		Lt Chaplin A.O.D. arrived to take over duties of D.A.D.O.S. under Authy IV Army No A 301/400	
VLAMERTINGHE	27		Moved to VLAMERTINGHE	
"	28		Took Lt Chaplin to A.D.O.S. who had not been of here.	
"	29		Received confirmation of move order to proceed to Havre on relief. Autd IV Army No A 301/400 at 24/7 8th Div No C/174/7	
"	30		Handed over A.D.O.S. Coyts	
"	31		Handed over duties of D.A.D.O.S. VIII Divn to Lt Chaplin A.O.D. & proceeds to Havre	

A.D. Semmens Captain
D.A.D.O.S. VIII Divn

Army Form C. 2118.

WAR DIARY
or
INTELLIGENCE SUMMARY.

(Erase heading not required.)

BANDS 8 Bn
9/1/37

WAR DIARY

JANY 1 — JANY 31 — 1918

Nº 33

DADOS VIII DIVN

Army Form C. 2118.

WAR DIARY
or
INTELLIGENCE SUMMARY.
(Erase heading not required.)

Instructions regarding War Diaries and Intelligence Summaries are contained in F. S. Regs., Part II. and the Staff Manual respectively. Title pages will be prepared in manuscript.

Place	Date	Hour	Summary of Events and Information	Remarks and references to Appendices
Vlamertinghe	1/7/18		Reported to ADOS VIII Corps on taking up duties of DADOS on departure of Capt Tennant ADOS	
"	9/7/18		Lorries withdrawn under VIII Corps R.O. 407 and G.S. wagons supplied from Train in lieu. A most unsatisfactory substitute.	
Steenvoorde	18/7/18		Moved from Vlamertinghe this day. Staff taken over from 50th Divn transport unit to an Omnibus Division.	
"	19/31/7/18		Routine - Refitting the Division.	

Ralph Kent A.C.D.
DADOS 8th Divn.

Army Form C. 2118.

WAR DIARY
or
INTELLIGENCE SUMMARY.
(Erase heading not required.)

WAR DIARY
Feby 1 – Feby 28 – 1918

No 34.

Army Form C. 2118.

WAR DIARY
or
INTELLIGENCE SUMMARY.
(Erase heading not required.)

Place	Date	Hour	Summary of Events and Information	Remarks and references to Appendices
Steenwoorde	1/10 2/18		Routine. Refitting the Division.	
Vlamertinghe	11 2/18		Moved from Steenwoorde this day. Took over stores from 29th Division dump situated in 'NISSEN HUTS'. Unsuitable for Ordnance Dump.	
—	15 2/18		Lieut. H.S. Chapten A.O.D., DADOS 9th Divn. Proceeded on leave to U.K. Capt. G.L. Bradley (0621 to Emp.Coy) a/DADOS leave from 16-2-18 to 2-3-18. Capt. G.L. Bradley (0621 to Emp.Coy) a/DADOS	
—	19 2/18		Three 6" Trench Mortars received under Q.M.G. 17/7 (Q.B.3) d/- 2-2-18 for X/87.T.M.B.	
—	20 2/18		Six 6" Trench Mortars received under Q.M.G. 17/7 (Q.B.3) d/- 2-2-18 for Y/87.T.M.B.	
—	21/28 2/18		Routine	

1/3/18.

L. J. Bradley, Captain
for D.A.D.O.S. 9th [Divn]

Army Form C. 2118.

WAR DIARY
or
INTELLIGENCE SUMMARY.

(Erase heading not required.)

WAR DIARY

March 1 — 31 1918

No. 35.

D.A.D.O.S.
8th DIVISION

M(ark-G...
D.A.D.O.S 8th Div

Army Form C. 2118.

WAR DIARY
or
INTELLIGENCE SUMMARY.
(Erase heading not required.)

Instructions regarding War Diaries and Intelligence Summaries are contained in F. S. Regs., Part II. and the Staff Manual respectively. Title pages will be prepared in manuscript.

Place	Date	Hour	Summary of Events and Information	Remarks and references to Appendices
Vlamertinghe	5/3		Capt H.S. Chaplin DADOS 8th Divn returned from leave - detained 2 days	
			hard from Vlamertinghe this day to Abeele. Stores located in offices &	
Abeele			vacated by C.E. XXII Corps.	
	19/3		Capt Robinson. Chief Clerk to DADOS proceeded to UK on 1 month leave.	
			Moved from Abeele this day. Store accommodation in Paper Factory.	
Wizernes	13/3			
Hazebrouck	22/3		Moved from Wizernes this day to V Army Area by road & rail - Stores discharged	
			from troop train at Chaulnes. Removed during the night to Hazebrouck.	
			DADOS to advanced Divn HQ at Villers Carbonnel & forward -	
			Stores moved from Hazebrouck. 158 Yukon packs left to transport not available	
Dorvast	24/3		to carry them. Reserve Stores J Box Respirators to Bovers Railhead	
			moved Stores from Dorvast. All Stores that could be dispensed with	
Jamechon	28/3		Ammunition Shop tools & Office records despatches to Bone from Poix railhead	
			under NCO.	
			On completion of rum issue Domart-sur-la-Luce stores & personnel were placed in	
			charge of 1st Cav. Divn DADOS. DAQS remaining at ADS Divn HQ to superintend the	
			supply of machine guns & parts to replace losses & arrival of branch to Bone in	
			company possible. Stores not yet arrived at railhead despatched to Bone	

T2183. Wt. W709-776. 500000. 4/15. Sir J.C. & S.

WAR DIARY
or
INTELLIGENCE SUMMARY.
(Erase heading not required.)

Army Form C. 2118.

Place	Date	Hour	Summary of Events and Information	Remarks and references to Appendices
Field	21/3		It is recorded that the withdrawal of the transports moved allowed to the Ordnance Officer in Durazzo to be done in the reverse of the same and towards him from taking the necessary steps to have always available a reserve of machine gun magazines and belts &c. When these stores were required the requisite transport for removing – he in some cases is withdrawn from ammunition supply – the stores had to be dumped; hence in order to prevent possible loss of the Stores to the enemy the number of Guns were reduced to a minimum – 600 magazines to some Vickers guns equivalent to 2 teams per gun were retained loose in hansel for this reason	

H. H. ? Captain
D. A. D. O. S. & Infy.

Army Form C. 2118.

WAR DIARY
or
INTELLIGENCE SUMMARY.

(Erase heading not required.)

WAR DIARY

APRIL 1 - 30 1918

No. 36

Army Form C. 2118.

WAR DIARY
or
INTELLIGENCE SUMMARY.
(Erase heading not required.)

Instructions regarding War Diaries and Intelligence Summaries are contained in F. S. Regs., Part II. and the Staff Manual respectively. Title pages will be prepared in manuscript.

Place	Date	Hour	Summary of Events and Information	Remarks and references to Appendices
Cotenchy	1/4		D.A.D.O.S with Advanced Div HQ at COTENCHY. Small advanced Store of Machine Gun found to supply immediate requirements of troops in action.	
Cavillon	3/4		Moved from COTENCHY this day, and also Stores and Personnel from FAMECHON.	
"	5/4		N.C.O. and Office recruits, Armourer's shop tools & returned from Base.	
"	4/4-11/4		Refitting the Division. Losses in Clothing & Equipment Machine Guns on the more important stores made good within this period.	
Hangest	12/4		Office Stores moved this day to HANGEST-SUR-SOMME. The Div Arty holding reserve line & Angatts being in reserve East of AMIENS. All Stores were arranged to suit by lorry.	
"	16/4		Conf. Reference Chief Clerk to Staff returned from leave, having been detained at Base.	
Longpre	18/4		Division less Arty relieved from reserve line. Office Stores moved to LONGPRE-L'AMIENS.	
"	19/4		Div Arty moved to Artillery concentration area tonight. W.O. = 2 O.R. detailed to accompany Arty HQ.	
Camon	20/4		Division taken over Section of front line, Office Stores moved to CAMON.	
"	22/4		Reported to C.R.A who had confirmed as to movements in which the refitting of his unit was being arranged. Saw D.D.O.S to have Army troops & arrange matters	

Army Form C. 2118.

WAR DIARY
or
INTELLIGENCE SUMMARY.
(Erase heading not required.)

Instructions regarding War Diaries and Intelligence Summaries are contained in F. S. Regs., Part II. and the Staff Manual respectively. Title pages will be prepared in manuscript.

Place	Date	Hour	Summary of Events and Information	Remarks and references to Appendices
Cannon	22/4		To satisfaction of C.R.A. Reported to A.D. of Corps viewing ammunition & lorries & clothing & stores generally.	
"	25/4		Owing to unsettled condition of affairs on the front held by the Div. had orders to bring ammunition stores to CAMON, and to store received munitions was to be dumped at LONGPRÉ-L'AMIENS. Permanent were forwarded appointments for reserve.	

H.S.Hughes Capt.
D.A.D.O.S. 2nd Div.
May 5/1918.

Army Form C. 2118.

WAR DIARY
or
INTELLIGENCE SUMMARY.

(Erase heading not required.)

WAR DIARY.

MAY 1 – 31 1918

No. 37

8th Division

Army Form C. 2118.

WAR DIARY
or
INTELLIGENCE SUMMARY.
(Erase heading not required.)

Instructions regarding War Diaries and Intelligence Summaries are contained in F.S. Regs., Part II. and the Staff Manual respectively. Title pages will be prepared in manuscript.

Place	Date	Hour	Summary of Events and Information	Remarks and references to Appendices
Camon	1/5.		Moved this day to HUPPY near ABBEVILLE, from CAMON and LONGPRÉ - 19 lorry loads of Stores, the accumulation of one week's receipts from Base.	
Huppy	3/5.		Lt. Snutshall A.O.D. attached for instruction, ordered to report to 47th Divn. The Divn. entrained commencing this day at SALEUX, to proceed to VI French Army Area.	
Chéry-Chartreuve	4/5		Detrained at FINARPUAUENUAIVSA FISMES & proceeded to CHÉRY-CHARTREUVE. Called on A.D.O.S. IX Corps who was out.	
"	5/5 – 11/5		Routine, refitting the Divn.	
Ventelay	12/5		Moved this day to VENTELAY, Divn. HQ being at ROUCY.	
"	15/5		8 lorries allotted the Divn. for General Purposes & attached to D.A.O.S. 2 for Post, 1 for Laundry, 1 for Canteen, 4 for Ordnance. These lorries were to be detailed for duty daily by Q. on application being made the previous evening.	
"	17/5		Conference of D.A.D's.O.S. at Corps HQ. convened by A.D.O.S. Discussion of General matters and of procedure on opening of IX Corps Gun Park.	
"	18/5 – 20/5		Routine.	
"	27/5		Enemy attack commenced 1 am. VENTELAY shelled continuously from nightfall. Considerable amount of gas in the village in the early morning that has not known till early morning –	

T2134. Wt. W708-776. 500000. 4/15. Sir J. C. & S.

Army Form C. 2118.

WAR DIARY
or
INTELLIGENCE SUMMARY.
(Erase heading not required.)

Instructions regarding War Diaries and Intelligence Summaries are contained in F. S. Regs., Part II. and the Staff Manual respectively. Title pages will be prepared in manuscript.

Place	Date	Hour	Summary of Events and Information	Remarks and references to Appendices
Venteley	27/5	8/30 a.m.	Instructions received for all available lorries to proceed to Div. HQ. Rovey; therefore have were available to move Ordnance Stores in the event of a retirement becoming necessary.	
"	"	11 noon	The Position was reported as being Serious. No lorries yet returned, or others received, so a written request for extra lorries was forwarded to HQ. Nor were following.	
"	"	2 p.m.	Sen. Supply Commandant undertaken the lorries were working & arranged to intercept the first one that returned to VENTELAY.	
"	"	3 p.m.	One lorry returned & moved to MONTIGNY, whither the Div HQ was moving, was commenced.	
"	"	4 p.m.	Two additional lorries were procured.	
"	"	7 p.m.	One lorry taken away to move Bavaria Framework.	
"	"	8 p.m.	Last load left VENTELAY. A lorry returning for an additional load arr 8/30 was hurriedly on the position was unsafe.	
Montigny	"	9 p.m.	Reported to Div.HQ ordered to move to LHÉRY with two lorries - States J.H.Q. 10 Lorries of Stores took, it was informed that extra lorries had been asked for from Corps & two would be allotted to me if they arrived.	

Army Form C. 2118.

WAR DIARY
or
INTELLIGENCE SUMMARY.
(Erase heading not required.)

Instructions regarding War Diaries and Intelligence Summaries are contained in F. S. Regs., Part II. and the Staff Manual respectively. Title pages will be prepared in manuscript.

Place	Date	Hour	Summary of Events and Information	Remarks and references to Appendices
MONTIGNY	27/5	10 p.m.	Two lorries located so far as possible with the most valuable Stores & Office were despatched to LHÉRY — with orders to return tomorrow a.m. if possible for more loads.	
"	28/5	3 a.m.	Personnel (less M.O. & 4 men) despatched to LHÉRY by march route under Capt. Robinson.	
"	"	5.30 a.m.	All transport having long left MONTIGNY & no lorries having returned, decided to abandon dumps & proceed to LHÉRY. One mile on met one lorry returning & forwarded to dumps for a load. Thence to LHÉRY — Dumps at MONTIGNY under shell fire from time of arrival there 27/5.	
LHÉRY	"	12 noon	Ordered to move to OEUILLY — with two lorries. That village being occupied by French troops, camped in BOIS DE RARREY, South of Rue written OEUILLY.	
B. de Rarrey	29/5	9 a.m.	Ordered to move to a position near OEUILLY, S. of Rv. MARNE. Camped near Regtl Transport line about X roads S.W. of OEUILLY.	
Nr Oeuilly	30/5	12 noon	Ordered to move to St MARTIN D'ABLOIS. Camped in wood near the town.	
VILLERS AUX BOIS	31/5		Moved this day from St MARTIN D'ABLOIS to VENTELAY & MONTIGNY are valued at about £5000. This loss is due entirely to Ordnance lorries being used for other services.	

PLEURS. 13/6/18.
K/Chatham Capt—
O.C. 5th D.A.C.

T2134. Wt. W708—776. 500000. 4/15. Sir J. C. & S.

Army Form C. 2118.

WAR DIARY
or
INTELLIGENCE SUMMARY.

(Erase heading not required.)

WAR DIARY

JUNE 1 – 30, 1918

No. 38.

H. Chaplin Major ADS
D.A.D.O.S. 8th Divn.

Army Form C. 2118.

WAR DIARY
or
INTELLIGENCE SUMMARY.
(Erase heading not required.)

Instructions regarding War Diaries and Intelligence Summaries are contained in F. S. Regs., Part II. and the Staff Manual respectively. Title pages will be prepared in manuscript.

Place	Date	Hour	Summary of Events and Information	Remarks and references to Appendices
VILLERS AUX BOIS	1/6		Visited units to ascertain what stores were unsuitable required to re-equip the personnel withdrawn from the line.	
BERBERES-les-VERTUS	3/6		Moved from VILLERS AUX BOIS this day. Called A.D.O.S.	
"	5/6		Called A.D.O.S. 16-18pm. 6.45 pm with Griggs + some covered lorry vans to DuS Artillery park for CONN ANTRE Railhead.	
PLEURS	10/6		Moved from BERGERES.	
SEZANNE	13/6		Entrained for IV Army area. Artillery repairs the bulk with Composite Brigade	
HUPPY	14/6		Arrived from IX Corps area.	
"	15/6		A.D.O.S. XIX Corps called. Visited R.A. units to ascertain the deficiencies in gun equipment.	
"	16/6		Called in A.D.O.S. + Gun Park in HQ RA.	
"	17/6		Visited all R.A. units.	
"	19/6		Attended at Gun Park + moved 10-18pm 5.45pm press Composite Brew	
PRIVILLE-ESCREBOTIN	22/6		Machine guns + transformers from Gun Park: Composite Bug left on IX Corps area arrived to repair the same. Moved HQ this day from HUPPY.	

Army Form C. 2118.

WAR DIARY
or
INTELLIGENCE SUMMARY.
(Erase heading not required.)

Instructions regarding War Diaries and Intelligence Summaries are contained in F. S. Regs., Part II. and the Staff Manual respectively. Title pages will be prepared in manuscript.

Place	Date	Hour	Summary of Events and Information	Remarks and references to Appendices
FRIVILLE	23/6		D.D.O.S. with A.D. D of S XIX Corps & called to ascertain re: provision of Officers in transport & machine for	
"	25/6		Called Gerrard & troops.	
"	26/6		Visited Army H.Q. re: issue of Returns & retransports. Called A.D.O.S re:	
"	27/6		C.H.Q. Abbeville re transfers — Visited Gerrard 6 horses 9.15 - 2.30pm outside Coiffis - Arrived post Port A.T. Depot. A.D.O.S. XXII Corps called. Visited 7pm Durham L.I & 23rd Div. Detachment. Work Progressing.	
"	28/6		Work progressing in amalgamation — Visited 23rd Divn. mech. work Progsng. 23 Vehicles received at Rubberg - Called this morning the day to ascertain how — Visited Loo Mienville to know of summer vehicle [?]. Visited IInd American Corps Reinforcement Depot at EU regarding issue of Returns & remuneration Stats. Also D.O. TREPORT & now of Blacoult. Returning vehicles & issued from A.D.M.T. Depot Abbeville.	
"	29/6 & 30/6			
"	30/6		2 Waggons E.S. Wakart for II American Corps Reinforcement Depot. Complete Transport Arriving from A.D. M.T. Depot & despatched to Aumerie.	Alex Major D.D.O.S XIX Corps

Army Form C. 2118.

WAR DIARY
or
INTELLIGENCE SUMMARY.
(*Erase heading not required.*)

WAR DIARY

July 1 - 31 - 1918

No. 34

Vol 43

Army Form C. 2118.

WAR DIARY
or
INTELLIGENCE SUMMARY.
(Erase heading not required.)

Instructions regarding War Diaries and Intelligence Summaries are contained in F. S. Regs., Part II. and the Staff Manual respectively. Title pages will be prepared in manuscript.

Place	Date	Hour	Summary of Events and Information	Remarks and references to Appendices
FRIVILLE	1/7		Called on D.D.O.S. IV Army re Supply of Air Flaps for R.A. units.	
"	4/7		M.D.O.S. XVII Corps Called on interview re. Visited R.A. units.	
"	5/7		C.R.E. called re delay in supply of Pontoon wagons & Pontoons.	
"	6/7		Called on D.D.O.S. & C.R.E. regarding R.E. wheeled equipment. Visited D.O.S. units.	
"	4/7		Visited 7th Durham L.I. with D.A.Q.M.G.	
"	12/7		Called on C.E. IV Army - & reported to C.R.E. the positive strength of the wheeled equipment which he was deficient.	
"	16/7		Visited R.A. units, under orders to entrain.	
"	17/7		Called C.O.O. Abbeville to try to obtain horse shoes for R.A. Now available. Artillery entrained for I Army Area.	
"	19/7		Remainder of Division commenced entraining for I Army. Stores despatched by rail. Horse shoes gone from Base this day Pit not arrive.	
MONT ST ELOY	20/7		Moved to I Army area this day Called A.D.o.S. VIII Corps. Drawing Officer situated at Mt. St. Eloy. 3 lorries withdrawn for use by Division. the lorry returned 21/7.	
"	23/7		Called on A.D.o.S. I Army - D.D.O.S. I Army - GunRoad -	

Army Form C. 2118.

WAR DIARY
or
INTELLIGENCE SUMMARY.
(Erase heading not required.)

Place	Date	Hour	Summary of Events and Information	Remarks and references to Appendices
MONT ST ELOY	26/7		Two lorries reported & complete establishment. Also VIII Corp called	
"	27/7		2 lorries withdrawn under orders from Div. Hqrs & another prior to demand for spare when required.	

Instructions regarding War Diaries and Intelligence Summaries are contained in F. S. Regs., Part II, and the Staff Manual respectively. Title pages will be prepared in manuscript.

WAR DIARY
or
INTELLIGENCE SUMMARY.

(Erase heading not required.)

Army Form C. 2118.

DADOS 8th Division

Vol 44

Place	Date	Hour	Summary of Events and Information	Remarks and references to Appendices

WAR DIARY

August 1 - 31, 1918.

No 40

[signature] Captain
for ADDOS 8th Division

[stamp: D.A.D.O.S. 1 SEP 1918 8th DIVISION]

Army Form C. 2118.

WAR DIARY
or
INTELLIGENCE SUMMARY.
(Erase heading not required.)

Instructions regarding War Diaries and Intelligence Summaries are contained in F.S. Regs., Part II. and the Staff Manual respectively. Title pages will be prepared in manuscript.

Place	Date	Hour	Summary of Events and Information	Remarks and references to Appendices
MT ST ELOY	3/8		A.D.O.S. VIII Corps called on Visit of inspection.	
"	6/8		Called VIII Corps. Army for authority for issue of flag material, and Gun Parts.	
"	7/8		M.O.E. I Army called. To Sot Pol to purchase Soap. Purchased Soft Soap on interview MGOE	
"	10/8		DA&QMG called re general matters & re complaints from huts repairing various matters.	
"	11/8		A.D.O.S. VIII Corps called	
"	23/8		A.D.O.S. (Major H.S. CHAPLIN) Confirm on Course proceeded to No 19 Ordnance Depot Capt G.J. BRADLEY acting for A.D.O.S.	

G.J.Bradley Captain
from A.D.O.S. 8th A
23/8/18

1

D.A.G.
    Base

Herewith War Diary No
41 for month of September.

                    [signature]
                    Lt Col i/c ADS

30/9/18

Army Form C. 2118.

WAR DIARY
or
INTELLIGENCE SUMMARY.
(Erase heading not required.)

DADOS 25
8th DIV 45

WAR DIARY.

September 1 – 30 1918

No. 41.

Army Form C. 2118.

WAR DIARY
or
INTELLIGENCE SUMMARY.
(Erase heading not required.)

Instructions regarding War Diaries and Intelligence Summaries are contained in F. S. Regs., Part II. and the Staff Manual respectively. Title pages will be prepared in manuscript.

Place	Date	Hour	Summary of Events and Information	Remarks and references to Appendices
Mont St Eloy	September 1/7		Routine	
	8		D.A.D.O.S. returned from Ammunition Course.	
	10/11		2Lt Timms A.P.O. Boot Expert. Found unit a Divisional Boot Shops not doing	
	12/27		Routine	
	28		A.D.O.S. VII Corps called & inspected certain clothing returned by units.	
	29/30		Routine.	

H Stephenson
D.A.D.O.S. 8th Div

[Stamp: D.A.D.O.S. 30 SEP 1918 8th DIVISION]

D.A.G.
  3rd Echelon –

Forward War Diary
No 42 of DADOS 8th
Div. for the month of
October.

                    H Chaplin
                       Major
1/11/18   DADOS 8 Div

Army Form C. 2118.

WAR DIARY
or
INTELLIGENCE SUMMARY.

(Erase heading not required.)

Vol 46

Unit 8 S.O.F.A.R

WAR DIARY

October 1 – 31, 1918

No 42.

Army Form C. 2118.

"WAR" DIARY
or
INTELLIGENCE SUMMARY.
(Erase heading not required.)

Instructions regarding War Diaries and Intelligence Summaries are contained in F. S. Regs., Part II. and the Staff Manual respectively. Title pages will be prepared in manuscript.

Place	Date	Hour	Summary of Events and Information	Remarks and references to Appendices
MONT ST ELOY	1/10		Inspected Workshop & Btn wksp C.	
VICTORY CAMP S18.g.3.b.	3/10		Moved from Mt St Eloy. Stores in Cinema S15 - g 3690.	
"	7/10		A D o S VII Corps called on inspection.	
"	9/10		Inspected all Transport of 1/33 Div Bde with A.E. & Div. Train. Condition generally satisfactory.	
STIRLING CAMP S18.G.13.b.	14/10		Moved from VICTORY CAMP. Stores forwarded to refilling point FAMPOUX for issues, by L.Ry. Main Stores remaining at VICTORY CAMP.	
LAURENT BLANGY	15/10		Moved from STIRLING CAMP. Office H.Q.5 personnel nil.	
"	16/10		Visited all Divisional units to ascertain their urgent requirements. Stores from Railhead forwarded to Dumps at S18 - I.13.a., for issue. Major portion of Stores sent up in our own lorries.	
"	18/10		Stores from railhead to Dumps at D 25.b., Divisional Stores remaining at I.13.a. were also forwarded. Very few issues made.	
PLANQUE	19/10		Office, H.Q. personnel & Brigade H.Q.s moved from LAURENT BLANGY. Stores remaining at D 25.b. moved to the Mairie AUBY on this & following days.	
RACHES	20/10		Office & H.Q. moved from PLANQUE to refilling point. A selected load of Stores was also moved up, but very few units collected. The Mairie AUBY being selected as forward store. Railhead Stores were forwarded here.	

Army Form C. 2118.

WAR DIARY
or
INTELLIGENCE SUMMARY.
(Erase heading not required.)

Instructions regarding War Diaries and Intelligence Summaries are contained in F. S. Regs., Part II. and the Staff Manual respectively. Title pages will be prepared in manuscript.

Place	Date	Hour	Summary of Events and Information	Remarks and references to Appendices
CATTELET	21/10		Office moved from RACHES. Transfer of main Stores from VICTORY CAMP to AUBY commenced.	
"	22/10		Rept. of 23rd Inf. Bde & 33rd Bde. R.F.A. commenced & completed on following day. Arranged for trains for 23/10 for transport of Stores from VICTORY CAMP to PLANQUE.	
"	23/10		Visited units of 24 & 25 Inf. Bdes. with DAGOHT. to investigate Complaints made to G.O.C. by units that the arrangements for mal & ordnance Stores were not working well. Reason of investigation being that units themselves were entirely responsible for not receiving Ordnance Supplies at refilling points & drawing their requirements, is instructed by D.R.O.	
"	24/10		Refilling point fixed at N.12. a sheet 44. Where advanced ordnance Stores were formed.	
"	27/10		Transfer of necessary Stores from VICTORY CAMP to AUBY & CATTELET. Moved office to from CATTELET. Commenced to concentrate all Stores here.	
MARCHIENNES	29/10		A.D.O.S. VIII Corps Called on inspection.	
"	31/10		A.D.O.S. VIII Corps again called. The moving warfare of the third week in October has forced that the present transport allowed to Divisional Tps. Divn. is inadequate. Although about 4 tons loads of Reserve Stores have since been kept upon him. (Box Respirators, Containers, Tool Caps.	

WAR DIARY
or
INTELLIGENCE SUMMARY.

Army Form C. 2118.

(Ground Carriers, antigas clothing &c) in addition has been made to the original allotment to Corps — one each for 3 Inf. Bdes. & Div. Troops. Then to bring Carriers Coy. with more than their own Brigade or stores in a phase of moving warfare extending over a week, or distances would then be too great to permit their 2-Stage forward the reserve or other stores held. The absence of a Box Car makes it impossible to shift mules temporarily withdrawn from the line, with Gun Park stores &c. Such a Car would be invaluable when the roads are hopeless for feeding units with stores urgently needed or finished. They cannot be used. It is considered that the addition of 2 lorries and 1 15cwt Box Car to the transport of a Brigade is absolutely essential for any phase of moving warfare.

A. Chapman Major
D.A.D.O.S. 3rd Div.

31/10/17

WAR DIARY
or
INTELLIGENCE SUMMARY

WAR DIARY
November 1-30 1918
No 43

DADOS 8th DIV

Army Form C. 2118.

WAR DIARY
or
INTELLIGENCE SUMMARY.
(Erase heading not required.)

Instructions regarding War Diaries and Intelligence Summaries are contained in F. S. Regs., Part II. and the Staff Manual respectively. Title pages will be prepared in manuscript.

Place	Date	Hour	Summary of Events and Information	Remarks and references to Appendices
MARCHIENNES	3/11		All Surplus Ordnance Stores left in VICTORY Camp returned to Base	
"	6/11		Inspected Transport of 2/4th Batty Bde with OC 8th Div Train	
"	8/11		Inspected Transport of 25th Batty Bde with OC 8th Div Train	
"	10/11		Move from MARCHIENNES	
ONNAING	12/11		Move from ONNAING	
THULIN	13/11		Move from THULIN - 3 additional lorries arranged for this move	
TERTRE	15/11		All Surplus Stores cleared from ONNAING to Base preparatory to advance -	
"	16/11		Move from TERTRE -	
TOURNAI	17-30 /11		Routine - Refitting Division -	

Army Form C. 2118.

WAR DIARY
or
INTELLIGENCE SUMMARY.

(Erase heading not required.)

WAR DIARY

DECEMBER 1-31. 1918

Nº 44.

Army Form C. 2118.

WAR DIARY
or
INTELLIGENCE SUMMARY.
(Erase heading not required.)

Instructions regarding War Diaries and Intelligence Summaries are contained in F. S. Regs., Part II. and the Staff Manual respectively. Title pages will be prepared in manuscript.

Place	Date	Hour	Summary of Events and Information	Remarks and references to Appendices
TOURNAI	1-11/Dec		Routine. Refitting &c.	
"	12/12		D.A.D.O.S. Major M.E. Chaplin to III Corps H.Q. for temporary duty	
"	13-16/Dec		Routine. Refitting &c.	
ENGHIEN	17/12		Moved from TOURNAI.	
	18-31/Dec		Routine. Refitting &c.	

[Signature] Captain
for A.D.O.S.

D.A.D.O.S.
2 - JAN 1919
8th DIVISION

Jan – June 1919

Exhibit "A"

Berwick War Diary for
January, for despatch.

J M Baphm
Mayor
Berwick NSW

1/2/19

Army Form C. 2118.

WAR DIARY
or
INTELLIGENCE SUMMARY.
(Erase heading not required.)

DADOS 87

Vol 49

WAR DIARY.

JANUARY 1 – 31 1919

No 45.

D.A.D.O.S. & DvP

Morgan Major RAVC

Army Form C. 2118.

WAR DIARY
or
INTELLIGENCE SUMMARY.
(Erase heading not required.)

Instructions regarding War Diaries and Intelligence Summaries are contained in F. S. Regs., Part II. and the Staff Manual respectively. Title pages will be prepared in manuscript.

Place	Date	Hour	Summary of Events and Information	Remarks and references to Appendices
ENGHIEN	1-5 Jany 1919		Daily Routine	
"	6.1.19		Major. H.S. CHAPLIN regressed from TT Corps	
"	7-10 Jany 1919		Daily Routine.	
"	11.1.19		Major. H.S. CHAPLIN proceeded on leave to the U.K.	
"	12-26 Jany 1919		Daily Routine	
"	27.1.19		Major. H.S. CHAPLIN returned from leave	
"	29.1.19		D.D.O.S. T Army moved called re instructions to proceed to forming Intermediate Collecting Station	
"	30-31		Routine.	

H.C. Clarke Major
D.A.D.G.S. T. Army

WAR DIARY

FEBY 1 – 28 1919.

No 48.

D.A.D.O.S. 8T DIV
Motor Lorry Park

Army Form C. 2118.

WAR DIARY
or
INTELLIGENCE SUMMARY.

(Erase heading not required.)

Instructions regarding War Diaries and Intelligence Summaries are contained in F. S. Regs., Part II. and the Staff Manual respectively. Title pages will be prepared in manuscript.

Place	Date	Hour	Summary of Events and Information	Remarks and references to Appendices
ENGHIEN	1/2 - 15/2		General Routine work.	
ATH	16/2		March from ENGHIEN – Stores + I.C.S located in Chemical Factory – ATH	
"	18/2		Visited D.D.V.S V Army	
"	27/2		D.D.V.S V Army called on inspection re	

H Stephenson
Major
D.A.D.V.S. II Corps
2/3/19.

Army Form C. 2118.

WAR DIARY
or
INTELLIGENCE SUMMARY.
(Erase heading not required.)

WAR DIARY.

March 1 - 31 1919

No 47

DADOS 8th Div

Instructions regarding War Diaries and Intelligence Summaries are contained in F. S. Regs., Part II. and the Staff Manual respectively. Title pages will be prepared in manuscript.

Place	Date	Hour	Summary of Events and Information	Remarks and references to Appendices

Army Form C. 2118.

WAR DIARY
or
INTELLIGENCE SUMMARY.
(Erase heading not required.)

Instructions regarding War Diaries and Intelligence Summaries are contained in F. S. Regs., Part II. and the Staff Manual respectively. Title pages will be prepared in manuscript.

Place	Date	Hour	Summary of Events and Information	Remarks and references to Appendices
ATH	11/3-11/3		General Routine work.	
"	12/3		D.D.O.S. V Army Called.	
"	13/3		Visited units of 332nd Bde R.F.A.	
"	14 -15/3		General routine work	
"	15/3		Lt. Workman R.F.A. reported for instruction	
"	17+18/3		General routine work	
"	19/3		Visited units Yeomanry R.F.A. — D.D.O.S V Army Called	
"	20/3		" 15th Bde R.F.A.	
"	21/3		A.D.S V Army Called	
"	22/3		Formal inspection of Equipment of R.E. WBBk R.E.A. 1. B. 5. O.S. Batteries	Lt Sontham A.I.A. left
"	23/3		Visited 1/1 Phn D.I. 1 & 156th Shermont parities	
"	24/3		Formal inspection of Equipment of R. 167th Shermont troght. 200th Rifle Bde	200th Regt Bear Regt at inchin R.A. left
"	25/3		Formal inspection of Equipment 8th Bn W.Y.R.	
"	26/3		Formal inspection of Equipment Le 90 Field Co R.E. 24th Field Co R.E.	
"	27/3		Formal inspection 1/1 Northern H (Rusion) 15th Field Co R.E. 25th Field Ambce	& 2/4th Etavo Regt.
"	28/3		D.D.O.S V Army called. Formal inspection Equipment of Dn G. Field Ambce.	
"	29/3+31/3		Routine work	

M Morkman Major
D.D.S V Army

Army Form C. 2118.

WAR DIARY
or
INTELLIGENCE SUMMARY.
(Erase heading not required.)

WAR DIARY
No 48
APRIL 1 - 30 1919

D.A.D.O.S. Supply

Army Form C. 2118.

WAR DIARY
or
INTELLIGENCE SUMMARY.
(Erase heading not required.)

Instructions regarding War Diaries and Intelligence Summaries are contained in F.S. Regs., Part II. and the Staff Manual respectively. Title pages will be prepared in manuscript.

Place	Date	Hour	Summary of Events and Information	Remarks and references to Appendices
ATH	3/4		Inspected Mobilization Equipment of 7/15th Inf. Bde.	
"	4/4		Inspected Mobilization Equipment of 230th Inf. Bde. 7th Bn. 3 Dot Not ava Called	
"	5/4		Inspected Mobilization Equipment of 231st Inf. Bde. 7th Bn. A Dot Not ava Called.	
"	7/4		A.D.M.S. IIIrd Cp. called. Visited Depot & Guard Room BASINGY	
"	11/4 14/4 15/4		Inspected Mobilization Equipment 2nd Duty Bn. & 1/1st Bn. Hereford Regt. Inspected Mobilization Equipment of 15th Cheltenham Regt. A.D.o.S IIIrd Cps. Called Inspected Mobilization Equipment of 1/1st Bn. London Regt. & 4/5th Lincoln Regt.	
"	16/4		Major H.E. Chaplin proceeded to HQ IIIrd Cps of Reserve Duty to A.D.o.S	
"	21/4		Inspected Mobilization Equipment of 2nd Bn. Wynch Regt.	
"	26/4		Each following unit proceeded to UK without equipment 2nd Suffolk R.E. 15th Welsh 2-17th Middlesex Rgt. 2- Bn. Midland Rgt. 2- Bn. Devon Rgt. 2- Bn. Wigan Rgt. 1 Bn. Worcester Rgt.	

A Chalstrapin
Brig. P. Com.

/ 49

Army Form C. 2118.

WAR DIARY
or
INTELLIGENCE SUMMARY.
(Erase heading not required.)

WAR DIARY
May 1 - 31 1919
No. 49

Army Form C. 2118.

WAR DIARY
or
INTELLIGENCE SUMMARY.
(Erase heading not required.)

Place	Date	Hour	Summary of Events and Information	Remarks and references to Appendices
ATH	2/5		Major R.S. Chaplin opened Journey of Duty. H.Q. 8th Div.	
	3/5		D.S. full duties proceeded home with equipment.	
	5/5		2nd Lt. Banks 1/4th Hunts Regt. & 2nd Lt. Ryt Bade Regt. ceased & ret proceeded home with equipment.	
	5/5		Inspected Mobility Equipment of 32nd & 45th Bde. R.F.A.	
	6/5		Inspected Mobility Equipment of 8th Div. Train, decided not to inspect The Tables as no Officers were available in 2 of the Corps to sign them.	
	8/5		Inspected Mobility Equipment of H.Q. 33rd Div. R.F.A. & 33–36th Bde. & the E. Lancs Regt. 8th Div 89th & 90th Regt. 15th/17th Steam Lorries proceeded home with equipment.	
			8th Div Signal Co. disbanded & Stores handed over to Indian Signal Co.	
	15/5		Inspected Mobilyation Stores of H.Q. & Section of 8th D.A.C.	
	16/5		Inspected Mobilyation Stores of J.B. Divn — H.Q. Div R.E. H.Q. D.A. R.A. H.Q. 23rd Inf. Bde.	
	28/5 29/5 30/5		Major R.S. Chaplin inspected Mob. Stores Station & depot ATH–TOURNAI Sub area – Administration of J & A Sub units of Ordnance Services mentioned herein up.	

R.C. Chaplin Major R.A.O.C.

Army Form C. 2118.

WAR DIARY
or
INTELLIGENCE SUMMARY.
(Erase heading not required.)

WAR DIARY
June 1 - 30 1919
No 50

DADOS ATH-TOURNM Sulphur
(5th Div)

Klaghi main Rate

WAR DIARY
or
INTELLIGENCE SUMMARY.

Army Form C. 2118.

Place	Date	Hour	Summary of Events and Information	Remarks and references to Appendices
ATH	June 11/7		General Routine Work	
"	" 9/11		Inspection of N.S.T.'s of 119 Army Bde RFA	
"	"	13	D.B.G. No 3 F.A. called - 24 + 26 Field Ambulances returned Stores to R.C.	
"	"	15	Vehicles of 119 D.A.C. O.M.R. & 115th Field Ambulance despatched to Base 119 DAC returned Stores to FCD	
"	"	17	H.Q. 86 Bn proceeded to ANTWERP for L.R.	
"	"		Units of 74th Divn for distribution Belgium Caunnies foreshore Stores -	
"	"	20	Visited units of 229 Inf Bde 74th Divn to inspect M.S.T. & handed over by DADOS 74th Divn	
"	"		Called to see ADS of 14 Corps	
"	"	21	Visited units + M.S.O. Corps 74th Divn Train to inspect M.S.T.?	
"	"	"	Visited units of 230 Inf Bde 74 Divn to inspect M.S.T	
"	"	"	Visited units of 231 Inf Bde 74 Divn to inspect M.S.T.	
"	"	26	Visited Corps Cavalry Collecting Camp - 137 Pow Coy & BELOEIL to inspect captured vehicles	
"	"	27	Visited BEATON Salvage Dump - Ammn Dump at PS4 (No 69 OFS) of Hq ATH Area.	
"	"	27	This day units of 7th 8 Bn completed hand in of Stores - following units had Returned Stores to F.C.R. 231 Field Ambce. 74 Infantry Coy, 74 M.M.G.C. 74 T.M.B.C. M.2nd D.H.C.	
"	"		DRtn 2nd ATH MGC - 44th Bde RFA Completed to B.H.G. - 447 + 463 Coys 7th 8 Bn Train - MGiments of our Rides. 229. 230.231 T.M. Bty. 5th Hyphry + 75 Monmouth Field Coys R.E.	
"	"	20	Visited D.D.V.L. London, V.C. to arrange for closing down of ordnance work in 30 inst	H. Charles Major RAOC

8TH DIVISION

A. D. V. S.
DEC 1914 - APL 1919

Index

APVS

SUBJECT.

No.	Contents.	Date.

Index

APVS

121/4044

ADVS. 8th Division.

Vol I. 13—26-12-14

apl 1919

Army Form C. 2118.

WAR DIARY
or
INTELLIGENCE SUMMARY.
(Erase heading not required.)

Instructions regarding War Diaries and Intelligence Summaries are contained in F.S. Regs., Part II. and the Staff Manual respectively. Title pages will be prepared in manuscript.

Hour, Date, Place	Summary of Events and Information	Remarks and references to Appendices
10 am. 13-12-14 LA GORGUE	Inspected 45' Brigade R.F.A. Ammunition Column found several animals suffering from Ringworm. Four cases of mange sent to M.V.S. Suspicious case of mange reported in 2/Middlesex by V.O. Inspected the animal and found it to be suffering from Ringworm, had it sent to M.V.S. for treatment. The D.D.V.S. called in the afternoon & I showed him the mange cases	
14-12-14	Had arranged to inspect all animals of the Blue Watch, but owing to have been much indifferent health was unable to do so. I then went to M.V.S. and inspected animal being to be sent to hospital. One horse belonging to H.Q. and in 23' Infantry Brigade suffering from sore every lame I ordered to be the hospital. Visited Headquarters horses. made out consolidated return.	
15-12-14 9.30 am	Inspected 33' Brigade R.F.A. Horses looking in good condition. The Lines are in an awful condition.	
" 2.30 P.m.	Visited Mobile Section and inspected mange cases. all doing well	
16-12-14	Inspected "J" Battery 3' Royal Artillery Brigade Mules & mules look quite [illegible]	

Army Form C. 2118.

WAR DIARY
or
INTELLIGENCE SUMMARY.
(Erase heading not required.)

Instructions regarding War Diaries and Intelligence Summaries are contained in F.S. Regs., Part II. and the Staff Manual respectively. Title pages will be prepared in manuscript.

Hour, Date, Place	Summary of Events and Information	Remarks and references to Appendices
16.12.14 LA GORGUE	and suffered all mules should be shod. Inspected horses at hostile Section to be sent to Hospital also hand cases.	
17.12.14 "	Inspected 118' Battery RGA and Ammunition Column. Sent three cases to Section also suspicious case of mange. Visited Mobile Section also Ordnance re clippers for Section.	to 36.
18.12.14	Attended D.D.V.S. Conference at G.H.Q.	
19.12.14	Inspected Amm Column Heavy Brigade Artillery also 119' Battery. Animals looking well. Inspected animals at M.V. Section.	
20.12.14	Visited Normanh Yromahry inspected horse reported lame by V.O. to horse received a severe injury.	
21.12.14	Inspected horses at Mobile Section. Such needed attendance for a fortnight.	
22.12.14	Inspected sick to be sent to Boulogne	
23.12.14	Inspected suspicious cases of mange in 2/Devons and Worcestershire Rg 5	
24.12.14	Inspected Headquarters Co. 6th Train and went thro' all the sick cases to be V.O.'s sick in bed. Many cases were fit to work and many were only fit for Hospital. Then inspected Sectn of Ammunition Column	

Forms/C. 2118/11.

Army Form C. 21

WAR DIARY
or
INTELLIGENCE SUMMARY.
(Erase heading not required.)

Instructions regarding War Diaries and Intelligence Summaries are contained in F.S. Regs., Part II. and the Staff Manual respectively. Title pages will be prepared in manuscript.

Hour, Date, Place	Summary of Events and Information	Remarks and references to Appendices
25.12.14. LA GORGUE	Visited hostile Section.	
26.12.14.	Visited sick case belonging to French Subenne item to hostile Section. Saw an V.O. at my office and lectured them on certain matters brought to my notice when inspecting.	
27.12.14.	Inspected 51 Seige Howitzer Battery. 3 suspected cases of mange sent to hostile	
28.12.14.	Lieut Gelard admitted sick. Lieut Blythe carrying on his duties.	
2-1-15.	Daily visited and inspected troops Horses.	

31-12-14

P J Harris Major
A.D.V.S. 8' Division

W.D.

121/4210

ADVS. 8th Division.

Vol II.

Confidential

War Diary
of
Major P.J. Harris
A.D.V.S. 8th Division

From 1-1-15 to 31-1-15.

WAR DIARY
or
INTELLIGENCE SUMMARY.
(Erase heading not required.)

Army Form C. 2118.

Hour, Date, Place	Summary of Events and Information	Remarks and references to Appendices
1st & 11th LA GORGUE		
12-1-15	Looking to record Brought to the notice of H.Q. the bad practice of letting horses on the pavé roads. Many cases of lameness have occurred from this cause, and orders have been issued to this effect. Inspected 45th Brigade RFA. Was not pleased with the attention paid to the sick. Ordered several cases to be sent to the M.V. Section. As they were needless being treated in the lines	Routine Orders 219 of 15-1-15
13-1-15	Inspected sick animals at M.V.S. proceeding to Hospital D.D.V.S. visited	
14-1-15	Inspected 33rd Brigade R.F.A. 12 bad cases I had sent to M.V.S. Horses working well. The Field Ambulance have a field forge and cart on board of their equipment but no farrier or shoeing smith, in fact nobody capable of removing a shoe. Have taken the subject up.	No 63 of 14-1-15
15-1-15	Inspected suspicious case of mange 13 London Regt. but Rushing itself more from a dirty coat, but ordered it to be sent to M.V.S. to be properly washed	

Army Form C. 2118.

WAR DIARY
or
INTELLIGENCE SUMMARY.
(Erase heading not required.)

Hour, Date, Place	Summary of Events and Information	Remarks and references to Appendices
15-1-15 LA GORGUE.	Inspected sick to be sent to Hospital to-day. Again the float, which has been prepared for the M.V. Section came in most useful. It took three very lame cases to Raulead, which could not have walked. I cannot understand why Horse Ambulances are not issued to Mobile Sections. Had the Section no float these very lame cases would have had to remain with the Mobile Section or be destroyed. By getting these cases to Hospital, their lives are saved and surely this is a saving. Take the value of 3 horses at £45 each, equalling £135, easily pays for a float. Lt. Hegarty V.O. 96 23 Infantry Brigade proceeded on leave from on the 13" inst for 7 days. Corps Routine Order No 96 having stated that horses not which are not veterinary cases, are to be handed over to M.V. Sections I have had orders published that I must be informed, when I will arrange for them to be sent	

WAR DIARY or INTELLIGENCE SUMMARY

Army Form C. 2118.

Hour, Date, Place	Summary of Events and Information	Remarks and references to Appendices
15-1-15 LA GORGUE	To the M.V.S. This I consider was necessary, otherwise many cast horses will be sent to the Section, filling up the stables; but if I am informed I can arrange for them to be sent on the day sick animals are being despatched to hospital.	Divisional Routine Orders 218 of 15-1-15.
16-1-15 "	Inspected/reported cases of suspicious mange at the Heavy Brigade Ammunition Column and Divisional Ammn. Column. Only one suspicious case which has been sent to Mobile Section. Gratefully our corps cannot supply clerks as those I have an old man is absolutely useless.	
17-1-15 "	Captain Pank VO? Northants/yeomanry granted leave of absence from 21st to 24th.	
19-1-15 "	Lieut. S. Hunter A.V.C. (SR) admitted to Hospital to-day. Inspected 46th Brigade 3 x 5" Battery, also suspicious case of mange. 13th Horse on Regiments. Am now deficient of 3 officers.	

WAR DIARY
or
INTELLIGENCE SUMMARY.
(Erase heading not required.)

Army Form C. 2118

Instructions regarding War Diaries and Intelligence Summaries are contained in F. S. Regs., Part II. and the Staff Manual respectively. Title pages will be prepared in manuscript.

Hour, Date, Place	Summary of Events and Information	Remarks and references to Appendices
20-1-15 LA GORGUE	Placed Lieut Nicholas in charge of 33 Brigade RFA in addition to his own duties, during Lt Hunter's absence on sick list. Took this officer round to the various batteries of the Brigade and showed him the sick cases.	
21-1-15 "	Visited No 6 Clearing Hospital at MERVILLE with the object of trying to get the RAMC to keep Lt Hunter so that he might return to his Brigade, as I was informed he would only be about 6 days on the sick list. My visit however was in vain as I found he had been evacuated. This is the third officer I have lost, who have not been seriously ill and have been told they would only be on the sick list for a few days.	
"	This is the admittance report of Lieut Hemmington (SR) 6 RHA Brigade = "Lieut. Z Battery. Greases Laminitis"	
"	Treatment. This mare may have some pus in the feet but as she was standing when I saw her, 1000 yds of the German trenches I did not stop to see."	

(9 29 6) W 2794 100,000 8/14 HWV Forms/C. 2118/11.

WAR DIARY or INTELLIGENCE SUMMARY.

(Erase heading not required.)

Army Form C. 2118

Hour, Date, Place	Summary of Events and Information	Remarks and references to Appendices
23.1.15 LA GORGUE	Captain Parks & Lieut Blyth granted leave to England 21-27" and 25"-31" respectively.	
25.1.15 "	The last few days, the armoured cars at the hostile section has brought in from the different units many cases. It however have been cruelly knocked, and which were too bad to treat with the units, where the horses are standing up to their knees nearly, in mud. I must army Emphasise the fact that a hospital should be part of the mobile section Equipment. I believe I was one of the first officers to command a mobile section when this unit of the Corps was established, and in every report after manoeuvres I always strongly recommended the issue of this vehicle	
29.1.15	Two batteries 190th 59th arrived last night. Visited the 59th this morning. Arranged for a V.O. to take charge This battery has had many horse cases have been cured	

WAR DIARY
or
INTELLIGENCE SUMMARY.
(Erase heading not required.)

Army Form C. 2118

Hour, Date, Place	Summary of Events and Information	Remarks and references to Appendices
29-1-15 LA GORGUE	Cont^d and returned to duty. I inspected the sick and sent into cured cases of mumps which I considered should be further treated, so had them sent to the Mobile Section. Some of the other cases were in an awful debilitated condition and I had these evacuated. Am inspecting the whole Battery tomorrow.	
30-1-15 —"—	Inspected 6b' Battery RFA - Horses very dirty and not looking at all well. As they are under orders in the field - they may improve. Reported on foot cases & called to by DDVS.	N^s 63 & 64.
31-1-15 —"—	Lt Fenton reported his arrival for duty. Went Div: Train. Inspected suspected case of mumps at 2/ sections, he arrival was not suffering from having. Lt Nicholls granted leave from 1-2-15 — 7-2-15.	

Confidential
War Diary
of
Major P.J. Harris
A.D.V.S. 8th Division
From 1-2-15 to 28-2-15.

121/4464

Vol III

WAR DIARY
or
INTELLIGENCE SUMMARY.

(Erase heading not required.)

Army Form C. 2118.

Hour, Date, Place	Summary of Events and Information	Remarks and references to Appendices
1-2-15. LA GORGUE	Drew attention to the indiscriminate way supply horses continuing nails are broken up & attention should be made at the various headquarters of the Battalions. There are too many cases of "picked up nails" in this Division and an Army Order published to the effect that more care must be taken, and broken nails are to be placed clear of the road. Inspected RE Companies and found horses looking well.	Routine Orders 247 of 31-1-15
3-2-15 — "—	Inspected Letterbird Field Co RE that arrived last night from St Omer. Horses looking well. Have 3 cases of mange. Arranged for veterinary attendance. Inspected 24th Infantry Brigade. Brought to the notice of Headquarters that the full ration of hay is not brought up to rivetted S.P.O states that it cannot be obtained. Subject taken up by IV Corps	1 (HC) Co R.E.
4-2-15.	Inspected 23rd Inf. Brigade. Visited CALONNE and ROBECQ. Inspect animal left behind by the 5B Battery RGA. When team chug to join this Division. The animal had died at work & place.	

WAR DIARY or INTELLIGENCE SUMMARY

Army Form C. 2118.

Hour, Date, Place	Summary of Events and Information	Remarks and references to Appendices
5.2.15. LA GORGUE	56 Howitzer Battery is moving to another Division tomorrow so inspected them and arranged for them to take some sick cases, that were at the M.V. Station, with them. They have a few bad influenza cases and am informing A.D.V.S. of their new Division of the fact. Inspected a suspected Glandered Case in a French horse. Our Train where a Battalion is billeted, found animal suffering from Strangles. As regards the shortage of Hay ration, am informed by Corps that 600 to 1000 quintals is to be issued and units are to requisition for same to make up the balance.	
8.2.15 "	Two deaths from Anthrax reported at Headquarters 4 Brigade R.F.A. Inspected cruel horses. Have had the horses, 10 in number, evacuated from the buildings and picketed in the open. Ordered the buildings to be dug up and quicklime put down, also the clearup of the buildings and of additional adjoining. The carcases where buried in quicklime.	

WAR DIARY or INTELLIGENCE SUMMARY.

Army Form C. 2118.

Hour, Date, Place	Summary of Events and Information	Remarks and references to Appendices
9.2.15 LA GORGUE	D.D.V.S. 1st Army visited. Inspected French farmer's horse that was suffering from Shingles. It had died early in the morning. Arranged for the burial of the carcase and had stables disinfected.	
10.2.15 " "	Inspected building where Anthrax case occurred, also inspected new battery (40th Howitzer Battery) which has joined this Division.	
12.2.15 " "	A French horse having died suddenly in the town and as the Local veterinary surgeon is ill, I visited the stables and have arranged to make a P.M. tomorrow. Extention who has joined the Division in relief of friend joined the Divisional train, has no knowledge of the duties of an officer attached to a unit with the result that great trouble is caused in rendering returns correctly. Would suggest that Officers going sick should, if possible, be sent back to their Division on discharge from Hospital.	

Army Form C. 2118.

WAR DIARY
or
INTELLIGENCE SUMMARY.
(Erase heading not required.)

Instructions regarding War Diaries and Intelligence Summaries are contained in F.S. Regs., Part II. and the Staff Manual respectively. Title pages will be prepared in manuscript.

Hour, Date, Place	Summary of Events and Information	Remarks and references to Appendices
13.2.15 LA GORGUE	Collected 5 horses from different farmers, some being many miles away. I always gave me the information after I had asked him if he knew of any farmers who had British horses. Two were in good condition but the other three were p.m. The P.M. on the French horse revealed Pneumonia.	Three sent to E.F.O. for details. The other two are being mallined will be issued a remount
14.2.15 — " —	Lieut. S. Hunter reported his arrival	
16.2.15 — " —	D.O.V's visited. Inspected several units.	
17.2.15 — " —	Inspected 25th Infantry Brigade.	
18.2.15 — " —	Inspected Heavy Artillery Brigade. As the full ration of hay is not being received and units are supposed to requisition for straw to make up the balance, I am arranging with the S.S.O. for the issue of Linseed Cake in lieu of the deficiency of hay on part of it. I consider this will be beneficial to the horses.	
20.2.15 — " —	Lt. Warren reported his arrival with the Headquarters 39 Howitzer Brigade	

WAR DIARY or INTELLIGENCE SUMMARY

Army Form C. 2118.

Hour, Date, Place	Summary of Events and Information	Remarks and references to Appendices
22.2.15 LA GORGUE	Inspected 31st and 35th Howitzer Batteries. Horses looking well and very few sick cases. These batteries have not joined this Division. 34th Brigade	
23.2.15 " "	Inspected Ammunition Column of above Brigade. Horse clippers which were indented for over two months ago have not yet been received.	
24.2.15 " "		
25.2.15 " "	Ammunition Column 5th R.H.A. reported that 2 of the recruits received were suffering from hernia. It was supported by V.O. Inspected them and found them suffering from same. Units can now draw linseed cake at the scale of 14 lbs for 120 of hay in lieu of straw, where it is requisitioned for to supplement the hay ration.	
27.2.15 " "	Inspected 40th Brigade R.F.A. Not well pleased with the Veterinary treatment and attention of sick animals.	

121/4779

A.V.D.

Confidential

War Diary.

of.

Major. P. J. Harris.
A.D.V.S. 8° Division

From 1-3-15   To 31-3-15.

Vol IV

121/4779

March 1915

WAR DIARY or INTELLIGENCE SUMMARY.

(Erase heading not required.)

Army Form C. 2118.

Hour, Date, Place	Summary of Events and Information	Remarks and references to Appendices
1-3-15 LA GORGUE	Units moving to different areas which will mean a rearrangement of veterinary duties. Mobile Section moved this morning to K 28 C Centre. Some units will have a great distance to send their sick, but this cannot be avoided owing to the large area taken up by the Division. The M.V. Section is situated centrally. A float would have been invaluable today, where some of the sick cases with mud, were moving.	
2-3-15 "	Inspected reported case of Mange. Ammunition Column 37 Howitzer Brigade. Annual suffering from Lice & Mange.	
4-3-15 "	Visited M.V. Section. They had to find fresh billets owing to the field Ambulance turning them out. Inspected Bents & Royal Irish transport	
5-3-15 "	Lt Le Geard (VC) reported his arrival. Posts to 25th Inf Bde	
6-3-15 "	Visited Doulieu to inspect horse left behind by British troops in accordance with orders from D.D.V.S.	
7-3-15 "	Collected horse at Doulieu.	

WAR DIARY or INTELLIGENCE SUMMARY.

Army Form C. 2118.

(Erase heading not required.)

Hour, Date, Place	Summary of Events and Information	Remarks and references to Appendices
8.3.15 LA GORGUE	Inspected the Divisional Ammunition Column at Invertergue. Horses looking remarkably well. I consider every executive V.O. should be allowed two chains; V O -p- of "O.W." train Amm. Column, Infantry Brigades and R.F.A. Brigades have just as much distance to travel as the V.O. 40 R.H.A. Brigade. I must also be remembered that officers have more charge than the mind to which they are attached viz Field Ambulances, R.E. Companies &c.	
10.3.15 "	Division ordered to move. Several horse collected by and of a float that were unable to move at the last minute. Had it not been two of our points to the necessity of a float horse collected today by the float, would in the ordinary course have had to be picked for something and perhaps in the end had to be destroyed, owing to not-	

WAR DIARY or INTELLIGENCE SUMMARY

Army Form C. 2118.

Hour, Date, Place	Summary of Events and Information	Remarks and references to Appendices
10.3.15 LA GORGUE	having veterinary attention, whereas these horses were collected at once, received veterinary attention and will be immediately despatched to Hospital. I am more convinced every day that if the hostile sector was equipped with a fleet belts still a motor horse Ambulance, more horses would be saved, and money saved to the Government.	
11.3.15 " "	Collected more horses. Visited mobile Section. Humane Cattle Killer should be available for some Several units are without them. I have repeatedly asked for them. A few that were issued in England had no ammunition.	
12.3.15 " "	More horse collected. Mule belonging to Sapper Hercules was wounded in shoulder with shrapnel, when Shrapnel to be so I personally collected same and brought him	

Army Form C. 2118.

WAR DIARY
or
INTELLIGENCE SUMMARY.
(Erase heading not required.)

Instructions regarding War Diaries and Intelligence Summaries are contained in F.S. Regs., Part II. and the Staff Manual respectively. Title pages will be prepared in manuscript.

Hour, Date, Place	Summary of Events and Information	Remarks and references to Appendices
12.3.15 LA GORGUE	In to La Gorgue where it was handed over to mobile Section to collect. Many units have no transport vans with the result that many items are not numbered on the feet. Also branding irons and laid down in Equipment, they were unable to be procured from Ordnance, before leaving for England	
13.3.15 "	Visited No 5 Mountain Battery to see mule shot in the knee. 1st London Territorial Regiment arrived	
14.3.15 "		
15.3.15 "	Inspected 1st London T Regt. Good draught horses Mules. Brought no veterinary equipment with them. 7th Middlesex Territorial Regiment arrived. There are now Six battalions to a Brigade. When made leave a Division to join another Division temporarily, should be informed as to rendering their returns to the A.D.V.S. of the Division they are attached to temporarily	
16.3.15 "	Personally collected two wounded Charges	

WAR DIARY or INTELLIGENCE SUMMARY

Army Form C. 2118.

(Erase heading not required.)

Hour, Date, Place	Summary of Events and Information	Remarks and references to Appendices
16.3.15 Ed Gorpue	Inspected 7 mule lines. Found six cases of ringworm. This unit has no cook stoves. Heavy draught horses out of light class.	
17.3.15 " "	Inspected 6 Siege Battery where a suspected case of Anthrax was reported. Investigation proved there was no foundation for this report and having made a P.M. on the animal that died suddenly found it had died from a perforated Colon. This animal was addicted to attacks of colic.	
18.3.15 " "	Visited East Lancs Transport Lines. Inspected carcase of horse that died which V.D. thought might be Anthrax. Held P.M. as there was no appearance of Anthrax. Death due to ulcerative intestine.	
19.3.15 " "	45 Brigade RFA horse, suddenly went dead lame outside Headquarters, was unable to move. Had the animal removed to Mobile Section in float.	

Army Form C. 2118.

WAR DIARY
or
INTELLIGENCE SUMMARY.
(Erase heading not required.)

Instructions regarding War Diaries and Intelligence Summaries are contained in F.S. Regs., Part II. and the Staff Manual respectively. Title pages will be prepared in manuscript.

Hour, Date, Place	Summary of Events and Information	Remarks and references to Appendices
19.3.15 LA GORGUE	Also another driver I was called in to see early this morning who had badly injured himself during the night.	
20.3.15 "	Inspected 4th Seige Brigade. This Brigade has recently arrived from England. The majority of them are suffering from catarrh	
21-3-15 "	Visited mobile Section. Informed O.C. that he was to proceed to England	
22.3.15 "	Inspected Suspected case of mumps - Westforts annual suffering from lice. Sent S. Hegarty reported his departure for Abbeville went to C. Lillers grantes 4 days leave owing to his son having been killed.	
23.3.15 "	Capt. J. Bone reported his arrival & takes over command of M.V.S.	
24.3.15 "	Inspected three horses left behind by 24th Infantry Brigade. Two of them would he required. Inspected new site for mobile Section. Then visited mobile Section and	

Army Form C. 2118.

WAR DIARY
or
INTELLIGENCE SUMMARY.

(Erase heading not required.)

Instructions regarding War Diaries and Intelligence Summaries are contained in F.S. Regs., Part II. and the Staff Manual respectively. Title pages will be prepared in manuscript.

Hour, Date, Place	Summary of Events and Information	Remarks and references to Appendices
25-3-15 LA GORGUE	Arranged with O.C. for the Section to move mobile 27th inst	
26.3.15 "	Arranged billets for the mobile section	
27.3.15 "	Moved to Sailly	
28.3.15 SAILLY	Lieut W.S. visited Lieut G.W. Wheeler reported his departure 4th Corps A.3034.1/27/3/15 to England	
29.3.15 "	Visited O.V.S. 7th Division and made preliminary arrangements for units which have been transferred to this Division. Visited Mobile Section.	
30.3.15 "	Lieut W. P. Reid reported his arrival. Posted to 23rd Infantry Brigade. Inspected 33rd Brigade R.F.A. Mules not looking so well as when I last saw them. This no doubt is the hard work they have had recently. Shoeing in the 32nd Battery not good. Shoes not fitting. Farrier says he cannot alter the shoes properly without an anvil. Supply of forge tools should, I consider, be carried by all batteries. One to a Brigade is insufficient	

Forms/C. 2118/11.

Army Form C. 2118.

WAR DIARY
or
INTELLIGENCE SUMMARY.
(Erase heading not required.)

Instructions regarding War Diaries and Intelligence Summaries are contained in F. S. Regs., Part II. and the Staff Manual respectively. Title pages will be prepared in manuscript.

Hour, Date, Place	Summary of Events and Information	Remarks and references to Appendices
30.3.15 SAILLY	Inspected as usual the batteries as a rule, are situated far apart. The shoes do not stand too much widening when cold. Here for the Gun be easily be carried - would not require any extra transport.	
31.3.15 "	Inspected 24th Infantry Brigade. Majority of Animals looking well	

121/5140

Confidential

AVD

War Diary

from 1-4-15   to 30-4-15

of

Major P. J. Harris
A.D.V.S.
8th Division

Vol V

Army Form C. 2118.

WAR DIARY
or
INTELLIGENCE SUMMARY.
(Erase heading not required.)

Instructions regarding War Diaries and Intelligence Summaries are contained in F.S. Regs., Part II. and the Staff Manual respectively. Title pages will be prepared in manuscript.

Hour, Date, Place	Summary of Events and Information	Remarks and references to Appendices
1-4-15 SAILLY	Inspected 45th Brigade RFA. Horses looking in fair condition	
2-4-15 "	Visited mobile Section	
3-4-15 "	Inspected 5 RHA Brigade. Horses looking well	
4-4-15 "	Visited 119 Battery & Battery — mobile Section	
5-4-15 "	D.D.V.S visited and interviewed O.C. units	
6-4-15 "	Inspected horse of Cavalry Division Ophthalmia to test if treatment would be necessary to collect it. Animal unable to work for inspector. Horse knee of Cavalry Division. Treatment required for	
7-4-15 "	all of them. Visited mobile Section	
8-4-15 "	applied for 1 days leave	
10.4.15 to 16.4.15	On leave to England	
17.4.15	Completed returns	
18.4.15	Office work. Visited mobile Section	
20.4-15	Visited 5 RHA & 33rd Brigade RFA. Lt Pennington Scotts Fusiliers reported their departure for England	
21-4-15	Lt Read reported sick. Then came in with 4 officers	

(9 29 6) W 2794 100,000 8/14 H W V Forms/C. 2118/11.

WAR DIARY or INTELLIGENCE SUMMARY.

Army Form C. 2118.

Hour, Date, Place	Summary of Events and Information	Remarks and references to Appendices
21-4-15 SALLY	Several R.F.A. Brigades have recently been attached to this Division, so he thought he could get an Inspection ~~transport~~ Arrangement for returning attendance. As far as possible, and have taken an Executive work myself, as he returning duties could not be carried out properly with only 4 Officers under me. More Officers being sent in relief so he will keep matters considered.	
22.4.15	Extend granted 14 days Cook Cairo Office	
23.4.15	Inspected Intrepid 1st Londons	
24.4.15		
25.4.15	Battery moving. Arrived Veterinary duties. O.P.J. Austin Church Motor Ambulance with 5 R.H.A. Brigade Indian	
26.4.15	Inspected D & Z Batteries also A Q & N Battery Cavalry Divn	
27.4.15	Visited Northumberland Heavies	
28.4.15	Visited 37' Brig R.F.A. As some of the batteries are moving Lieut R.N.M. Williams reported his arrival and is posted to 25th Infantry Brigade for duty	

Army Form C. 2118.

WAR DIARY
or
INTELLIGENCE SUMMARY.
(Erase heading not required.)

Instructions regarding War Diaries and Intelligence Summaries are contained in F. S. Regs., Part II. and the Staff Manual respectively. Title pages will be prepared in manuscript.

Hour, Date, Place	Summary of Events and Information	Remarks and references to Appendices
29.4.15 SAILLY	Visited 5th Mountain Battery Murlite Section.	
30.4.15	Reported Head quarters re watering of horses	28

Confidential

War Diary
of
Major P.J. Harris
ADVS. 8' Division

From 1-5-15 to 31-5-15

Vol VI

Army Form C. 2118.

WAR DIARY
or
INTELLIGENCE SUMMARY.
(Erase heading not required.)

Instructions regarding War Diaries and Intelligence Summaries are contained in F.S. Regs., Part II. and the Staff Manual respectively. Title pages will be prepared in manuscript.

Hour, Date, Place	Summary of Events and Information	Remarks and references to Appendices
1-5-15 SALLY	Visited I Corps H.A.R. was ordered to send Worcester T 2.3.3 Ambulance into working district, for the loss of two chargers to V.O.S All problem have been reduced distance to hazel and uphill would not have they incurring into consequently they cannot with all our rents as has happened as more than the occasion also with to authority for the loss of horse etc. been. It is intended for this Division to have received any at all. The more casualled units should have East film Annual suffering from lies can only be positively dealt with by clipping	
3-5-15	Visited 3' Brigade R.G.A	
4-5-15	Visited 7 Siege Brigade IV Corps replied to my application for two Chargers to V.O. that now this Division to more plus stationary, we have to a good many chargers or horses that are only being excised and V.O. erred was these. This is absolutely understandable	

WAR DIARY or INTELLIGENCE SUMMARY.
(Erase heading not required.)

Army Form C. 2118.

Hour, Date, Place	Summary of Events and Information	Remarks and references to Appendices
5-5-15 SAILLY.	Visited Mobile Section.	
6-5-15 "	Inspected 1st C. (1/O) RE Horses not looking well but this mud brought very inferior animals with them. Attended Conf at Bn Hd qrs 5th RA. also 37th Bn F.A. RA as these units are at present in close proximity. Coy Office	
7-5-15 "	Inspected horses at mobile section.	
8-5-15 "	Office work	
9-5-15 "		
10-5-15 "		
11-5-15 "	Inspected Divisional Train. Veterinary charge and treatments are always promptly received on incidents but there are a good many items not sent owing to not being in stock. haq Sheff. Capt Cough Bukhay Brarch and some of the drugs which are difficult to be obtained. Also Wallets, nozzles for syringes & others do not viewed.	

Army Form C. 2118.

WAR DIARY
or
INTELLIGENCE SUMMARY.
(Erase heading not required.)

Instructions regarding War Diaries and Intelligence Summaries are contained in F.S. Regs., Part II. and the Staff Manual respectively. Title pages will be prepared in manuscript.

Hour, Date, Place	Summary of Events and Information	Remarks and references to Appendices
12.5.15 SAILLY	Batteries on the move arranged for veterinary attendance	
13.5.15 "	Inspected Highland Division (Heavy Battery) they brought several cards of ammunition with them. Visited 3 R.H.A Brigade which had been attached to this Division	
14.5.15 "	Return	
15.5.15 "	Inspected men under training for each shoer fitting the new pattern (filled up toe) shoe, so different was experienced	
16.5.15 "	Visited mobile section inspected Remounts	
17.5.15 "	P.M. Visited 5" Mountain Battery Headquarters	
18.5.15 "	A.M. Visited 6" Mountain Battery Headquarters	
19.5.15 "	Inspected 1 (#C) Co R.E. with reference to a number of animals they wish to get. Visited 5 M.B. H.Q. 21st mobile Section	
20.5.15 "	H.Qrs 5" Mountain Battery. Also attended hora of French Division	
21.5.15 "	Office visited mobile section	
22.5.15 "	Inspected 23rd Infantry Brigade in Company with O.C. Train	

Army Form C. 2118.

WAR DIARY
or
INTELLIGENCE SUMMARY.
(Erase heading not required.)

Instructions regarding War Diaries and Intelligence Summaries are contained in F.S. Regs., Part II. and the Staff Manual respectively. Title pages will be prepared in manuscript.

Hour, Date, Place	Summary of Events and Information	Remarks and references to Appendices
22-5-15 SAILLY	Horses of 2/Scottish Rifles looking in poor condition. Stable management bad. Horses daily + no proper supervision. Reported to Head quarters. Horses of other battalions looking remarkably well more especially the Wexfords Reserve	
23-5-15 "	Visited 1st & 2nd Lines + 5th M. Battery. Interviewed Staff Capt. Div. RA with regard to not notifying us when Brigades Batteries suddenly move. Visited mobile Section	
24-5-15 "	Visited ADVS W. Riding Division in connection with the veterinary charge of some of their batteries.	
25-5-15 "	Visited 1st & 2nd : 5 Mountain Battery. West Riding Battery 2, 3rd C. RE and mobile Section	
26.5-15 "	Inspected Ringworm cases Highland Division A Battery	
27.28.29. "	Visited mules in list charge and mobile Section	
30. "	Inspected both area establishes 2 3 C RE	
31- "	Reported the way the mule drivers of the W Riding Division drive their mules. They never let their animals break up a fast trot or gallop.	

8th Division

ADS

Confidential

121/5497.

War Diary

of

Major P.J. Harris
ADMS 8' Division

From 1st June To 30 June

Vol VII

Army Form C. 2118.

WAR DIARY
or
INTELLIGENCE SUMMARY.

(Erase heading not required.)

Instructions regarding War Diaries and Intelligence Summaries are contained in F.S. Regs., Part II. and the Staff Manual respectively. Title pages will be prepared in manuscript.

Hour, Date, Place		Summary of Events and Information	Remarks and references to Appendices
1-6-15	SAILLY	Inspected 25th Infantry Brigade.	
2-6-15	"	Inspected Remounts. Two or three debilitated and in bad condition, three broken away and the cold sheen will find great difficulty in showing our	
3.6.15	"	Inspected horses of Mobile Section	
4.6.15	"	Office	
5.6.15	"	Inspected Rifle Brigade and 1st London wagon lines. Visited Mobile Section	
6.6.15	"	Office	
7.6.15	"	Inspected horses of 45 Brigade RFA brought forward for Casting. Inspected two unpoisonous cases of 45 Bde. Dying Cpl. had them evacuated at once.	
8.6.15	"	Inspected all horses of Ammunition Column 45 Brigade and 1st Battery	
9.6.15	"	Inspected all horses of 3 & 5 Batteries 45th Brigade. Interviewed owner of stud with regard to hiring same when required.	

WAR DIARY or INTELLIGENCE SUMMARY

Army Form C. 2118.

Hour, Date, Place	Summary of Events and Information	Remarks and references to Appendices
10.6.15 Sailly	Inspected all horses of Signal Co. majority of animals in fit condition. Evacuated one with suspected mange. Interviewing C.O. on its apparent want of supervision. Visited M.V.S.	
11.6.15 "	Inspected 3" Battery R.F.A. mobile section.	
12.6.15 "	Visited 10 Brigade (Amm. Col.). Inspected two Horses of Landing party. Inspected Reo also of the two others also Rifle Brigade. Inspected crew also of the two Colns and depots of Div. Amm. Col.	
13.6.15 "	Wrote to Prect&Rts. for A.V.C. number to be given to a man who has been transferred to the Corps and now with the section. This man has been numbered for nearly a month and no number has yet been allotted him.	
14.6.15 "	Inspected all lines of 33 Brigade Ammunition Column and 36" Battery R.F.A. Two cases picked out in the Battery to be moved with No Cartus as they were slightly itchy.	

Forms/C. 2118/11.

WAR DIARY
or
INTELLIGENCE SUMMARY.
(Erase heading not required.)

Army Form C. 2118.

Hour, Date, Place	Summary of Events and Information	Remarks and references to Appendices
14 6.15 SAILLY	The horses of the battery are not at all well groomed and the O.C. states he cannot procure dandy brushes no body brushes from Ordnance	
15. 6.15 "	Inspected all horses of the 33rd & 32nd Battery and Headquarters 33 Brigade RFA: Visited M.V. Section	
16. 6.15 "	Inspected all horses Amm Column 5 RFA. Visited 53rd Battery and Mobile Section.	
17. 6.15 "	Inspected all horses of 0 & 2 Batteries also Headquarters 5 RFA	
18. 6.15 "	DDVS visited. VO reviewed retiring personally	
19. 6.15 "	Inspected all horses of the Highland 5th Battery Amm: Column also Amm Column Headquarters of Heavy Brigade Artillery are retained. Authority for issue of Body brushes Inspected two Skin cases in Div: Amm Column	

Army Form C. 2118.

WAR DIARY
or
INTELLIGENCE SUMMARY.
(Erase heading not required.)

Instructions regarding War Diaries and Intelligence Summaries are contained in F.S. Regs., Part II. and the Staff Manual respectively. Title pages will be prepared in manuscript.

Hour, Date, Place	Summary of Events and Information	Remarks and references to Appendices
19.6.15 SAILLY	Reported on 1st Bde quality & distribution of Units that are now being issued	
20.6.15 "	Visited Mobile Section	
21.6.15 "	Inspected all Guns of 114" 118" Heavy Bryds. Horses looking remarkably well. Visited 5" RGA Amm Col. and Mobile Section	
22.6.15 "	Reported on the use of sandbags for protection of horses against fire. Did not advise their use	V/11/15 V/22.6.15.
23.6.15 "	Reported on the issuing of heavy draught horses by Cold Stream. Recommended the issue of feed for 50 ac Coy Horses to be unsatisfactory	
24.6.15 "	Visited Mobile Section	
25.6.15 "	Office Returns	
26.6.15 "	Mobile Section had to move owing to this part of Sailly area being taken by another Division. Hunted all day for suitable place. Have chosen one but not yet secured	

(9 29 6) W 2794 100,000 8/14 H W V Forms/C. 2118/11.

WAR DIARY or INTELLIGENCE SUMMARY.

Army Form C. 2118.

(Erase heading not required.)

Hour, Date, Place	Summary of Events and Information	Remarks and references to Appendices
26.6.15 SAILLY	A battalion is billeted here. Section bivouac'd close by.	
27.6.15 — —	Advanced about Mobile Section is its new position. McLeod was having been changed. attended Field Ambulance horses which were badly wounded by shell fire the Ambulance being attacked by my office. Inspected wounded horses and visited Mob. Section.	
28.6.15 — —		
29.6.15 — —	Proceeded on seven days leave to England	

8th Division

AVD

187/6210

Confidential

War Diary

of

Major. P. J. Harris
A.D.V.S. 8th Division

From 1st July to 31st July.

Vol VIII

Army Form C. 2118.

WAR DIARY
or
INTELLIGENCE SUMMARY.
(Erase heading not required.)

Instructions regarding War Diaries and Intelligence Summaries are contained in F. S. Regs., Part II. and the Staff Manual respectively. Title pages will be prepared in manuscript.

Hour, Date, Place	Summary of Events and Information	Remarks and references to Appendices
5.7.15 SAILLY	Returned from Leave.	
6.7.15 — " —	Took over charge of Mobile Section during absence on leave of Capt. Bone. Inspected some sick of 2" Middlesex	
7.7.15 — " —	Office and Section	
8.7.15 — " —	Visited Divisional Mounted Troops & section. Went into the cause of and ache eyes trouble, was sanctioned months ago, no one can be blamed	
9.7.15 — " —	Inspected suspicious cases of Mumps at Sherwood Foresters 148 Brigade Amm. Column. Attended Mob. Section compiled returns	
10.7.15 — " —	Inspected suspicious case of Mumps in 2" Field C. RF Visited Mobile Section and attended ordinary sick after drill held	
11.7.15 — " —	Visited Mobile Section	
12.7.15 — " —	Visited Mobile Section and 33 Brigade RFA weapon lines	

WAR DIARY or INTELLIGENCE SUMMARY

Army Form C. 2118.

(Erase heading not required.)

Instructions regarding War Diaries and Intelligence Summaries are contained in F.S. Regs., Part II. and the Staff Manual respectively. Title pages will be prepared in manuscript.

Hour, Date, Place	Summary of Events and Information	Remarks and references to Appendices
13.7.15 SAILLY	Visited mobile section. Divisional train. O.2 Battery and 55th & 57th Battery.	
14.7.15 "	Visited mobile section. Rifle Brigade & Bomb Wagon Line.	
15.7.15 "	Visited mobile section. Inspected suspicious case of mange in 59 Battery. Orders received for Capt Bone to take A.D.V.S. 5th Division. On detailing B. Taylor S.R. I take over temporary command, he being the only suitable officer for this duty. He however had no experience and am issuing a regular officers will soon be detailed for.	
16.7.15 "	Completing returns.	
17.7.15 "	Visited mobile section. and A.D.V.S. 27 Div. with reference to 8 Heavy Brigade being administered by him. Capt. T. Bone reported his departure.	
18.7.15 "	Spent the morning at mobile section instructing B. Taylor	
19.7.15 "	Inspected suspicious case of mange 8 Signal Co. Visited H/Q section.	

Army Form C. 2118.

WAR DIARY
or
INTELLIGENCE SUMMARY.
(Erase heading not required.)

Instructions regarding War Diaries and Intelligence Summaries are contained in F.S. Regs., Part II. and the Staff Manual respectively. Title pages will be prepared in manuscript.

Hour, Date, Place	Summary of Events and Information	Remarks and references to Appendices
20/7/15 SAILLY	Visited Mobile Section Northumberland Hussars	
21.7.15 " "	Visited H.Q. Section & Div. Ammn Column	
22.7.15 " "	Visited Mob. Section Northumberland Hussars. The 19' Infantry Brigade is now in our area and complains that for a Division this Brigade belongs to no Division and is without a veterinary officer. As this a very strong Brigade comprising 5 battalions, Signal Section, Cyclist Platoon, C.o. Amm. Supply Column Section, Field Ambulance, and Ammunition Column I have asked that a V.O. could not be permanently attached to this a.brig. unit. As regards horses not numerically perhaps but quickly up and taking up a large area.	34/46 ⌐ 17/23.7.15
23.7.15	Visited Mobile Section and B' Divisional Howitzer Brigade RFA Inspected horses brought forward for casting. V.O. rendered returns	
24.7.15	Visited Wagon lines of 19' Infantry Brigade and arranged for veterinary charge. The Field Ambulance	

WAR DIARY
or
INTELLIGENCE SUMMARY.
(Erase heading not required.)

Army Form C. 2118.

Instructions regarding War Diaries and Intelligence Summaries are contained in F.S. Regs., Part II. and the Staff Manual respectively. Title pages will be prepared in manuscript.

Hour, Date, Place	Summary of Events and Information	Remarks and references to Appendices
24.7.15 SALLY	Being a food division away amongst the Lahore Division. Men have asked the ADVS what Division to many.	
25.7.15 — " —	Visited Secn with Lt Taylor to witness demonstration of new method of maintaining horses	
26.7.15 — " —	Visited mobile section and Highland (Rifle) Battery	
27.7.15 — " —	Visited Highland (Rifle) Brigade = 10" Infantry Brigade and Supply Column.	
28.7.15 — " —	Visited mobile section, 19 Field Ambulance and ADMS Lahore Div with reference to this mud. Visited Northumberland Hussars. Called out in the evening to see horse with badly contused leg caused by accident belonging to Highland (Rifle) Heavy Battery	
29.7.15 — " —	Visited mobile section and Highland Battery	
30.7.15 — " —	Handed over charge Highland Battery to Lt Reed. Returns rendered	
31.7.15	Handed over charge N Hussars to Lt Quilter. Orders received 2 PM from 2nd Corps Sanitary Officer to proceed to Vet Hospital Rouen. Am quite in the dark about this as I have not applied for his transfer.	

(9 29 6) W 2794 100,000 8/14 H W V   Forms/C. 2118/11.

8th Division

W.D. /121/6598

Confidential

War Diary

of

Major P. J. Harris
A.D.V.S. 8' Division

From 1st Aug. 15.   To 31 Aug. 15.

Vol IX

WAR DIARY
or
INTELLIGENCE SUMMARY.
(Erase heading not required.)

Army Form C. 2118.

Instructions regarding War Diaries and Intelligence Summaries are contained in F.S. Regs., Part II. and the Staff Manual respectively. Title pages will be prepared in manuscript.

Hour, Date, Place	Summary of Events and Information	Remarks and references to Appendices
1. 8.15 SAILLY	Visited Mobile Section Lt Austin reported his departure	
2. 8.15 — —	Visited 19' Field Ambulance	
3. 8.15 — —	Visited Mobile Section	
4. 8.15 — —	Orders received for Lieuts of ? to proceed to 27 Division. Lt Lewis no not 4 officers for the Division which on Etna Brigade attached to it. Have asked that an officer be sent at once to command Section so that I can release Lt Taylor from that duty	
5. 8.15 — —	DDMS informs me I can return to Reid pending arrival of officer nominated for OC Section	
6. 8.15 — —	DDMS visited. Inspected Mob Section. Visited 59 Infantry Brigade HQ and conferred when I had sent to mob section Lieutenant Relation rendered by VD	
7. 8.15	Visited 84 Field Co RE ambulance to attend sick horse by request of ADVS of 28 Division The 27 Division Ord was now informed I or ?	

Forms/C. 2118/11.

WAR DIARY or INTELLIGENCE SUMMARY.

Army Form C. 2118.

(Erase heading not required.)

Instructions regarding War Diaries and Intelligence Summaries are contained in F.S. Regs., Part II. and the Staff Manual respectively. Title pages will be prepared in manuscript.

Hour, Date, Place	Summary of Events and Information	Remarks and references to Appendices
7.8.15 SAILLY	Must arrange with A.D.V.S. of this Division completed returns	
8.8.15	Visited Mobile Section & 26th Field Ambulance	
9.8.15	Visited Mobile Section, Northumberland Hussars and Cyclist Company. Have been informed that the 1/Glamorgan Field Co. R.E. were in Morques. I visited them but found they were in the 27th area. As the A.D.V.S. of this (27) Division says they destroy in his area I visited visiting this much myself to save see future correspondence. Visited Mobile Section. Major of this town asked if I could render help to a farmer horse which was suffering from tetanus. As I believe we are to render every help to the inhabitants I felt justified in having horse removed dealt with & carrion.	
10.8.15		
11.8.15	Visited Mobile Section & Glamorgan Field Co. R.E.	

WAR DIARY or INTELLIGENCE SUMMARY

Army Form C. 2118.

(Erase heading not required.)

Hour, Date, Place	Summary of Events and Information	Remarks and references to Appendices
12.8.15 SAILLY	Visited Northumberland Hussars Turb Section	
13.8.15 — " —	G O C inspected Section. Visited Mobile Section and 96' Field Co RE (xx Division) also inspected some Calves that were ill on the farm this Co is billeted. V.O's rendered opinion Horse Show Jumping all day. Animals looked Ifound	
14.8.15 — " —		
15.8.15 — " —	Office work	
16.8.15 — " —	Handed over Northumberland Hussars to Lt Lewis found the different positions of wagon lines of the horse Brigade of 20' Division and Field Ambulances that have been attacked and in that area inspected charge of 2. Jr Co RE	
17.8.15 — " —	Visited Campbell 50 Co RE and inspected Sick Animals of 36' Battery RFA. Two Ivl horse sent to hospital Section Inspected CRA' charge which has skin eruption	
18.8.15 — " —	Visited Vet Section and inspected Sick of 32, 33 Batteries	

WAR DIARY or INTELLIGENCE SUMMARY.

Army Form C. 2118.

(Erase heading not required.)

Hour, Date, Place	Summary of Events and Information	Remarks and references to Appendices

18-8-15 SAILLY — Had two horses sent to mobile Section

19 8 15 — Visited mob: Section 19 Inf: Bde Amm Column so two
sick horses evacuated. Arranged for the move of Mob: Section.
Motor position went to the front and being required
by Corps. Inspected two New Cases on 53 + 59 Battalion
have been concealed.

20 8 15 — Mobile Section moved to new position. Inspected 3
Suspected mange Cases in 45 Bde Ammn Col Evacuating
two VO rendered returns.

21 8 15 — Visited Mot: Section. Compiled returns
22 9 15 — Office work
23 8 15 — Visited Mobile Section not probably in position will
have to move to another position. Two P.M. on cow
supposed to have died from Su poisoning. No
examinations are fresh on owners farm.

24 8 15 — Visited mobile Section Headquarters 55 Brigade RFA

WAR DIARY or INTELLIGENCE SUMMARY.

(Erase heading not required.)

Army Form C. 2118.

Hour, Date, Place	Summary of Events and Information	Remarks and references to Appendices
24 8/15 SAILLY		
25 8/15	Visited 1st Co. R.E. Visited 36 Battery RFA inspected w/t wire proposed for aerial testgrades 5 RFA – 45 Brigade RFA Inspected 23rd Inf. Brigade where I found a semaphore signaller supposed to be visible tower but in a shock with another heavy horse had it sent to w/t section for treatment	
26 8/15	Visited Mob. Section. Inspected Renard 64th Battery RFA but section too afraid to move and at present there seems great difficulty in finding a suitable place. Applied for car to go round in the afternoon but there were none available.	
27 9/15	Arranged move of mobile section, having found a suitable position. V.O. rendered returns	
28 8/15		
29 8/15	Visited Inspection Compiled returns Office	

Army Form C. 2118.

WAR DIARY
or
INTELLIGENCE SUMMARY.
(Erase heading not required.)

Instructions regarding War Diaries and Intelligence Summaries are contained in F.S. Regs., Part II. and the Staff Manual respectively. Title pages will be prepared in manuscript.

Hour, Date, Place	Summary of Events and Information	Remarks and references to Appendices
30.8.15 SAILLY.	Inspected annuals of Middlesex proposed for Casting 25" Field Ambulance very short of horses made inquiries at Headquarters and found that Included for horses had been overlooked.	
31.8.15 —"—	Inspected annual (Signal Co) proposed for Casting for Vice - advised transfer to old mobile Section	

8th Division

121/6923

Confidential

War Diary.
of
Major. P. J. Harris
A.D.V.S. 8th Division

From 1-9-15   To 30.9.15

Vol X

Army Form C. 2118.

WAR DIARY
or
INTELLIGENCE SUMMARY.
(Erase heading not required.)

Instructions regarding War Diaries and Intelligence Summaries are contained in F. S. Regs., Part II. and the Staff Manual respectively. Title pages will be prepared in manuscript.

Hour, Date, Place	Summary of Events and Information	Remarks and references to Appendices
1.9.15 SAILLY	Visited Cannongere Co. R.E. also Sotterers Coys and accus with excavator. Visited Mob. Section	
2.9.15 — " —	Visited Mobile Section 112th Battery RGA	
3.9.15 — " —	Visited Mob Section 10th rendered returns.Head Conference	
4.9.15 — " —	Visited Mob Section. Compiled Returns. Attended CRE's Conference	
5.9.15 — " —	Visited Mob Section. Office work	
6.9.15 — " —	Visited new positions of Amm. Columns. Inspected Canvas to R.E.	
7.9.15 — " —	Visited Mob. Section. Office work. Have arranged for all units to be issued with Smoke Helmets for Horses at behalf of 10%. Brought up at Conference the question of Shortage of Hay issued at Refilling point. I am (substantiate) my statement by fact. Inspected Sick of Div. Amm. Col. Visited M.V. Section	
8.9.15	Informed DAZVS that the Head Quarters Staff received a shortage	

Forms/C. 2118/11.

Army Form C. 2118.

WAR DIARY
or
INTELLIGENCE SUMMARY.
(Erase heading not required.)

Instructions regarding War Diaries and Intelligence Summaries are contained in F.S. Regs., Part II. and the Staff Manual respectively. Title pages will be prepared in manuscript.

Hour, Date, Place	Summary of Events and Information	Remarks and references to Appendices
8.9.15 SAILLY	Of Straw today nearly 200 lbs delivered. Have had orders issued that all horses are to be picketed wheel pegs owing to the large number of kicks.	
9.9.15	Inspected all sick of Divisional Train. Visited Mobile Section of Hants Fus. 3d Co RE, and ADVS of Division with reference to the East treatment went Eating wood into the Divisional Area	
10.9.15	Inspected sick at M Section. VO rendered returns and held conference of Veterinary officers returned from leave	
11.9.15	Inspected sick at M Section. ADVS visited	
12.9.15 "	Compiled returns	
13.9.15 "	Inspected sick at Section. Inspected horses 25" Field Ambulance	
14.9.15 "	Inspected sick at Section. Have evacuated 46 animals in the last five days in accordance with DDVS order	Strictly Confidential No 293. V.S. of 9.9.15
15.9.15 "	Inspected sick at Section	

WAR DIARY or INTELLIGENCE SUMMARY.

Army Form C. 2118.

(Erase heading not required.)

Hour, Date, Place			Summary of Events and Information	Remarks and references to Appendices
16.9.15		SAILLY	DDVS visited and interviewed all V.O's in their Sub-Area.	
17	9.15	"	Visited Mob.Section. V.O. Conference	
18	9.15	"	Inspected sick at Mob.Section. Inspected sick 8th Spares Co. Completed returns.	
20	9.15	"	Visited 5th R.M.R. Brig. Ammn. Col. 128 Brig Ammn Col. and Mobile Section. Went to inspect horses of the Canadian Div. Ammn. Col. (1 Section) which had just arrived but found they had not left.	
21	9.15	"	Inspected sick Mobile Section and visited A.D.V.S 27 Div. with reference to animal admitted to my Mob.Section.	
22	9.15	"	Inspected sick Mob. Section. Visited advanced dressing post.	
23	9.15	"	Visited 3rd Canadian Brigade R.F.A. also A.D.S. 23 Division and instructed him as regards to routine work.	
24	9.15	"	Visited Mob.Section and advanced dressing post. V.O.s rendered returns.	

Army Form C. 2118.

WAR DIARY
or
INTELLIGENCE SUMMARY.
(Erase heading not required.)

Instructions regarding War Diaries and Intelligence Summaries are contained in F.S. Regs., Part II. and the Staff Manual respectively. Title pages will be prepared in manuscript.

Hour, Date, Place	Summary of Events and Information	Remarks and references to Appendices
25.9.15 SAILLY	Visited Sector Advanced Post. No CRITS answering. Adversely Completed return. An extra wagon has been added to the Mobile Section transport. The reason given for the refusal of my application for a tent for the Mr Section was the increase in transport which was undesirable. It would have been much more preferable if a tent had been added as this could have been used as a supply wagon thereby acting for a dual purpose and not increasing the transport.	
26.9.15 — " —	Visited Advanced Post and Mobile Section.	
27.9.15 — " —	Visited Advanced Post. Mobile Section. 8th Field Decces. R Berts.	
28.9.15 — " —	Visited Advanced Post. M.T. Section. 5th Battery. T. of D. coms. Lieut Williams reports sick at 24th Field Ambulance	
29.9.15 — " —	Visited 45 Brigade R.F.A.	

Army Form C. 2118.

WAR DIARY
or
INTELLIGENCE SUMMARY.

(Erase heading not required.)

Instructions regarding War Diaries and Intelligence Summaries are contained in F. S. Regs., Part II. and the Staff Manual respectively. Title pages will be prepared in manuscript.

Hour, Date, Place	Summary of Events and Information	Remarks and references to Appendices
30.9.15 SAILLY	Inspected both Sections. Visited ADVS 23rd Division with reference to her Div. Ammunition Column that was in the area.	

8th Division

121/7933

Confidential

War Diary

of

Major. P. J. Harris
A.D.V.S. 8th Division

From 1-10-15   to 31-10-15.

Vol XI

Army Form C. 2118

WAR DIARY
or
INTELLIGENCE SUMMARY.
(Erase heading not required.)

Instructions regarding War Diaries and Intelligence Summaries are contained in F.S. Regs., Part II. and the Staff Manual respectively. Title pages will be prepared in manuscript.

Hour, Date, Place	Summary of Events and Information	Remarks and references to Appendices
1-10-15 SAILLY	Visited Section. V.O's rendered returns.	
2.10.15 "	Compiled returns. Visited 33rd Bde; 45 Bde; 5 RHA Brigade Ammunition Column	
3.10.15 "	Visited Mobile Section. Also 3rd Battery RFA.	
4-10.15 "	Office	
5.10.15 "	Lieut PARMITER F. reported his arrival. Visited Mobile Section; 45 Bde. Ammn Column and 128th Ammn Column	
6.10.15 "	DDVS visited. Visited Mobile Section.	
7.10.15 "	Visited Mobile Section. Inspected Remounts 45 Brigade RFA with G.O.C. RA	
8.10.15 "	Visited Section. V.O's rendered returns	
9.10.15 "	Visited Section. Compiled returns	
10-10-15 "	Left for England on leave	
18-10-15 "	Returned from leave	
19-10-15 "	Office and visited Mobile Section.	

WAR DIARY or INTELLIGENCE SUMMARY.

Army Form C. 2118

Hour, Date, Place		Summary of Events and Information	Remarks and references to Appendices
20.10.15	SAILLY	Inspected 1/London Regt Transport animals. Majority of mules suffering from a depleted condition of the skin, patches of hair falling away, hepatic revel from scrapings taken. In doubt a variety of Ringworm and have ordered treatment as such. Have also DOV's to inspect.	
21.10.15	SAILLY	Inspected Ringworm Cases. Visited mobile section	
22.10.15	"	D.D.V.S visited suspected Ringworm cases. V.O. returned	
23.10.15	"	Visited 11 & 2nd Co. Div Train with reference to man attacked to Co having been admitted to hospital suffering from Anthrax. Inspected 24th Field Ambulance Supplies return.	
24.10.15	"	Inspected Ringworm Cases 1/London & machine gun sect.	
25.10.15	"	Visited Heavy Batteries in 23rd area.	
26.10.15	"	Visited M. Victn A.V.S. 20 & 23 Division Veterinary officers with their divisions.	

Army Form C. 2118.

WAR DIARY
or
INTELLIGENCE SUMMARY.
(Erase heading not required.)

Instructions regarding War Diaries and Intelligence Summaries are contained in F. S. Regs., Part II and the Staff Manual respectively. Title pages will be prepared in manuscript.

Place	Date	Hour	Summary of Events and Information	Remarks and references to Appendices
SAILLY	27.10.15	—	Visited mobile Section. Attended to Civilian force.	
	28.10.15	— " —	Visited and inspected Registration huts but cattle and mouvements to Casualty courts. Inspected him.	
	29.10.15	— " —	Inspected Rainform Case. V.O's rendered returns	
	30.10.15	— " —	Inspected h h Police force. Attended D.D.V's Conference	
	31.10.15	— " —	Inspected proposed cast case 5th HtA Ann Column. Visited mobile section. Completed returns	

121/7636

Confidential

War Diary.

of.

Major. P. J. Harris

A.D.V.S. 8ᵗʰ Division

From 1-11-15   to 30-11-15.

Vol XII

Army Form C. 2118.

WAR DIARY
or
INTELLIGENCE SUMMARY.
(Erase heading not required.)

8th Division

November 1915

Place	Date	Hour	Summary of Events and Information	Remarks and references to Appendices
SAILLY	1st		Inspected proposed gun horse of Z Battery. Concealed 5" Straight away, one debility case being suspicious of tuberculosis. Have asked the DDVS of question, could not be obtained for a fired Jorj to be issued to mobile section. The J Emeries is a recently as the are always a review pattern shoes to be made. Visited mobile section. Attended usual Regimental Conference and brought to the notice of practice of butting Every on the pavé roads. British horses accustomed to hard roads any the Commanders they must receive to only a minimum of bone diseases.	
"	2nd			
"	3rd		Inspected Pick 33 Bde Amm Col. This unit is very behind with their Grooms Standings. The present standings are in a frightful condition. Visited MVS.	
"	4		Visited 32 Battery Headquarters 5 Petts 3 mpais, 33/5 rifled Bde and DWRA Headquarters	
"	5		Visited mobile veterinary section. VO received returns	
"	6		Completed petition. Inspected horses proposed for casting horse E RE	

Army Form C. 2118.

WAR DIARY
or
INTELLIGENCE SUMMARY.
(Erase heading not required.)

Instructions regarding War Diaries and Intelligence Summaries are contained in F. S. Regs., Part II. and the Staff Manual respectively. Title pages will be prepared in manuscript.

Place	Date	Hour	Summary of Events and Information	Remarks and references to Appendices
SAILLY	7		Visited Mobile Section. Inspected horses 1/5 Black Watch with a view to classifying them, as this battalion brought some Clydesdales out with them.	
"	8		Visited 32nd Battery and interviewed J. 2. M.S. Preston with reference to his transfer to the A.V.C. Am having evacuated all bad cracked heels and wounds about the feet, as I consider it hopeless trying to treat them under the muddy conditions experienced at the front.	
"	9		Inspected all animals of the 25th Infantry Brigade.	
"	10		Inspected all animals of the 23rd Infantry Brigade. 2/Scottish Rifles very backward in making cover for their animals, due to not being able to let any trees.	
"	11		Inspected all horses of 7th Infantry Brigade. All animals of this Division are fed four times a day, the last feed of the day being about 8 o'clock at night, thus preventing the long hours of fasting if the last feed is at "Léantime".	

Army Form C. 2118.

WAR DIARY
or
INTELLIGENCE SUMMARY.
(Erase heading not required.)

Place	Date	Hour	Summary of Events and Information	Remarks and references to Appendices
SAILLY	11		arrival at railhead. Yes, I think a greatly the hay ration is only 10 lbs. As all units are allowed to requisition for straw, to make up the deficiency many will not fuel the time to go and head it, owing to the stack being miles away. A great deal of straw has been used for making roofs for the covered standings and I cannot keep trucking it would have been cheaper more serviceable to have covered tarpaulins or sail cloth. The straw does not keep the rain out and when it becomes sodden, it continually drips on the horses, notwithstanding the weather being dry.	
"	12		Visited Mobile Section. DDVS. called but missed him. V.O. rendered returns	
"	13		Compiled returns	
"	14		DDVS. accompanied by Lt. Col. E.S. martin visited. Inspected horse S¹ Signal Co	
"	15		Inspected horses of the 33rd Brigade R.F.A. One battery having 20 4th made the no evidence for evacuation. I ordered these cracked heels cases to be evacuated. I am trying an afterwards treatment, preserving grease of all heels with Anti-frostbite grease.	

Army Form C. 2118.

WAR DIARY
or
INTELLIGENCE SUMMARY.
(Erase heading not required.)

Place	Date	Hour	Summary of Events and Information	Remarks and references to Appendices
SAILLY	17		Inspected all horses 5th R.H.A. Brigade. Animals of this Brigade have not been looking at all well, but since the majority have at last got under cover standings an improvement has been noticed. A better system of watering and feeding has also taken place with good results. It is rather unfortunate that owing to the Brigade moving into a new area the animals will again be in the open, as it only means they will feel free effects conditions.	
"	18"		Visited Mobile Section.	
"	19"		Visited A.D.S. Section and arranged the handing over Command to Lt Taylor. Lt Lewis reported his departure to ROUEN	
"	20"		Lt Taylor assumed Command of the Mobile Section. Inspected horse lines. Amm: Column work then Lessons then visited Mob: Section and helped Lt Taylor in his various duties. Completed returns.	
"	21"		Inspected all horses of the 24th Field Ambulance. This unit has to be well watched as there is nobody who really knows anything about horses	
"	22"		Visited Mobile Section. Lieut Brie reported his Arrival.	
"	23		Office closed down on moving to new area	

Army Form C. 2118.

WAR DIARY
or
INTELLIGENCE SUMMARY.
(Erase heading not required.)

Instructions regarding War Diaries and Intelligence Summaries are contained in F. S. Regs., Part II. and the Staff Manual respectively. Title pages will be prepared in manuscript.

Place	Date	Hour	Summary of Events and Information	Remarks and references to Appendices
SAILLY	24		Left at 8 am and rode to new area.	
BLARINGHEM	24	1.30	Arrived. Inspected O.C. Clubs which had been badly kicked its right fore arm.	
"	25		Rode out and inspected farm, which has been allotted to mobile Section. He arriving would not allow me to go and choose a suitable place but a farm who picked for the map I consider the site is suitable but the place is unsuitable. No cover for the horses	
"	26		Visited Site of Inspection – Completed returns	
"	27		Visited Signal Co. R.E. horses of Staff.	
"	28		Rode over to mobilization site. Met D.D.V.S. here. Decided that the building would be unsuitable for the time being.	
"	29		Mobile Section arrived but billeted in the wrong farm P	
"	30		Visited Mobile Section, which has now got into the farm allotted to them. Owner very decent and there is every chance of working it fairly nice place. Orb.	

Confidential

WAR. DIARY

of.

Major. P.J. Harris
A.D.V.S. 8th Division

121/7929

From 1st December 1915   To 31st December 1915.

Vol XIII

Army Form C. 2118.

WAR DIARY
or
INTELLIGENCE SUMMARY.
(Erase heading not required.)

8th Division

DECEMBER 1915

Place	Date	Hour	Summary of Events and Information	Remarks and references to Appendices
BLARINGHEM	1st		Visited waggon lines of the 33 Brigade R.F.A.	
"	2nd		Visited "D" Battery and inspected mule Cephas suffering from Laminitis. Would like to have removed the animal to Mobile Section but cannot do so owing to being unable to obtain a Stead in any of the Brigades in Divisional Area. Visited Mobile Section and classified all sick animals being evacuated	
"	3rd		Rode to Lynde with two A.V.C. men and collected mule suffering from Laminitis. The animal was much better and was able to travel. V.O. rendered returns. Inspected & classified sick animals being evacuated. Completed returns	
"	4th			
"	5th			
"	6th		Searched for 1/5 Blackwatch Transport lines as the V.O. could not find them. Found their position and informed V.O. Visited Mobile Section.	
"	7th		Visited Mobile Section. In view of any Horse Clippers being handed over being issued H. books as if the same thing is going to happen as Cropped, when mans clippers were authorized but never received, units cannot carry out the orders on clipping if they are not supplied with machines. And it is not much use having them issued when the	

Army Form C. 2118.

WAR DIARY
or
INTELLIGENCE SUMMARY.

(Erase heading not required.)

Instructions regarding War Diaries and Intelligence Summaries are contained in F.S. Regs., Part II. and the Staff Manual respectively. Title pages will be prepared in manuscript.

Place	Date	Hour	Summary of Events and Information	Remarks and references to Appendices
BARINGHEM	7.		The clipping season is over.	
"	8.		Have clippers have not been issued. Inspected verified description of horses that clippers have not been issued being evacuated.	
"	9.		Inspected V.O.s at the Mobile Section and gave them a practical demonstration in the practical method of inoculation. Each officer then practised by inoculating 15 mobile section horses	
"	10.		V.O.s rendered returns	
"	11.		Compiled return	
"	12.		Inspected horses to be evacuated. Wired to Veterinary Stores to know when drugs indented for on the 1st inst. might be expected. Reply received that they were despatched per M.F.O. on the 5th inst. So a great delay takes place in having brought up by the returning Conducting the old system of having brought up by the returning Conducting brutes was done away with. This System was much more satisfactory in every way. One received the things very much quicker and there was never any chance of the package going astray. Am collecting several horses of the 33rd Division which cannot the Division is on the move and the Animals are unable to march.	

2333 Wt W2344/1454 700,000 5/15 D.D.&L. A.D.S.S./Forms/C. 2118.

Army Form C. 2118.

WAR DIARY
or
INTELLIGENCE SUMMARY.

(Erase heading not required.)

Instructions regarding War Diaries and Intelligence Summaries are contained in F. S. Regs., Part II. and the Staff Manual respectively. Title pages will be prepared in manuscript.

Place	Date	Hour	Summary of Events and Information	Remarks and references to Appendices
BLARINGHEM	13th		Inspected officers charger at R.A. Head quarters, suffering from skin eruptions on withers. An informed this animal suffered from skin eruptions on the legs during last winter. As I did not like the appearance of it I had the animal evacuated. Visited Aire to interview the D.D.V.S. but he was not in.	
"	14th		Inspected sick at 5th R.H.A. Amm: Column and "Z" Battery	
"	15th		Visited the various stables in and around Blaringhem.	
"	16th		Inspected M.M.P. horses also sick animals at mobile section to be evacuated	
"	17th		"Machine" Stores mobile section horses. V.O.s rendered returns	
"	18th		Inspected sick to be evacuated. Compiled returns	
"	19th		Prepared for manoeuvres.	
"	20th		Left for manoeuvres.	
"	23rd		Returned from manoeuvres. An informer Operation Orders should be issued to A.D.V.S. to enable them to communicate with first arrivals, which cannot be done otherwise.	
"	24th		Visited Cate manoeuvres area and inspected sick animals left by Corps of inhabitants. If a float was available these animals could at once be collected. V.O.s rendered returns.	

2353 Wt. W2544/1454 700,000 5/15 D.D.&L. A.D.S.S./Forms/C. 2118.

Army Form C. 2118.

WAR DIARY
or
INTELLIGENCE SUMMARY.

(Erase heading not required.)

Instructions regarding War Diaries and Intelligence Summaries are contained in F. S. Regs., Part II. and the Staff Manual respectively. Title pages will be prepared in manuscript.

Place	Date	Hour	Summary of Events and Information	Remarks and references to Appendices
BLARINGHEM	25th 26th		Visited Mobile Section. Visited Mobile Section and Military Mounted Police. Created two animals belonging to 38th Division. The O.C. of their Mobile Section being sick I have hired a seat for the Section as here are a few animal that require ambulance, having been left behind on manoeuvres.	
"	27		Visited Mobile Section.	
"	28		Inspected Sick at Mobile Section. Inspected animals of 33rd Brigade R.F.A. Lilled with Mallein.	
"	29		Inspected Sick at Mobile Section. also arrival of 33rd Brigade Lilled with Mallein.	
"	30		Inspected Sick at M.S. to be evacuated — Sick at 1st Battery and again to Mobile Section to meet D.D.V.S.	
"	31st		Visited Mobile Section of the Division we are taking over from at the front line. Consider it a much worse place than my own position, both as regards buildings & position. Will therefore go back to my old place which is also a very much cleaner place. V.O's rendered returns.	

Confidential

War Diary
of
Major P. J. Harris
ADVS. 8th Division

Vol XIV

From 1-1-16   To 31-1-16.

Army Form C. 2118.

WAR DIARY or INTELLIGENCE SUMMARY.

(Erase heading not required.)

JANUARY 1916. 8th DIVISION

Place	Date	Hour	Summary of Events and Information	Remarks and references to Appendices
BLARINGHEM	1st		Inspected sick to be evacuated. Compiled returns	
"	2nd		Reported to H.O. 2/c that during manoeuvres the 70th Inf Brigade did not feed their transport animals from early morning until late in the evening. Transport Officers stated that they had no Brigade to turn to. The B.G. commanding the Brigade states that in case of a march with no long halts, he has given instructions for nose bags to be used at the 10 minute halt. He remarks that it would be better if required feeding time could be arranged. The G.O.C. states that he does not consider it practicable to lay down fixed hours for a long halt during a march in contact with the enemy. Every advantage must be taken of the 10 minute halt when practicable. The probable duration of the halts will be given. Personally I do not see how nose bags can be put on and taken off in a 10 minute halt. In my opinion, whatever happen, will be many nose bags being lost owing to the men having hurriedly to fasten on the nose bags. However, now that I have taken the question up letter arrangements, let us hope, will be made by the Brigade in the future.	V/27/4/5
"	3rd		Inspected sick animals to be evacuated, also two cows reported to be sick.	
"	4th		Inspected M.H. Ponies	
"	5th		Inspected horses of 1/- Black Watch which are leaving the Division tomorrow.	

Army Form C. 2118.

WAR DIARY
or
INTELLIGENCE SUMMARY.
(Erase heading not required.)

JANUARY 1916 8th DIVISION

Place	Date	Hour	Summary of Events and Information	Remarks and references to Appendices
BLARINGHEM	6th		Inspected several animals of different units which were reported the doubtful cases after inoculation. Only one animal of the many whom I considered should be looked upon as doubtful and intend to have it retested again in 3 weeks time. In the meantime the animal is to be isolated.	
"	7th		Inoculated all the Headquarters Staff Charters.	
"	8th		Inspected animals mallein'd. V.O. rendered returns.	
"	9th		Inspected animal to be evacuated at M.V.S. Visited 26th F. Ambulance. Investigate a case of very sudden death in a horse. Complies returns.	
"	10th		Visited mobile section and inspected animal to be evacuated.	
"	11th		Visited Sailly and arranged about taking over.	
"	12th		Inspected animal to be evacuated. Headquarters move tomorrow to Sailly.	
SAILLY	13th		Arrived at Sailly.	
"	14th		Visited mobile Section which arrived to-day.	
"	15th		Visited mobile Section. V.O. rendered returns. Visited Headqt 70th Inf Brigade. Inspected animal with skin eruption a French.	

Army Form C. 2118.

WAR DIARY
or
INTELLIGENCE SUMMARY.
(Erase heading not required.)

JANUARY 1916.   8th DIVISION

Place	Date	Hour	Summary of Events and Information	Remarks and references to Appendices
SAILLY	16th		Mattered the remaining horses of the Headquarters Staff. The Hay ration has been cut down to 6 lbs p. horse, which is very small quantity, especially as no unhusked straw can be obtained. Inspected horses to be evacuated and verified their description.	
-"-	17th 18th		Mattered the M.M.P. horses. Visited A.D.V.S. Guards Division to inquire the nature of the reaction the horses which were destroyed for Glanders in the Division.	
-"-	19th		Inspected horses to be evacuated.	
-"-	20th		Mattered remaining horses of Headquarters Staff. D.D.V.S. visited and inspected 2 doubtful reactors in 2/Lincs. Decided to destroy them. Visited mobile section, and took over temp. command during absence of O.C. on leave.	
-"-	21st	10.00	Made P.M. on 2 reactors 2/Lincs. One case which had joined the unit about 4 or 5 months ago had numerous nodules in the lungs, some of which had become encysted or encroded. The other case had been with the unit since the Division came out and only one nodule could be found. V.O. rendered returns.	
-"-	22nd		Carried on with section work all morning. Compiled returns	

Army Form C. 2118.

WAR DIARY
or
INTELLIGENCE SUMMARY.
(Erase heading not required.)

JANUARY 1916   8' Division

Instructions regarding War Diaries and Intelligence Summaries are contained in F. S. Regs. Part II. and the Staff Manual respectively. Title pages will be prepared in manuscript.

Place	Date	Hour	Summary of Events and Information	Remarks and references to Appendices
SAILLY	23"		Called up during the night to attend to a bad case of colic at M.M.P. On arrival I could see the animal had ruptured and could not live very long. Died within ½ an hour. P.M. this morning revealed an extensive rupture of the double colon. The whole of the intestinal tract was full of grit & sand(?). There have been a previous case of Enteritis and ruptures and I put it down to the dirt the animals eats, when eating the corn off the ground, also to the dirty oats and hay which is issued. Owing to the shortage of hay, ordinary straw is being issued to make up the deficiency. I am inclined to think this is being issued to Spencer & Co, Cabio	
"	24"		inspection and cabio	
"	25"		Mobile Section.	
"	26"		Mobile Section.	
"	27"		Mobile Section. Destroyed M.M.P horse, which was very old and futtock becoming ancylosed. Horse sending these cases to the Base	
"	28"		Mobile Section. Inspected 2/ Lincs horses which were retested. Mobile Section. V.O. redeemed returned	

Army Form C. 2118.

JANUARY. 1916. 8' Division

WAR DIARY
or
INTELLIGENCE SUMMARY.
(Erase heading not required.)

Place	Date	Hour	Summary of Events and Information	Remarks and references to Appendices
SAILLY.	29th		Attended Mobile Section. Compiled returns	
"	30th		Inoculated Sutherne horses with Mallein. Visited M.V. Section	
"	31st		Inspected Gendarme horses. Visited Mobile Section	

Confidential

War Diary

of

Major. P. J. Harris
A.D.V.S. 8th Division

From 1-2-16.   To 29-2-16.
                Vol 15

Army Form C. 2118.

WAR DIARY
or
INTELLIGENCE SUMMARY.
(Erase heading not required.)

FEBRUARY 1916   8th Division

Place	Date	Hour	Summary of Events and Information	Remarks and references to Appendices
SAILLY	1st		OC Mobile Section returned from leave yesterday and I handed over this morning.	
"	2nd		Visited 2/ Rine Brie and inspected Animals. Inspected sick animals to be evacuated.	
"	3rd		Visited D/2, 1, 3 & 5th Battery Wagon Lines.	
"	4th		Visited R.1 Rifle Transport & 25th Brigade Machine Gun Company Transport and inspected all animals. VO's rendered returns.	
"	5th		Inspected sick to be evacuated. Completed relative brought to the notice of the 8th the way Officers took their horses into the main road, also had put in orders the number of P.V.N. cases and tending to notice the habit of putting wagon with mules in into the field entrance.	
"	6th-14th		On leave	
"	15th		Office work all day.	
"	16th		Inspected sick to be evacuated	
"	17th		Visited 110th Battery R.G.A. Lines, being in our area.	
"	18th		Inspected sick to be evacuated. VO's rendered returns	
"	19th		Inspected 36th & 32nd Battery Wagon Lines	

Army Form C. 2118.

WAR DIARY
or
INTELLIGENCE SUMMARY.
(Erase heading not required.)

FEBRUARY 1916   8th DIVISION

Place	Date	Hour	Summary of Events and Information	Remarks and references to Appendices
SAILLY	20		Visited A.D.V.S. 23rd Division. Completed returns.	
"	21st		Inspected 31st Battery wagon lines. Also sick animals to be evacuated	
"	22nd		Inspected "O" & "Z" Battery wagon lines	
"	23rd		Visited C.R.E. and inspected Remounts.	
"	24		Inspected 25th Infantry Brigade fm Divisional Section.	
"	25		Inspected R.I. Rifles & 2/Lincolns Transport lines. Ordered skin and debilitated cases to be evacuated. V.O.s received returns.	
"	26		Visited Mobile V. Section. Owing to snow and frost the roads are in a very bad state and have noticed Infantry transport have not "roughed" their horses. Have brought it to the notice of the Headquarters.	
"	27		Completed returns	
"	28		Inspected horses of 2/Lincolns which were inoculated. (3rd listing) Inspected 57th Battery wagon lines. Majority of animals looking in poor condition, due in to the bad standings. They have not got a roof, and 2 lines are attached by rope. The bad with no protection from the wind and the infantry cooks standing one them than being in the open. The horses which are standing under than being in the open. They have about 30 in the open. They are unable look very much better. They have no rugs either. Reports made to Headquarters.	

Army Form C. 2118.

WAR DIARY
or
INTELLIGENCE SUMMARY.
(Erase heading not required.)

FEBRUARY 8th Division

Place	Date	Hour	Summary of Events and Information	Remarks and references to Appendices
SAILLY	29th		Visited Mobile Section. Inspected 55th Battery R.F.A. wagon lines	

Confidential

War Diary
of
Major. P. J. Harris
A.D.V.S. 8th Division

From 1-3-16   To 31. 3. 16.

Vol XVI

Army Form C. 2118.

WAR DIARY
or
INTELLIGENCE SUMMARY.
(Erase heading not required.)

MARCH 1916 8th Division

Place	Date	Hour	Summary of Events and Information	Remarks and references to Appendices
SAILLY	1st	P.M.	Inspected 5", 3" and 1st Battery wagon lines. Two sections of the 5th Battery are not looking too well. Had 6 sick animals in the 3rd Battery sent to mobile section.	
"	2nd	A.M.	Inspected sick to be evacuated. Also 128th Brigade Amm. Column wagon lines. Found an animal suffering from tetanus and ordered its destruction.	
"	3rd	P.M.	Inspected 45 Brigade RFA wagon lines. VO's rendered returns.	
"	4th	P.M.	Compiled returns.	
"	5th	P.M.	Inspected 33rd Brigade R.F.A. and 5th Extra Rng. Ammunition Column wagon lines. The former's lines are in a filthy condition and I am reporting the fact. When the 20th Division took over our lines during our absence in Reserve Area, they have never attempted in any of their wagon lines to remove the manure, only shovelling it to the rear of the animals. On taking over the lines again it took weeks merely to clear away the manure and in many cases it still remains, especially in this the case in the Ammunition Column wagon lines.	

Army Form C. 2118.

WAR DIARY
or
INTELLIGENCE SUMMARY.
(Erase heading not required.)

MARCH 1916. 8th Division

Place	Date	Hour	Summary of Events and Information	Remarks and references to Appendices
SAILLY	5th	PM	Inspected sick to be evacuated.	
"	6th	PM	Inspected No 2.3 M.T Company. Div. Train wagon lines	
"	7th	PM	Inspected 25th Infantry Brigade Machine Gun Detachment wagon lines	
			Also Home Counties R.E. transport lines.	
"	8th	PM	Inspected H.Q 26. D.R.A. Div. Signal Co and 2nd Field C.R.E. wagon lines. The Signal Co lines are in a neglected state and am bringing the matter forward	
"	9th	PM	Inspected No 1 + 2 Section Div. Ammt Column wagon lines	
"	10th	PM	V.O.s rendered returns	
"	11th	PM	Visited mobile Section and inspected Horse Ambulance. Not at all suitable for a Mobile Section. Action taken	
"	12th	PM	Visited D.D.V.S. Took sample of oats with a peculiar seed in which I wished to have identified. An animal which died from Colic revealed suppurative hepatitis typhlitis and the stomach contained a number of these seeds, which at first looked like like Conch Grit. On examining the oats these seeds were found	

Army Form C. 2118.

WAR DIARY
or
INTELLIGENCE SUMMARY.
(Erase heading not required.)

MARCH 1916 8th Division

Place	Date	Hour	Summary of Events and Information	Remarks and references to Appendices
SAILLY	13th	P.M.	V.O. reported that 2 horses of the D.A.C. 39th Division had died during the night one suffering from Septic Pneumonia and the other being suspicious of such. Another horse was taken ill showing same symptoms. At once visited the unit and inspected all animals. Took blood smears from the line inspected and took to the laboratory at Merville where I had arrived and took to the Laboratory at Merville where I had examined with a negative result. As these animals have only just landed in the country and have had very hard work I have come to the conclusion they are suffering from exhaustion with lung trouble. All precautions have been taken and animals showing any dullness with high temperature to be segregated 39th Divn.	
"	14th	P.M.	The horses of the Div Amn Col. are suffering from Septic Pneumonia. Several other cases belonging to other units of this Division, have occurred.	
"	16th	P.M.	Inspected No 3 Section Div Amn: Col: Visited Mobile Section called in V.O.s of 39th Division and showed them position of the various units they are placed up & nearly the whole of this Division	

Army Form C. 2118.

WAR DIARY
or
INTELLIGENCE SUMMARY.
(Erase heading not required.)

MARCH 1916   8th Division

Place	Date	Hour	Summary of Events and Information	Remarks and references to Appendices
BAILLY	15th	PM	have moved into our lines but their Headquarters with the A.D.Vs. are right back in Divisional Reserve Area so I am practically A.D.V.S. to both Divisions. I have given everyhelp to the A.D.V.S. as regards his duties and have arranged for him to come to my Office on Friday and meet his V.O's with their returns.	
"	16th	PM	Visited Mobile Section and inspected sick to be evacuated. D.D.V.S. visited and took him round Wagon Lines of 55th & 3rd Battery. Then visited Mobile Section.	
"	17th	PM	Inspected Wagon Lines of 2/Royal Irish Rifles accompanied by D.Z.W.S. as I have reported this unit on the condition of their lines and horse management. V.O's rendered returns. I also had the A.D.V.S. of the 39th Division in my Office and arranged for his Officers to come and meet him and accompanied by their returns so that I could indicate in the general routine. On nearly the whole of his Division is attached I thought it would be better for him to render his own returns.	

Army Form C. 2118.

WAR DIARY
or
INTELLIGENCE SUMMARY.
(Erase heading not required.)

Instructions regarding War Diaries and Intelligence Summaries are contained in F. S. Regs., Part II. and the Staff Manual respectively. Title pages will be prepared in manuscript.

Place	Date	Hour	Summary of Events and Information	Remarks and references to Appendices
SAILLY	18th	P.M.	The ADMS 39th Division has rendered me to include his returns in my consolidated returns acting on DDS Cir memo No 45 of 25.8.15 which states that when a unit from one Division is temporarily attached to another, the A.F. A 2000 should be rendered to the ADMS of the Division to which attached and included in his returns. I do not think this memo intends to this effect where practically the whole Division is attached. As it has first arrived in the country it is absolutely impossible to get completed returns from the V.O.'s partly from experience of what is required and being detached from unit on the journey from home straight up to the front. Inspected wagon lines of 26th Field Ambulance. Completed returns inspected wagon lines of Div Train and 24th Field Ambulance wagon lines.	
SAILLY	19th	P.M.	Inspected 21 Co Div Train and 15 Co RE wagon Lines.	
"	20th	P.M.	Inspected 25th Field Ambulance and 15 Co RE wagon Lines.	

Army Form C. 2118.

WAR DIARY
or
INTELLIGENCE SUMMARY.

(Erase heading not required.)

Instructions regarding War Diaries and Intelligence Summaries are contained in F.S. Regs., Part II. and the Staff Manual respectively. Title pages will be prepared in manuscript.

Place	Date	Hour	Summary of Events and Information	Remarks and references to Appendices
SAILLY	21st	P.M.	Visited M.V. Section and inspected Animals to be evacuated. Inspected Northumberland Troops (Div'l Troops) Picked out a suspicious case of mange and had it sent to M.V. Section.	
"	22nd	P.M.	Visited mobile section and examined scabs from Dermatitis case. Have written O.C. Veterinary Hospital asking that I might be informed whenever a case of dermatitis sent down to hospital as many incorrectly reported. Should help one a lot, as one would know what particular mis-work on in carrying out preventative measures.	
"	23rd	P.M.	Orders have been received that the Division is to remain in for a new area on the 27th, 28th & 29th inst. Visited Mobile Section and arranged about evacuation.	
"	24th	P.M.	Visited M.V. Section. M.V.S. 19th Division and the A.D.V.S. of that formation and arranged for the evacuation of our sick. V.O's rendered returns.	
"	25th	P.M.	Compiled returns. Office work. Visited Mob. Section.	
"	26th	P.M.	"	
"	27th	P.M.	"	
"	28th	P.M.	Entrained at 5.5 P.M. for new area.	
FLESSELLES	29th	A.M.	Arrived in new area.	
"	30th	P.M.	Visited section	
"	31st	P.M.	V.O's rendered returns	

P.J. Harris Major
A.D.V.S. 8th Div.

Vol XXII

Confidential

War Diary
of
Major. P. J. Harris
A.D.V.S. 8th Division

From 1-4-16.   To. 30. 4-16.

Army Form C. 2118.

WAR DIARY
or
INTELLIGENCE SUMMARY.
(Erase heading not required.)

APRIL 1916   8th DIVISION

Instructions regarding War Diaries and Intelligence
Summaries are contained in F.S. Regs., Part II.
and the Staff Manual respectively. Title pages
will be prepared in manuscript.

Place	Date	Hour	Summary of Events and Information	Remarks and references to Appendices
FLESSELLES	1st	P.M.	Visited Mobile Section. Went over to Headquarters new area and arranged about billets &c. Completed returns	
-"-	2nd	P.M.	Office work	
-"-	3rd	P.M.	Visited Mob. Section. N°26 Div. Train. Arranging about move.	
-"-	4th	P.M.	Marched to new area. Attended 24th Field Ambulance before starting	
HÉNENCOURT	5th	P.M.	Visited 3rd Corps and attended sick animals. Cannot get Motor ambulances for this duty until the whole of the Division is in. Met the D.B.V.S. Visited BRESLE and chose quarters for mobile Section. Visited ALBERT.	
"	6th	P.M.	Visited 3rd Corps and attended sick.	
-"-	7th	P.M.	Mobile Section arrived. Visited same. V.O. reported return.	
-"-	8th	P.M.	Visited 3rd Corps and attended Sick. Completed returns	
-"-	9th	P.M.	Visited Railhead.	
-"-	10th	P.M.	Visited Mobile Section. 33 Brigade RFA. 4.45	
-"-	11th	P.M.	Visited Mot. Section	
-"-	12th	P.M.	Visited Mot. Section. and hunted around area for straying units	

2333 Wt. W.3544/1454 700,000 5/15 D.D. & L. A.D.S.S./Forms/C. 2118.

Army Form C. 2118.

WAR DIARY
or
INTELLIGENCE SUMMARY.
(Erase heading not required.)

APRIL 1916   8th Division

Place	Date	Hour	Summary of Events and Information	Remarks and references to Appendices
HENENCOURT	13	P.M.	Visited motor section. As the section has got no cover now, visited LAVIEVILLE to see if there were anywhere available places there. I do not like the idea of sick animals being in the open and in this case there would be a certain amount of work entailed in fetching water.	
—"—	14	P.M.	Have obtained a fairly decent place at LAVIEVILLE where there will be a little cover and water near at hand. Have received consent from Headquarters to put the section there when we have to give up BRESLE. V.O's received returns.	
—"—	15	P.M.	The place at LAVIEVILLE has been taken by the Gunners, and as there is no other place available. Am afraid the section will have to move into the woods. I hunted high and low in LAVIEVILLE but could find no other suitable place. Compiled returns.	
—"—	16	P.M.	Rode over to Fourth Army to explain about returns. V.O. 45th Brigade RFA reports 1 horse died and 4 others ill belonging to 53rd Battery. Am visiting tomorrow.	

Army Form C. 2118.

WAR DIARY
or
INTELLIGENCE SUMMARY.
(Erase heading not required.)

APRIL 1916.   8th Division

Place	Date	Hour	Summary of Events and Information	Remarks and references to Appendices
HENENCOURT	17"	P.M.	Visited 55 Battery. The 4 animals are much better. Careful nursing gave no results. As the animals were standing alongside one another the one sub-section, it points to them having received some virulent bacilli has been given but I have told them to stop serum it.	
- " -	18"	P.M.	Visited mobile section.	
- " -	19"	P.M.	Visited mobile section. Called Headquarters of M.D. Section Conference in BRESLE but ---- as I considered the wood was not a suitable place for a mobile section. Col. ---- said No!, the section must be in the area. Then informed to try BAIZEUX. So immediately went over this morning and interviewed the Town Major and walked round the village with him. Have chosen a farm which will be suitable, and has the making of a good place, if a little work is put into it. One thing, there is water handy and some covering for the sick animals.	
"	20"	P.M.	Visited D.D.V.S.	
"	21"	P.M.	Visited M.D section and arranged for its moving to BAIZEUX. V.O. returned.	

Army Form C. 2118.

WAR DIARY
or
INTELLIGENCE SUMMARY.
(Erase heading not required.)

APRIL 1916   8th Division

Place	Date	Hour	Summary of Events and Information	Remarks and references to Appendices
HENENCOURT	22nd	P.M.	Visited ADVS 32nd Divn re visits in my area. Visited Newport &c of Mobile Section. Compiled returns	
"	23rd	P.M.		
"	24th	P.M.	Visited mobile Section. Wagon lines moving into BAIZIEUX. Inspected their various lines.	
"	25th	P.M.		
"	26th	P.M.	Inspected animals for be evacuated.	
"	27th	P.M.	Inspected 36' Battery have several debility cases that should be evacuated	
"	28th	P.M.	Visited Mobile Section. V.O. rendered returns	
"	29th	P.M.	DDVS visited. Inspected mobile Section and 45"Bde "Amm" Column	
"	30th	P.M.	Inspected 15 Co, 12 Co and Home Counties R.E.	

Confidential

War Diary
of
Major P.J. Harris
A.D.V.S. 8th Division

From 1-5-16   To 31-5-16

Army Form C. 2118.

WAR DIARY
or
INTELLIGENCE SUMMARY.
(Erase heading not required.)

MAY 1916. 8th Division

Instructions regarding War Diaries and Intelligence Summaries are contained in F. S. Regs., Part II. and the Staff Manual respectively. Title pages will be prepared in manuscript.

Place	Date	Hour	Summary of Events and Information	Remarks and references to Appendices
HENENCOURT	1st	P.M.	Visited mobile Section. Inspected 128" Brigade Ammunition Column.	
"	2nd	P.M.	Visited DERNANCOURT and looked at the Northumberland Hussars transport. Being Yeomanry they are just they have only a 25 that chot. Hussars. Being Yeomanry they are often detached from their Division, and appears in consequence without veterinary attendance. At time owing to moving into the Divisional area under these circumstances as they have no Sergt. A.V.C. attached to them I remarked they should be supplied with a veterinary wallet as part of their veterinary equipment. Have written R.D.V.S. on the subject. Owing to the scarcity of water, and the long distance some animals have to go for water, some of the animals of the Division have mild foot condition. Have brought the matter forward.	
"	3rd	P.M.	Visited mobile Section. also the Divisional train which has moved to a new position in a wood. There is no water here and I suggested will be laid on but Corps will not Sanction it. During bombardment the other night, Lehydration sheds were used by the enemy and it was noticed that the fumes made the horses cough.	
"	4th	P.M.	Visited ALBERT and inspected site for proposed wagon lines	

Army Form C. 2118.

WAR DIARY
or
INTELLIGENCE SUMMARY.
(Erase heading not required.)

MAY. 1916. 8th Division

Place	Date	Hour	Summary of Events and Information	Remarks and references to Appendices
HENENCOURT.	5th	P.M.	Visited Mobile Section, 282 A.T. Co. R.E. and Employed for Heavy Brigade. V.D's rendered returns.	
— " —	6th	P.M.	Visited Mob Section. "O" Battery and Divisional Train. Compiled returns. Sex' Munty cow admitted hospital yesterday.	
— " —	7th	P.M.	Visited Mobile V. Section	
— " —	8 – 18" P.M.		On Leave	
— " —	19th	P.M.	Visited Mobile V. Section. V.O's rendered returns.	
— " —	20th	P.M.	Inspected all animals of 33rd Brigade R.F.A. Compiled returns.	
— " —	21st	P.M.	Visited Albert and inspected dog suspected of Rabies. also inspected animal belonging to Rifle Brigade suffering from Arthritis Rock Orland. Ordered distruction as I feel sure it would have been, if evacuated to Hospital.	
— " —	22nd	P.M.	Visited Mobile Section	
— " —	23rd	P.M.	Visited Mobile Section and Ordnance workshops with reference to repair of Hunt. This vehicle has not stood the work well. Both wheels have been renewed and the shafts have broken.	
— " —	24th	P.M.	Inspected 1st and 3rd Battery. Inspected proposed site for an advanced dressing & Collects	

Army Form C. 2118.

WAR DIARY
or
INTELLIGENCE SUMMARY.
(Erase heading not required.)

MAY 1916   8th Division

Place	Date	Hour	Summary of Events and Information	Remarks and references to Appendices
HENENCOURT	24th	P.M.	Collecting station in the event of a forward movement. Site has already been chosen and prepared for collecting station during active operations	
"	25th	P.M.	Visited transport lines of new Pioneer Battalion. Final inspection of infected mules. Inspected transport lines of 2/ Rifle Brigade. Visited H.Q.G. lines.	
"	26th	P.M.	Visited mobile section. O.C. being on leave V.O.s tendered returns. A.S.C. clerk arrived. Having trained my A.V.C. clerk thoroughly and he is now to be transferred to the mobile section.	
"	27th	P.M.	Mobile Section	
"	28th	P.M.	Mobile Section	
"	29th	P.M.	Mobile Section	
"	30th	P.M.	Mobile Section. Saw sick evacuated attended.	
"	31st	P.M.	Mobile Section. Inspected 123rd Heavy Battery wagon lines	

P.J. Harre Major
AVC

Vol 19

Confidential

War Diary

Major. P. J. Harris
A.D.V.S. 8th Division

From 1-6-16   To 30-6-16.

Army Form C. 2118.

WAR DIARY
or
INTELLIGENCE SUMMARY.
(Erase heading not required.)

June 1916.   8' Division

Place	Date	Hour	Summary of Events and Information	Remarks and references to Appendices
HENENCOURT	1st	P.M.	Mobile Section	
-"-	2nd	P.M.	Mobile Section. D.D.V.S. visited. V.O. rendered helpless. On having horse attached to horse ambulance, a heavy vehicle and a sever strain on the animal in this hilly country.	
-"-	3rd	P.M.	Mobile Section.	
-"-	4th	P.M.	Mobile Section. 21 animals evacuated.	
-"-	5th	P.M.	Mobile Section. Visited A.D.V.S. 34' Division with reference to R.F.A. Brigade changing. Ordered head of dog, which was shot owing to it supposed to be mad, to be sent to the Laboratory to have the brain examined. French people would not allow it until the carcase had been inspected by a French Veterinary Surgeon. I pointed out that it was to the interest of the public that a definite decision could be obtained as to whether it was suffering from Rabies, as it has mauled 4 other dogs, which I have ordered to be tied up & separated. Inspected carcase of French farmers horse that died suddenly before being buried, in case it was suffering from a contagious disease. Capt Taylor O.C. M.V. Section returned from leave.	
-"-	6th	P.M.	Handed over to Captain Taylor.	

Army Form C. 2118.

WAR DIARY
or
INTELLIGENCE SUMMARY.
(Erase heading not required.)

JUNE 1916   8th Division

Place	Date	Hour	Summary of Events and Information	Remarks and references to Appendices
HENENCOURT.	7th	P.M.	All wagon lines are moving forward preparatory to operations but as usual I have received no information from HeadQuarters except from the C.R.A. with reference to Artillery movements. Have asked D.D.V.S. to relieve me of 3rd Corps charge as it is much too far for my V.O. to visit now that this forward move has taken place.	
-do-	8th	P.M.	Visited 23rd Infantry Brigade wagon lines, as they had just moved into a new position and had immediately been shelled, causing many animals to stampede. Were again shelled during my visit. Walked over to Divisional Train to see animals which were reported to me (walking to death owing to the movement of the various units – they could not find their V.O.	
-do-	9th	P.M.	Visited A.D.V.S. 34th Division to meet D.D.V.S. Arranged about relieving charge of 3rd Corps V.O.s rendered returns. Complies return visits mobile Section.	
-do-	10th	P.M.		
-do-	11th	A.M.	Visited D.D.V.S.	
-do-	12th	P.M.	Visited Mob: V. Section. Also lines of new Heavy Batteries just arrived in area.	
-do-	13th	P.M.	Inspected sick to be evacuated. Called on Corps Workshops re Stort.	

Army Form C. 2118.

WAR DIARY
or
INTELLIGENCE SUMMARY.
(Erase heading not required.)

JUNE 1916. 8th Division

Place	Date	Hour	Summary of Events and Information	Remarks and references to Appendices
HENENCOURT	13.	9.PM	Knowing that active operations are shortly to take place I sent to Head Quarters a draft concerning preliminary arrangements for publication in operation orders. The A.D.M.S. sent it back asking why it was submitted? I replied that it was submitted for publication in the event of active operations taking place. I seem to be unduly bitter being an Administrative officer in the Headquarter Staff, one is not warned of any forthcoming operations so as to allow one to prepare orders but according to have their own conclusions as regards the future. I drew conclusions from what was happening in the Division and prepared accordingly, knowing full well if anything went wrong with my branch of the service and I was to be asked the reason why and replied I was not informed, I should then be told I should have looked or foreseen. This I consider is a wrong principle. Being an Administrative officer I am bound to see everything there is being informed as I cover ore should and saving one a deal of trouble. If I had wanted to be informed I should never have been cleanses. I have to carry out my duties as an Administrative officer at the base.	
-do-	14.	P.M.	Mobile V. Section inspected sick to the Evacuated	
-do-	15.	PM	Visited this and Sweeping officer. Inspected work of Veterinary officer attached to Headquarters	

Army Form C. 2118.

WAR DIARY
or
INTELLIGENCE SUMMARY.
(Erase heading not required.)

JUNE 1916   8th Division

Place	Date	Hour	Summary of Events and Information	Remarks and references to Appendices
HENENCOURT	16"	P.M.	Inspected Sick at M.V.S. VO rendered returns	
-"-	17"	P.M.	Inspected sick at M.V.S. Compiled returns. Am endeavouring to obtain revolvers for M.V.C. Sergeants. The D.D.V.S. informs me they are part of their equipment, the being so, they were not properly equipped when sent from the Base.	
-"-	18"	P.M	Attended D.D.V.S. Conference	
-"-	19"	P.M.	Took O.C. Mob: Section out to see proposed site for Advanced Dressing Station in event of forward movement.	
-"-	20"	P.M.	Inspected Battle Wagon lines in front area. Inspected Sick to be evacuated	
-"-	21"	P.M.	Visited Mobile Section	
-"-	22"	P.M.	Visited front line where Mobile Transport are to be, in the Event of an advance. VO rendered returns	
-"-	23"	P.M.	V D.D.V.S visited	
-"-	24"	P.M.	Rode over to see A.D.V.S. 19th Div: and the O.C. M.V.S. of that Division to arrange about Evacuation of sick at railhead during active operations. Inspected sick to be evacuated	
-"-	25"	P.M.		

Army Form C. 2118.

WAR DIARY or INTELLIGENCE SUMMARY.
(Erase heading not required.)

JUNE 1916 8' Division

Place	Date	Hour	Summary of Events and Information	Remarks and references to Appendices
HENENCOURT	26"	P.M.	As the bombardment commenced on the 24th inst. and not receiving any instructions as regards opening the Advanced Collecting Station as I was informed I should be personally sounds as I am and informed him that I considered it absolutely necessary that I should open the A.C. Station on the bombardment (ie, wounded) as troops and I expected any moment a few many casualties. He answered when you receive orders SEE the D.A.D.M.S. to let you see operation orders you should have opened it until the D.A.D.M.S. asked the D.A.D.M.S. if I could see operation orders and 24" Every day I had asked the D.A.D.M.S. had let me know that there was no hurry he informed me that the A.D.M.S. had letters that there was no hurry and it comes to late. I am recording this in my diary to substantiate my argument as we far do not receive any receiving orders as an Administrative Officer should do.	tled
—"—	27"	P.M.	Inspected sick at M.V.S. to be evacuated. One wounded annual. Only admitted to Advance Dressing Station.	
—"—	28"	P.M.	Visited A.D. Station and mobile V. Section.	
—"—	29"	P.M.	Visited the battle wagon lines. Only one wounded case so far. Inspected sick to be evacuated.	
—"—	30"	1 P.M.	V.O. tendered return. Conference to-morrow "Z" day.	

Vol 20

Confidential

War Diary
of
Major P.J. Harris
A.D.V.S. 8th Division

From 1st July 1916.   To 31st July 1916.

Army Form C. 2118.

WAR DIARY
or
INTELLIGENCE SUMMARY.
(Erase heading not required.)

JULY 1916. 8th Division.

Place	Date	Hour	Summary of Events and Information	Remarks and references to Appendices
HENENCOURT	1st	9 A.M.	"Z" day. Remained at rendezvous and received advance dressing Post. No wounded in up to present hour 7 P.M.	
-"-	2nd	2 P.M.	Sudden orders to move Division (brought out of firing line with exception of Artillery and R.E. again received a verbal message from the A/2446. My section would move by march route with the trains. No time had my section word to proceed to the trains to find out what times given of their intention so I had to proceed to the trains to find out what times they were moving and whether they were going to. The 12th Division relieved us and the section took over from my sector lines. Also the sick. V.V.R. wrote to and its station with their units. Informed them by wire that RA Brigade & D.A.C. left with their Division all returns should be sent. They were now under A.D.S. 12th Division.	
BELLOY	3rd	9 P.M.	Arrived here at 1 a.m. Section at ST. SAUVEUR. Moving again tomorrow	
CAVILLON	4th	P.M.	Arrives 12 m.d. Section at SOUES. Artillery rejoining us tomorrow. Today I ordered the Horse Ambulances should not be made a transport when on the march as it was unfair to use it for an Ambulance Vehicle suddenly called upon as it means unloading it, which cannot be done when orders are received to keep [yourself] in readiness to move in a quarter of an hours notice.	

Army Form C. 2118.

WAR DIARY
or
INTELLIGENCE SUMMARY.
(Erase heading not required.)

JULY 1916.   8th Division

Instructions regarding War Diaries and Intelligence Summaries are contained in F. S. Regs., Part II. and the Staff Manual respectively. Title pages will be prepared in manuscript.

Place	Date	Hour	Summary of Events and Information	Remarks and references to Appendices
CAVILLON	5th	P.M.	Visited Mobile Section and arranged about collecting sick animals left at various villages in this area.	
" "	6th	P.M.	Orders to move troops to 1st Army area. Visited mobile Section. Entrained at 2.30 a.m.	
BRUAY	7th	P.M.	Arrived 12 m day.	
" "	8th	P.M.	Visited Mobile Section and arranged for it to hold over the sick at BRUAY received for a Mobile Section. Visited various other Ques.	
" "	9th	P.M.	Visited Mobile Section in its new lines.	
" "	10th	P.M.	Inspected sick animals to be evacuated.	
" "	11th	P.M.	Visited M.V.S. Pioneer Battn and Reserve Park.	
" "	12th	P.M.	Inspected 70th Infantry Brigade. Animals looking in good condition after their severe work for the last month.	
" "	13th	P.M.	Received orders to move on Saturday the 15th inst.	
" "	14th	P.M.	Compiled return. Inspected sick to be evacuated.	
BETHUNE.	15th	P.M.	Arrived 11.30 a.m. No orders received re moving mobile section, so went round to No 25 and asked if it was intended that the M.V.S. should move with the Division. (who tried they should move to BETHUNE and billet work)	

Army Form C. 2118.

WAR DIARY
or
INTELLIGENCE SUMMARY.
(Erase heading not required.)

Instructions regarding War Diaries and Intelligence Summaries are contained in F. S. Regs., Part II. and the Staff Manual respectively. Title pages will be prepared in manuscript.

Place	Date	Hour	Summary of Events and Information	Remarks and references to Appendices
BETHUNE	16th	P.M.	would be coming there on arrival. As this next in point thought of to buy was I instructed the O.C. March at 2 P.M. and I would meet them en-route and conduct them to the M.V.S. knowing there would be no place. On arriving at BETHUNE I received a wire from the D.D.V.S. informing me the position so there was no trouble as the M.V.S. marched straight in.	
"	16th	P.M.	Visited mobile section and then went on to ANNEZIN (to 24th Inf. Brigade Headquarters. The 70th Brigade has returned to the Oxford Division and the 24th, on original Brigade, has returned home.	
"	17th	P.M.	Visited 1st Army Infirmals and Advanced Remount Depot.	
"	18th	P.M.	Inspected sick to be evacuated. Visited Field Ambulances. his arrival cancelled that was daily and has only been with the Brit. Six weeks Visited headquarters 24th Inf. Brigade and inspected animal with Donaldite. She arrived has been kept and tested when with the 23rd Division. Decided to evacuate it	
"	19th	P.M.	Visited RUITZ and inspected 24th Field Ambulance. Sent two in the trench at mobile section.	
"	20th	P.M.	Visited ALLOUAGNE and inspected 25th Field Ambulance.	
"	21st	P.M.	Other forme.	

Army Form C. 2118.

WAR DIARY
or
INTELLIGENCE SUMMARY.
(Erase heading not required.)

JULY 1916   8th Division

Place	Date	Hour	Summary of Events and Information	Remarks and references to Appendices
BETHUNE	22nd	P.M.	Left at 1.30 P.M. for SAILLY LA BOURSE. M.V.S. remains at same position.	
LA BOURSE	22nd	P.M.	Arrived - took over office of 15th Division A.D.V.S.	
"	23rd	P.M.	Visited M.V.S.	
"	24th	P.M.	Visited M.V.S. and 1st Corps.	
"	25th	P.M.	Visited M.V.S. and 33 Brigade R.F.A.	
"	26th	P.M.	Inspected both Echelon D.A.C. Interviewed A.V.C. Sergeants who have recently arrived. Inspected Veterinary wallets.	
"	27th	P.M.	Inspected sick to be evacuated. Attended sick horse of "D" Battery, do both the V.D and farrier where away. Attended funeral of Company R.E. whilst in Divisional area.	
"	28th	P.M.	Visited M.V.C. V.O.s rendered return.	
"	29th	P.M.	Inspected 25th Infantry Brigade. Animals looking well on the whole. Visited 7-8 Section Mt Pontoon Park	
"	30th	P.M.	Inspected 23rd Infantry Brigade. Vet animals looking very well. Visited M.V.S.	
"	31st	P.M.	Inspected sick to be evacuated.	P Harris M/N

Vol 21

Confidential

War Diary
of
Major P.J. Harris
A.D.V.S. 8th Division

From 1-8-16   To 31-8-16.

Army Form C. 2118.

WAR DIARY
or
INTELLIGENCE SUMMARY.
(Erase heading not required.)

AUGUST 1916.

Place	Date	Hour	Summary of Events and Information	Remarks and references to Appendices
LA BOURSE	1st	P.M.	Visited D.I.W.T with reference to evacuating sick by train. Visited M.V.S.	
" —	2nd	P.M.	Inspected 6th R.H.A. Brigade — Animals looking well. Interviewed A.V.C. Sergeant recently joined. Inspected sick to be evacuated.	
" —	3rd	P.M.	Visited Quay in morning and witnessed the evacuation of horses by barge to St Omer. Animals soon settled down and were easily put on board. Inspected 33 Brigade R.F.A. The Animals of this Brigade have improved. Interviewed the A.V.C. Sergeant and inspected veterinary equipment	
" —	4th	P.M.	Visited M.V.H. V.O's rendered returns.	
" —	5th	P.M.	Inspected Sick D/Lys Bo.614 and saw them embarked on barge. Inspected three Remounts of Network by order of A.D.V.S. Compiled returns.	
" —	6th	P.M.	Visited M.V.Section. Attended D.D.V.S. Conference	
" —	7th	P.M.	Visited Field Companies also Pioneer Battalion. Was not pleased with Latter Lines as they were in a boggy place and of any rain came the animals would soon be up to their knees in mud. Ask O.R.E.M.S if he could arrange to lengthen bell ties. Bethune was heavily shelled to-day so it went over early in the day to see if they were all right. The men had a narrow escape. As whilst they were at dinner a shell fell & their billet which is in a Brewery. There were no casualties happily

Army Form C. 2118.

Army Form C. 2118.

WAR DIARY
or
INTELLIGENCE SUMMARY.
(Erase heading not required.)

AUGUST 1916

Instructions regarding War Diaries and Intelligence Summaries are contained in F. S. Regs., Part II. and the Staff Manual respectively. Title pages will be prepared in manuscript.

Place	Date	Hour	Summary of Events and Information	Remarks and references to Appendices
LA BOURSE	8th	P.M.	Witnessed evacuation of sick by barge. 38 animals were put on board. The 2 V.M.S. tried putting six animals aside but I have seen others have them much worse before as it practically runs one of the ends. Animals under the side of the barge which causes it to become restive and may become cast. By ends where the horse backs and not required for one animal only, can be carried easily.	
"	9th	P.M.	Visited ABBEVILLE and went round three Hospitals, which was most interesting. The D.V.S. kindly gave us lunch and the O.C. Hospitals were most hospitable.	
"	10th	P.M.	Inspected sick at M.V.S.	
"	11th	P.M.	Inspected Divisional Train, including Section Reserve Park and 25th F. Ambulance. Animals looked well. Inspected Veterinary Equipment. The Hay Cart Shafts are very heavy and it's a pity there is no means of relieving the weight when the Carts are stationary. The animals are in the Shafts for many hours at a stretch. V.Os tendered relative. Brought to the notice of the DDVS. He instructed the bales of Hay receive when in the Indian Lorries.	

2353 Wt. W2544/1454 700,000 5/15 D. D. & L. A.D.S.S./Forms/C.2118.

Army Form C. 2118.

WAR DIARY
or
INTELLIGENCE SUMMARY.
(Erase heading not required.)

AUGUST. 1915.

Place	Date	Hour	Summary of Events and Information	Remarks and references to Appendices
LA BOURSE	12th	P.M.	Visited Gray Gate and saw animals evacuated by the bay.	
"	13th	A.M.	Visited M.V.S. Inspected horse at 55 Battery with slight skin lesions and took scrapings.	
"	14th	P.M.	Inspected animals to be evacuated.	
"	15th	P.M.		
"	16th	P.M.	Inspected 45th Brigade R.F.A. - Animals looking well. Inspected veterinary equipment. Visited Mobile Section.	
"	17th	P.M.	Inspected 2nd Infantry Brigade and 2nd & 16th t Home Counties Field Co. R.E. all animals looking well. Visited Mobile Section.	
"	18th	P.M.	Visited A.D.V.S. 30th Div. work reference to evacuating sick by tram, having very few sick to send from M.V.S. of this and 32nd Division, have arranged with I.T.O. to send train; up to day of these are not sufficient sick to send to render return and keep conferred.	
"	19th	P.M.	Inspected sick to be evacuated.	
"	20th	A.M.	Inspected 24th Machine Gun Co. also all animals manually of the 55th Battery. The latter unit having had a case of sarcoptic mange the animal having been isolated by me. The animal joined about 2 months ago as a remount. Disinfection and all necessary precautions have been taken.	

Army Form C. 2118.

WAR DIARY
or
INTELLIGENCE SUMMARY.
(Erase heading not required.)

AUGUST 1916.   8th Division

Instructions regarding War Diaries and Intelligence Summaries are contained in F. S. Regs., Part II. and the Staff Manual respectively. Title pages will be prepared in manuscript.

Place	Date	Hour	Summary of Events and Information	Remarks and references to Appendices
LA BOURSE	21st	P.M.	Visited Home Counties R.E. and inspected animal suffering from Dermatitis from Scratches. Have ordered animal to be evacuated as the Vy informs me that. Visited A.D.S. of 16th + 19th Division and arranged that there divisions evacuate some of their sick by Barge. Our fractious cases difficult to send 30 three times a week.	
-"-	22nd	P.M.	Visited Guy Cdr BETHUNE at 8 a.m. and saw animals evacuated by Barge, sick animals from 30, 32 & 16th Divisions. Visited D/5 Battery and took Scratches from an animal which had a scurfy patch on the abdomen and inspected & rubbing Guide below satisfaction to the animal. Examined seaparys from Home Counties R.E. animals behaved find no acari.	
-"-	23rd	P.M.	Inspected animals (the evacuated). An ADVS of a certain Division and his two chargers suffered in the section scales. On examining the 2 was suspicious of mange, so he separated the officers two seen it and he had ordered any treatment, both in reply he wrote in the negative. Went temporarily and on examination this evening found he claims parasot. Visited ADVS 16th Division and met the D.DVS there. As the Div: is arranging mark certain arrangement as regards evacuation of sick and fatigue arms (and parade) the M.V.S Levies.	

2353 Wt. W2544/1454 700,000 5/15 D. D. & L. A.D.S.S./Forms/C. 2118.

WAR DIARY or INTELLIGENCE SUMMARY

Army Form C. 2118.

August 1916   8th Division

Place	Date	Hour	Summary of Events and Information	Remarks and references to Appendices
LABOURSE	24th	P.M.	Attended Quay Side and Superintended Evacuation of sick by Barge. Judged at Divisional Horse Show	
"	25th	P.M.	Visited M.V. Section. Met A.D.V.S. there, who walked round Section lines. Judged at Divisional Horse Show.	
"	26th	P.M.	Visited Quay Side and saw sick embarked on Barge. Visited Mobile Section.	
"	27th	P.M.	Visited Mobile Section of 16th Division, where I have taken over for the time being, until the other Division arrives in the area. Visited Mobile Section.	
"	28th	P.M.		
"	29th	P.M.	Visited Quay Side. Inspected Surplus Animals handed over from 16th Divn. Evacuated one. Inspected D.L.I. Pioneer Battalion horses. Many having been machines. Suggested to D.A.D. that a transport Sergt. should be detailed as Transport Sergt. to the Battn. At present a lance Corporal is in charge, who has very little knowledge of horses. Being a Pioneer Batt. it has many more animals than other infantry units. They have not been in the country long and have some very nice H.D. horses.	
"	30th	P.M.	Inspected two animals of 2nd & 175th Co. R.E. respectively reported as being dirty. Took Serapings. Isolated the Suspect cleanse in one Case, Necessary orders issued.	

Army Form C. 2118.

WAR DIARY
or
INTELLIGENCE SUMMARY.
(Erase heading not required.)

AUGUST 1916 8th Division

Instructions regarding War Diaries and Intelligence Summaries are contained in F. S. Regs., Part II. and the Staff Manual respectively. Title pages will be prepared in manuscript.

Place	Date	Hour	Summary of Events and Information	Remarks and references to Appendices
LA BOURSE	30'	P.M.	Visited M.V.S. Inspected arrivals to the evacuated.	
— " —	31'	P.M.	Visited Quay side and saw arrivals evacuated. Visited M.V.Section and received its D.V.S. DO's and American Dr's. Visited 57. Battery and inspected animal work. Glen horses. Suspicious case and ordered it to the out to M.V.Section. Examination of feedpumps gave hopeless results	

Vol 22

<u>Confidential</u>

War Diary
of
Major P.J Harris
ADVS. 8th Divn

from 1.9.16   to 30.9.16.

Army Form C. 2118.

WAR DIARY
or
INTELLIGENCE SUMMARY.
(Erase heading not required.)

SEPTEMBER 1916. 8th Division.

Place	Date	Hour	Summary of Events and Information	Remarks and references to Appendices
LABOURSE	1st	P.M.	Visited Mobile Section. V.O. rendered returns. Conference held. Attended funeral. Guards horse practically the whole day. Died 7.30 P.M.	
- " -	2nd	P.M.	Quay-side to see animals to be practically evacuated. A.D.V.S. 3rd Division with reference to evacuation of sick.	
- " -	3rd	P.M.	Visited M.V. Section. Attended D.D.V.S. weekly conference.	
- " -	4th	P.M.	Steward inspecting 25th Inf. Brigade, but postponed it owing to the rain. Corps have disallowed the horse purchases of Chaffeuters. Considering their chaplain. I wrote to V. works by Re-state in the line by purchasing them, as the Division's wound limited up the deficiency of Pay Ration to so much, not which is raised limited up the deficiency of Pay Ration to so much, not xxxxx unless entered into chart. A.D.V.S. wanted to move to M.V. Section from Bethune. As I was near Bri. Rainbard but found out all animals were evacuated from Bethune by Barge and containers mere transported by rail from Bethune Station. As the space to exist remain in importent proximity. Visited Mobile V. Section and examined the Sharpeners now standing aside. The M.V.S. has been issued with the fresh have Sharpeners and not the small one which is attached to the clipping machine and wheel, from all accounts is the better one.	
- " -	5th	P.M.	Inspected 26th Infantry Brigade. And machine gun Co. All transport animals looking well, with the exception of the Irish Rifles.	

Army Form C. 2118.

WAR DIARY
or
INTELLIGENCE SUMMARY.
(Erase heading not required.)

SEPTEMBER 1916. 8th Division

Place	Date	Hour	Summary of Events and Information	Remarks and references to Appendices
LA BOURSE	6th	P.M.	Inspected 23rd Infantry Brigade Machine Gun Co. All animals looking well	
"	7th	P.M.	Visited 5th Mobile V. Section reference evacuation by Barge. Inspected animals (Evacuated) at M.V. Section. Inspected 24" machine gun Co. and two horse of 33" Battery and Ent ??? with suspicious skin lesions	
"	8th	P.M.	Visited M.V. Section. V.O.s rendered returns. Conference held	
"	9th	P.M.	Inspected 24th Inf. Brigade. Animals looking well. Drew attention to the insanitary state of the stables belonging to Headquarter East Lancs. Visited Mobile Section.	
"	10th	P.M.	Attended evacuation of sick by Barge. Visited M.V. Section.	
"	11th	P.M.	Inspected Signal Co. 2nd/15th Home Counties RE Companies. Visited M.V. Section.	
"	12th	P.M.	Visited Mobile V. Section.	
"	13th	P.M.	Inspected 33rd Brigade RFA. Visited M.V. Section	
"	14th	P.M.	Inspected 5th R.F.A. Brigade. Capt. Hurdle proceeded Special Leave. Visited M.V.S.	
"	15th	P.M.	Visited M.V.S and inspected sick to be evacuated. V.Os rendered returns.	
"	16th	P.M.	Attended evacuation officer at Quay Side. Owing to Barge being held up by traffic it did not load until 9 am instead of 8 am.	

Army Form C. 2118.

WAR DIARY
or
INTELLIGENCE SUMMARY.
(Erase heading not required.)

Instructions regarding War Diaries and Intelligence Summaries are contained in F. S. Regs., Part II. and the Staff Manual respectively. Title pages will be prepared in manuscript.

Place	Date	Hour	Summary of Events and Information	Remarks and references to Appendices
LABOURSE	17th	P.M.	Visited Mobile V. Section And Inspected Sick.	
-"-	18th	P.M.	Visited mobile Section twenty-one and took over from DDVS during his absence on leave	
-"-	19th	P.M.	Arrived at first Army to take over duties of O.D.V.S., during this Officers absence on leave	
LILLERS	20th	P.M.	Visited 24th Division which had just arrived in Army area, with No DDVS, made arrangements with A.D.V.S. and handed him over Standing Orders &c	
-"-	21st 22nd 23rd	P.M.	Visited my Division and attended to Office work and Animals undergoing chop.	
LILLERS	24th	P.M.	Returned to my Division the D.D.V.S. having returned from leave	
LABOURSE	30th	P.M.	Visited M.V.S and inspected animals to be evacuated. Compiles returns	

Vol 23

<u>Confidential</u>

War Diary.
of
Major P. J. Harris
ADVS. 8° Divn.

From 1° Oct 1916.   To 31st Oct 1916.

Army Form C. 2118.

WAR DIARY
or
INTELLIGENCE SUMMARY.
(Erase heading not required.)

OCTOBER 1916.

Place	Date	Hour	Summary of Events and Information	Remarks and references to Appendices
LABOURSE	1st	P.M.	Visited Section and inspected Animals to be evacuated	
" "	2"	P.M.	Proceeded on leave to England	
" "	11"	P.M.	Returned from leave.	
" "	12"	P.M.	Division moving. Proceeded to BETHUNE	
BETHUNE	13"	P.M.	Left by train for PONT REMY at 4 A.M. 14.10.16. Proceeded to Station CHOQUES at 10 P.M.	
PONT REMY	14"	P.M.	Arrived 10.30 A.M. marched to HALLENCOURT	
HALLENCOURT	15"	P.M.	Visited M.V. Section at LONGPRÉ it having just arrived	
HALLENCOURT	16"	P.M.	Left for AILLY-SUR-SOMME at 10 A.M. Arrangements for M.V.S. to move a day after column has moved to accom. of any sick being sent in. Arrived at AILLY 6.30 P.M.	
AILLY-SUR-SOMME	17"	P.M.	Left for TREUX 6.30 A.M. Called on the D.D.V.S. en route and wrote/wrote in time for conference. Arrived at TREUX at 5 P.M. Arrangements ticked for M.V.S.	
AILLY	18"	P.M.	M.V.S. arrived. Only two Animals have as yet been reported. Having been left behind on line of march. viz 2 at AILLY-SUR-SOMME. Rode over to forward area and interviewed A.D.V.S. 6" Div. where Div" we are relieving. Rations having been changed. Am arranging for the M.V.S. to be met at and furnished with the Divl. train.	

Army Form C. 2118.

WAR DIARY
or
INTELLIGENCE SUMMARY.
(Erase heading not required.)

OCTOBER 1916

Instructions regarding War Diaries and Intelligence Summaries are contained in F. S. Regs., Part II. and the Staff Manual respectively. Title pages will be prepared in manuscript.

Place	Date	Hour	Summary of Events and Information	Remarks and references to Appendices
AILLY	18th	P.M.	As our heavy float will never be able to travel on the side track. Am arranging with the A.P.M. to allow it to proceed on the metal track. The body being low and the vehicle of great weight it would sink in the mud.	
AILLY	19th	P.M.	Left at 9 a.m. for MINDEN POST. The M.V.S. moved same time.	
AILLY	21st	P.M.	Arrived 1 a.m. MVS went up position of advanced dressing post of the 6th Division.	
MINDEN POST	21	P.M.	As the new trench head is quite near here have arranged for the M.V.S. to remain where it is, as however the area is somewhat swell have taken another position a few yards further along the road on the other side. A few sick animals have been left behind by the 6th M.V.S. These will be evacuated as soon as possible. The new trenches not yet having received a name. The M.V.S. having absolutely no cover, and tents being impossible, have arranged for a few bivouac cover, and tents being impossible, have arranged for a few bivouac cover, and until these being broken, horses on the cliff cord to be issued. Owing to the water pipe being broken, horses cannot be watered until 6 P.M.	

WAR DIARY or INTELLIGENCE SUMMARY

Army Form C. 2118.

OCTOBER 1916

Place	Date	Hour	Summary of Events and Information	Remarks and references to Appendices
MINDEN POST	22nd	P.M.	Attended several cases. Visited Mobile Section and then went on Brigade wagon lines. Have applied officially for the road to travel on the metal roads. Today when it was ordered off the roads by the Police, but shafts were broken.	
MINDEN POST	23rd	P.M.	Visited M.V.S. and wagon lines. Went over to 4th Division Mobile A.D.S. but he was away. Am having pamphlets in orders circulated to the effect that everybody should endeavour to remove any article from the roads that are likely to be injurious to animals.	
MINDEN POST	24th	P.M.	Visited M.V.S. Reinforcing camp has been made by the Section, which was yesterday for evacuating Railhead not having one ready to R.T.O. has asked for the Evac. of one as Remounts have arrived. Had this camp not been made by the Section, it would have been impossible to detain the Remounts. To be on the safe side, so that any unit will not be kept up for the want of horses, am arranging for Remounts to replace those which are showing signs of the very hard work, as these animals will eventually have to be evacuated. The work the animals have to perform nearly loaded vehicles thro' the mud on the side tracks and over shell holes is prodigious-	

WAR DIARY or INTELLIGENCE SUMMARY.

Army Form C. 2118.

Place	Date	Hour	Summary of Events and Information	Remarks and references to Appendices
MINDEN POST	24th	P.M.	Carrying on my usual are for hourly ended and easy much above the weight that laid down. The battlefields are strewn with tins, horse shoes, nails, cartridges clips and other articles which are a danger to animals. Shell holes are also a danger although also in the daytime when covered up with mud as they cannot be seen.	
MINDEN POST	25	P.M.	The O.C. M.V.S. having been rieded entertainer, the M.O. ordered him to remain in bed. So I took over the Section for the day.	
MINDEN POST	26	P.M.	Visited M.V.S. O.C. now fit again. Information received from Army that I have been appointed D.D.V.S. Cavalry Corps.	
MINDEN POST	27	P.M.	Visited Advanced Head quarters also M.V.S.	
MINDEN POST	28	P.M.	Office work. Returns rendered.	
MINDEN POST	29	P.M.	Division moving tomorrow. If the M.V.S. has to move the float will have to be left behind, a new shaft have not yet been received from Ordnance.	
MINDEN POST	30	P.M.	Headquarters move tomorrow.	
TREUX	31	P.M.	Capt B M^cC arrived and took over. Proceeded to H. the Cavalry Corps.	

WAR DIARY
or
INTELLIGENCE SUMMARY.

(Erase heading not required.)

Army Form C. 2118.

A.D.V.S.
8th Division
Vol 24

Place	Date	Hour	Summary of Events and Information	Remarks and references to Appendices
TREUX	1/11/16	—	Took over the duties of A.D.V.S. 8th Division from Major P.J. Hannan.	
"	2/11/16		Visited Mobile Veterinary Section and arranged with O.C. M.V.S. to establish a collecting post consisting of 1 N.C.O. and 2 men at DERNANCOURT. Informed all Veterinary Officers of the Division of my office.	
"	3/11/16		Inspected horses of D.H.Q. Visited MEAULTE and inspected horse convalescent depot of the 24th & 26th Inf. Bdes. 26th Field Ambulance and No 3 Cy. A.S.E. Found all animals in satisfactory condition.	
"	4/11/16		Visited Mobile Veterinary Section and inspected all sick for evacuation.	
"	5/11/16		Discussed with D.D.V.S. methods received of casualties amongst horses chiefly due to Rose Hostetter as a result of informing the O.C. M.V.S. with reference to the hundred cases in hospital of further casualties. Inspected 2nd Field Cy. R.E. & found all animals in good condition.	
"	6/11/16		Office Routine. In respect of a post Lyt arr. received a detailed return of the Army Area, Horse Transport for this Division.	
"	7/11/16		D.H.Q. moved from TREUX to advanced area near MONTAUBAN.	
MONTAUBAN	8/11/16		Visited 25th Field Ambulance and also Artillery Horse Lines.	
"	9/11/16		Visited M.V.S. and inspected sick horses for evacuation. Survey to the large numbers that cannot be admitted I consulted if necessary to arrange at once with the D.A.Q.M.G. Division for the Corps C.O. carriage of casualties from artillery units to the rear of the Division. Examined all Veterinary officers and explained in the working of any casualties of artillery arms.	
"	10/11/16		Office Routine. Visited 4th Labour Battalion who asked to be examined. 1 N.C.O. and three men of 25th Inf. Bde. sent for duty R.M.V.S. from Div. H.Q.	
"	11/11/16		There were four artillery T.M. were sent to the Mob. Vet. Section and inspected. M.V.S. was shifted owing to animals in billet, owing to enemy - shells which were 7 feet high. Advanced for recapitulation was delayed owing so that the end of the formation & avail condition.	

WAR DIARY
or
INTELLIGENCE SUMMARY.
(Erase heading not required.)

Army Form C. 2118.

Instructions regarding War Diaries and Intelligence Summaries are contained in F.S. Regs, Part II. and the Staff Manual respectively. Title pages will be prepared in manuscript.

Place	Date	Hour	Summary of Events and Information	Remarks and references to Appendices
MONTAUBAN	12/11/16		Inspected Horses of the D.A.C. and found the animals looking fairly well considering the condition of work & weather.	
"	23/11/16		Inspected Horses of the 39 Div. R.F.A. & discussed the recent Command of the Division regarding the increase in his wagon teams to the best which will allow.	
"	24/11/16		Inspected Remounts at Veterinary Station in conjunction with 4th Division artillery for the inspection of this remount which we due Remounts held M.V. section.	
"	25/11/16		Attended conference of D.D.V.S. at 4th Army Head Quarters	
"	26/11/16		Arranged with S.S.O. for the medicine supply to mule Vet. Section holding mine to next area purchased pack & but before arranged with 29th Division & kits on side of M.V.S. Both Sections & work together untill the Divisions move	
"	27/11/16		Inspected DH Guards pit. Instructions issued all Vet. Officers of the Division re. engaged with Horses of the Division. Showing feeding issue, exercise clothing M.V. & grooming also instruction for economy & next issue	
"	28/11/16		D.H.Q. moved to TREUX.	
TREUX	29/11/16		Examined all H.Q. animals before they moved by road to new area.	
TREUX	30/11/16		Moved to BELLOY ST LEONARD with D.H.Q.	
BELLOY ST LEONARD	21/11/16		Officer Patrole of district D.H.Q. Horses. Instructed O.C. M.V.S. instructing to new billet and arranged with him to establish a collecting Post at ST.MAULVIS occupied by the Division having Horses un in large area. Also arranged a post Hosp. for animals if sick.	

WAR DIARY
or
INTELLIGENCE SUMMARY.

(Erase heading not required.)

Army Form C. 2118.

Instructions regarding War Diaries and Intelligence Summaries are contained in F. S. Regs., Part II. and the Staff Manual respectively. Title pages will be prepared in manuscript.

Place	Date	Hour	Summary of Events and Information	Remarks and references to Appendices
BELLOY	22/11/16		Inspected No 4 Co, A.S.C. Office Routine.	
" "	23/11/16		Office Routine	
" "	24/11/16		Commenced movement of the Divisions before Christmas. Inspected horses of the 25th Infantry Div, a Bde & Field Ambulances. 9 veterinary rest Officers of the Infantry Div.	
" "	25/11/16		Arranged with S.S.O. for the supply of Forage to the Infantry Div.	
" "	26/11/16		Office Routine.	
" "	27/11/16		Office Routine. Arranged with D.A.Q.M.G. for the training on Cable shoes of his men from each unit. Pde with the Bri. Inspected our L. O.C. M.V.S. Details of A.D.V.S. on proceeding to England. Handed over to his charge Canine. N.B. we Manyou A.V.C. A.D.V.S. 8th Division.	
" "	28/11/16		Took over from Major Bean duties of A.D.V.S.	
" "	29/11/16		Office Routine. Examined Mtg Sick horses.	
" "	30/11/16		Office Routine. Examined Mtg sick horses.	

J. C... AVC
for Major A.D.V.S. & D...

Army Form C. 2118.

Vol 26

WAR DIARY
or
INTELLIGENCE SUMMARY.

Diary of A.D.V.S. 8th Division

(Erase heading not required.)

Instructions regarding War Diaries and Intelligence Summaries are contained in F. S. Regs., Part II. and the Staff Manual respectively. Title pages will be prepared in manuscript.

Place	Date	Hour	Summary of Events and Information	Remarks and references to Appendices
BRAY-SUR-SOMME	1/1/17		Office routine	
"	2/1/17		" " Visited M.V.S.	
"	3/1/17		" " " "	
"	4/1/17		Visited M.V.S. Inspected No 1 Section D.A.C.	
"	5/1/17		" " " No 3 Section D.A.C.	
"	6/1/17		Visited M.V.S. Inspected No 1 Section and 'B' Echelon D.A.C.	
"	7/1/17		Received all Vet Officers and weekly sick returns	
"	8/1/17		Attended Veterinary Conference at Army Headquarters	
"	9/1/17		Visited M.V.S. and inspected 15th Field Coy R.E.	
"	10/1/17		" Inspected Headquarters Horses and 1st Divisional Train	
"	11/1/17		" Office Routine	
"	"		" "	
"	"		" "	
"	"		Divisional Headquarters moved to BELLOY ST LEONARD	
BELLOY	12/1/17		Office Routine	
"	13/1/17		Examined Headquarters sick. Office Routine	
"	14/1/17		General inspection of all Headquarters horses, M.M.P. and Signals & Divisional Train	
"	15/1/17		Office Routine. Visited R.A. Headquarters. Pneumonia work.	
"	16/1/17		Visited M.V.S. Inspected 15th Field Coy R.E. and B Echelon D.A.C.	
"	17/1/17		" " "	
"	18/1/17		Inspected No 4 Coy Divisional Train. Office Routine	
"	19/1/17		Inspected Divisional Signals and Headquarters horses, 24th M.G. Coy and 1st Divisional Train	

Army Form C. 2118.

WAR DIARY
or
INTELLIGENCE SUMMARY.
(Erase heading not required.)

Instructions regarding War Diaries and Intelligence Summaries are contained in F. S. Regs., Part II. and the Staff Manual respectively. Title pages will be prepared in manuscript.

Place	Date	Hour	Summary of Events and Information	Remarks and references to Appendices
BELLOY	20/1/17		Attended Veterinary Conference at Army Headquarters.	
"	21/1/17		Visited M.V.S. Inspected all horses of No 3 Section 33 D.A.C. at ALLERY. Inspected horse lift behind at FONTAINE LE SEC. by No 3 Coy Divisional Train	
"	22/1/17		Visited O.C. M.V.S. at ST SAUVEUR and inspected lift store by No 2 Section D.A.C. Inspected 25th Bg. Rle Transport in Rte Area. G. mud.	
"	23/1/17		Divisional Headquarters moved to CHIPILLY. D.D.V.S. 4th Army visited as a horse evacuated from Forward Hospital of AIRAINES and No 3 Section D.A.C. at ALLERY.	
CHIPILLY	24/1/17		Visited M.V.S. Interviewed all veterinary officers of Division during the day and arranged for interchange	
"	25/1/17		Inspected 22nd D.L.I. and 5th Bde R.H.A. Ammunition Column. General parade of all M.M.P. and Headquarters horses. Visited M.V.S.	
"	26/1/17		Inspected 2nd Field Coy R.E. and Rte Sub for remounts at M.V.S. Conference of Veterinary officers arranged for transfer of Lieut. S. Andrew, A.V.C.	
"	27/1/17		5th Bde R.H.A. now Army Troops. Office Routine. Visited No 2 Section D.A.C.	
"	28/1/17		Inspected 22nd D.L.I. and 5th Bde R.H.A. Conference attended 33rd Division with a Cry proceeding to Rest visited truck a Through inspection at G.H.Q. Inspected M.V.S.	
BRAY	29/1/17		Divisional Headquarters moved from CHIPILLY to Bay Forward Area	
"	30/1/17		Inspected No 2 Section D.A.C. and visited 40th D.A.C.	
"	31/1/17		Office Routine. Attended Vet. Conference at Army Headquarters.	

J. Byrne Major
A.D.V.S. 8th Division

WAR DIARY or INTELLIGENCE SUMMARY

Army Form C. 2118.

(Erase heading not required.)

A.D.V.S. 4th Division

Vol 27

Instructions regarding War Diaries and Intelligence Summaries are contained in F.S. Regs., Part II. and the Staff Manual respectively. Title pages will be prepared in manuscript.

Place	Date	Hour	Summary of Events and Information	Remarks and references to Appendices
BRAY	1/2/17		Inspected 45th Bde. R.F.A. Inspected M.V.S. 33rd Bde. R.F.A., 2nd Section D.A.C. and II Bty. 181 Bde. R.F.A. 40th Div.	
"	2/2/17		Office Routine. Inspected M.V.S. Inspected No 1 Section D.A.C. Conference of Vet. Officers of Division.	
"	3/2/17		Inspected M.V.S. and E. Echelon D.A.C.	
"	4/2/17		Inspected 23rd Inf. Bde. and Field Ambulance of the Division. Inspected M.V.S.	
"	5/2/17		Inspected 137th Heavy Battery R.G.A. returns attached of mange in that unit. Inspected 8th Division Signal Coy. Horses.	
"	6/2/17		Inspected 181st Bde. R.F.A. for Stomatitis. Inspected M.V.S.	
"	7/2/17		Office Routine. Inspected M.V.S. Inspected No. 1 Section D.A.C.	
"	8/2/17		Inspected 25th Infantry Bde.	
"	9/2/17		Inspected M.V.S. Inspected No 2 Coy Divisional Train. Conference of Vet. Officers.	
"	10/2/17		Inspected 137th Bty. R.G.A. and carried on with the Salving Officers for the mancurin of Mange Cases. Inspected M.V.S.	
"	11/2/17		Office Routine.	
"	12/2/17		Divisional Headquarters move to CORBIE - Drew own	
CORBIE	13/2/17		Office Routine. Inspected all Headquarters horses.	
"	14/2/17		Office Routine. Conference of returning Officers at Army Headquarters.	
"	15/2/17		Visited M.V.S. Visited 28th Machine Gun Coy and Irish Rifles.	
"	16/2/17		Inspected Div. Signal Coy and 2nd Devonshire Regiment. Conference of Vet. Officers	
"	17/2/17		Office Routine. Inspected A.D.V.S. 4th Division reference bringing mange cases into his area	

Army Form C. 2118.

WAR DIARY
or
INTELLIGENCE SUMMARY.
(Erase heading not required.)

Instructions regarding War Diaries and Intelligence Summaries are contained in F. S. Regs., Part II. and the Staff Manual respectively. Title pages will be prepared in manuscript.

Place	Date	Hour	Summary of Events and Information	Remarks and references to Appendices
CORBIE	18/2/17		Inspected H.Qrs. Northumberland Regt. Transport, Wounded and Starved Funerals also H.Qr. 24th Inf. Bde. and No 3 Coy. A.S.C.	
-"-	19/2/17		Officer Routine. Visited 136 Regiment of Infantry (French Territorials) at FOUILLOY and arranged for veterinary attendance of that unit at request of D.D.V.S. 4th Army	
-"-	20/2/17		Visited 25th Infantry Bde. and M.V.S.	
-"-	21/2/17		Divisional Headquarters moved to forward area.	
SUZANNE	22/2/17		Inspected Headquarters horses and visited M.V.S.	
-"-	23/2/17		Officer Routine. Conference of Veterinary Officers.	
-"-	24/2/17		Inspected 24th Machine Gun Coy and 2nd East Lancs. transport.	
-"-	25/2/17		Visited M.V.S. Office Routine	
-"-	26/2/17		Visited advanced Headquarters and interviewed C.R.A. reference clipping of horses in artillery units.	
-"-	27/2/17		Officer Routine. Visited D.D.V.S. re movement of units affected with STOMATITIS	
-"-	28/2/17		Attended conference of A.D.V.Ss. at 4th Army Headquarters	

A. Bruce Mayw.
A.D.V.S. 8th Division

Army Form C. 2118.

WAR DIARY
or
INTELLIGENCE SUMMARY.
(Erase heading not required.)

A.D.V.S. 8th Division

Vol 28

Instructions regarding War Diaries and Intelligence Summaries are contained in F.S. Regs., Part II. and the Staff Manual respectively. Title pages will be prepared in manuscript.

Place	Date	Hour	Summary of Events and Information	Remarks and references to Appendices
SUZANNE	1/3/17	—	Inspected 33rd Bde. R.F.A.	
"	2/3/17	—	Officers routine conference of Vet. Officers. Inspected M.V.S.	
"	3/3/17	—	Visited M.V.S. and installed all horses for evacuation. Officers Routine	
"	4/3/17	—	Inspected No 2 Cry. Div. Train. Visited M.V.S.	
"	5/3/17	—	Inspected No 2 Section D.A.C.	
"	6/3/17	—	Officers Routine. Visited M.V.S.	
"	7/3/17	—	Inspected 45th Bde. R.F.A. 2nd 16th 9490th Field Coy R.E. Div Sig. Coy. & 22nd D.L.9.	
"	8/3/17	—	Moved to BRAY. Inspected No 1, 3 & 4. Coys. Div. Train	
BRAY	9/3/17	—	Visited M.V.S. Officers routine conference of Vet. Officers	
"	10/3/17	—	Officers Routine. Visited M.V.S. and Headquarters D.A.C.	
"	11/3/17	—	" " Inspected horses for evacuation and visited advance	
"	12/3/17	—	Divisional Headquarters - Inspected 'B' Echelon D.A.C.	
"	13/3/17	—	Inspected Headquarters and No 1 Section D.A.C. Visited M.V.S.	
"	14/3/17	—	Visited D.D.V.S. 4th Army informa implements by O.C. units of arrival of forage. Visited M.V.S.	
"	15/3/17	—	Inspected 23rd R.F.R de. 25 M.S. Coy. and 22nd D.L.9.	
"	16/3/17	—	Visited M.V.S. Conference of Vet. Officers	
"	17/3/17	—	Officers Routine. Schedules attainment of sick horses. Inspected Rear H.Q. 4 Coy. Div. Train	
"	18/3/17	—	Visited M.V.S. Inspected No 2 Section D.A.C. Div. Signal Coy. & 5th Bde. R.H.A. A.C.	7, Bde. major A8/18 Brig.

2353 Wt. W3141/1454 700,000 5/15 D. D. & L. A.D.S.S./Forms/C. 2118.

Army Form C. 2118.

WAR DIARY
or
INTELLIGENCE SUMMARY.
(Erase heading not required.)

A.D.V.S. 8th Division

Instructions regarding War Diaries and Intelligence Summaries are contained in F.S. Regs., Part II. and the Staff Manual respectively. Title pages will be prepared in manuscript.

Place	Date	Hour	Summary of Events and Information	Remarks and references to Appendices
BRAY	19/3/17		Officer routine. Visited M.V.S. Attended a conference at 4th Corps Headquarters.	
"	20/3/17		Superintended entrainment of sick horses. Inspected 46th D.A. R.F.A.	
"	21/3/17		Office routine. Inspected horses of 92nd Battery R.F.A. Visited M.V.S.	
"	22/3/17		Inspected No 2 Coy. A.S.C. and 24th Field Ambulance. Visited M.V.S. and Divisional Headquarters.	
"	23/3/17		Visited M.V.S. and inspected Nos. 1,3 & 4 Coys. Divl. Train. Conference of Veterinary Officers.	
"	24/3/17		Office Routine. Supervised entrainment of sick horses. Inspected 24th Infantry Bde.	
"	25/3/17		Inspected 2/8 M.G. Coy. and arranged for its visit, the unit having recently arrived from England. Inspected 25th Field Ambulance, 32nd Battery R.F.A. and visited No 2 Section of 40th D.A.C.	
"	26/3/17		Visited M.V.S. and watched entrainment of sick horses. Inspected D.H.Q. to make arrangements for evacuation. Visited Divl. Train Headquarters and D.H.Q. to make arrangements for Veterinary nurse to new area.	
"	27/3/17		Supervised entrainment of sick horses. Moved to Curlu 161 new area.	
CURLU	28/3/17		Visited M.V.S. Inspected Remount. Inspected 265 Field Ambulance convoy at CERISY.	
"	29/3/17			
"	30/3/17			
"	31/3/17		Office Routine. Conference of Vet. Officers. Inspected No 1 Coy. A.S.C. and M.V.S.	

WAR DIARY or INTELLIGENCE SUMMARY

Army Form C. 2118.

A.D.V.S. 8th Division

Place	Date	Hour	Summary of Events and Information	Remarks and references to Appendices
CURLU	1/4/17		Inspected 23rd and 25th Infantry Bde. Transport	
" "	2/4/17		" 1st Battn. R.F.A., No.1 Section R.A.S.C. and Cable Section R.E. Also Headquarters and Police horses.	
" "	3/4/17		Office Routine. Informed advancement of Sub. at Railhead.	
" "	4/4/17		Inspected all Supply-Transport with D.A.Q.M.G. and interviewed A.A. & Q.M.G. at Divisional Headquarters reference the bad standing of the units. Arranged with him for the formation of a central Supply-Pole, sub-base at HAUT ALLAINES where more favourable standings and fields are to be found for flight cars.	
" "	5/4/17		Inspected HAUT ALLAINES with a view to selecting a site for the 16th Mob. Vet. Section. Inspected 8th Divisional Train.	
" "	6/4/17		Inspected M.V.S. Inspected 8th Div. Signals. Held interview of Vet. Officers of the Division.	
" "	7/4/17		Inspected 36th Battery R.F.A. Office Routine.	
" "	8/4/17		Inspected M.V.S. and Divisional Train. Went to a visit to motor-inspection at the unit expressed whether it was possible to move the Supply Park nearer the Units. The was a great inconvenience caused by bad state of the roads and consequent difficulty of motor transport carrying them. Supply hours were long, on average 7 hrs/day, and we had much ill and money cases of exhaustion mortality amongst wood draught horses.	
" "	9/4/17		Visited MOISLAINS to arrange for our Office and billet for myself. Inspected Mob.Vet. Section and 33rd Bdr. R.F.A.	

Army Form C. 2118.

WAR DIARY
or
INTELLIGENCE SUMMARY.
(Erase heading not required.)

Place	Date	Hour	Summary of Events and Information	Remarks and references to Appendices
CURLU	10/4/17		Moved Office to MOISLAINS. Adminst. D.D.V.S. 4th Army by arrangement at CURLU, and referred to him what 2 considered to be the causes of the heavy wastage amongst the horses of the Division. Suspended attainment of Sick at Railhead MARICOURT.	
MOISLAINS	11/4/17		Inspected 46th Bde R.F.A. and 150th Heavy Battery (15th Corps Artillery.)	
" —	12/4/17		Inspected 2nd Field Coy. R.E., 490th Field Coy. R.E. and 8th D.A.C.	
" —	13/4/17		Visited M.V.S. Arranged for a half-way halt for sick horses evacuated to Railhead. Every facility about to be made for the much required attention.	
" —	14/4/17		Inspected 23rd and 26th Infantry Bde Transport.	
" —	16/4/17		Inspected 8 D.A.C., 218th Machine Gun Coy. and M.V.S. Noted that the Mobile Gun Coy. animals which had recently arrived from England had lost condition considerably. Reorganised/Rearrangements the sub-diet them were shewn to refreshment, reduced diet, and my hot meat.	
" —	16/4/17		Office Routine. Inspected 25th Field Ambulance.	
" —	17/4/17		Inspected M.V.S. and cell refreshing Rides, Transport.	
" —	18/4/17		Office Routine. Inspected 46th Bde R.F.A.	
" —	19/4/17		Inspected M.V.S. Arranged with Pte Drummond Salvage Officer for a supply of Petrol Tins to M.V.S. to be used for watering the sick horses during their Journey by Lorries to Base Hospital.	

Army Form C. 2118.

WAR DIARY
or
INTELLIGENCE SUMMARY.
(Erase heading not required.)

Instructions regarding War Diaries and Intelligence Summaries are contained in F. S. Regs., Part II. and the Staff Manual respectively. Title pages will be prepared in manuscript.

Place	Date	Hour	Summary of Events and Information	Remarks and references to Appendices
MOISLAINS	20/4/17		Officer Routine. Inspected M.V.S. and inspected all substituted lines of the infantry Transport.	
"	21/4/17		Inspected 33rd D. de R.F.A.	
"	22/4/17		Officer Routine. Inspected M.V.S.	
"	23/4/17		" "	
"	24/4/17		Inspected 26th Field Ambulance, 22nd D.L.9, No 1 Coy. A.S.C., & 127th Heavy Battery. Arranged for evacuation of Sick from Peronne Railhead, about 1½ miles from Mont St Lotrin.	
"	25/4/17		Inspected 23rd Ag. Bde. & 218 M.G. Coy.	
"	26/4/17		" 3 & 4 Coys. 8th Div. Train.	
"	27/4/17		Officer Routine. Conference G.20/C G Division.	
"	28/4/17		Inspected M.V.S. Officer Routine.	
"	29/4/17		Inspected 45th Bde. R.F.A.	
"	30/4/17		" 33rd " " and D.L.9.	

A. Rowe Morgan
A.D.V.S. 8th Division

WAR DIARY
INTELLIGENCE SUMMARY

Army Form C. 2118.

ADVS 8th Division

Vol 30

Place	Date	Hour	Summary of Events and Information	Remarks and references to Appendices
MOISLAINS	May 1		Office routine.	
"	2		Office routine. MVS – Artillery Rest Station was visited.	
"	3		Office routine. Inspection of 24th Machine Gun Coy.	
"	4		Conference of ADsVS at 4th Army H.Q.	
"	5		Conference of N.C.O.'s of division. Inspection of M.V.S.	
NURLU	6		Office routine. Office moved to NURLU.	
"	7		Inspection of 24th Infantry Bde and 24th Field Ambulance.	
"	8		Inspection of 26th Field Amb. 24th Field Amb. and 45th Bde R.F.A.	
"	9		Inspection of all the remaining units of the division. All are showing great improvement in the condition of this horses	
"	10			
"	11			
"	12			

Army Form C. 2118.

WAR DIARY
or
INTELLIGENCE SUMMARY. A.D.V.S. 8th Div.

(Erase heading not required.)

Instructions regarding War Diaries and Intelligence Summaries are contained in F. S. Regs., Part II. and the Staff Manual respectively. Title pages will be prepared in manuscript.

Place	Date	Hour	Summary of Events and Information	Remarks and references to Appendices
NURLU	May 28		Office routine. Inspected 2 & 3 Corps A.S.C. & 2nd Devons.	
"	29		Office routine.	
"	30		Preparations for move.	
HEILLY	31		Moved to HEILLY.	

J. W. Capron
for A.D.V.S. 8th Div.

Army Form C. 2118.

WAR DIARY
or
INTELLIGENCE SUMMARY.
(Erase heading not required.)

ADVS. 8th Div.

Place	Date	Hour	Summary of Events and Information	Remarks and references to Appendices
NURLU	13/5		I took over duties of ADVS from Major Bone who proceeded on leave to England.	
"	14/5		Visited Mobile Vety Sect. & Horse Rest Station. Inspected 2nd Sco Rif.	
"	15/5		Office routine. Inspected 2nd Middlesex & 1, 2, & 4 Coys Divisional Train	
"	16/5		Visited M.V.S. Returned all horses from station Horse Rest station to duty	
"	17/5		Inspected Div Hd Qrs & Signal Coy & Bechelon DAC. Inspected Artillery Horse rest station returned horses to work	
"	18/5		Inspected 5th Bde R.F.A. Conference of N.C.O.'s in afternoon	
"	19/5		Inspected 45th Bde R.F.A. & BDAC horse to division moving out of 7th area	
"	20/5		Inspected 33rd Bde R.F.A on line of march. Met 309 remounts at LA CHAPELLETTE. They were a very good class of animals in good condition	
"	21/5		Visited M.V.S. Office Routine	
"	22/5		Visited M.V.S. Inspected 11 Field Ambulance	
"	23/5		Office Routine. Inspected 3 Coy Div Train - 24th Inf Bde	
"	24/5		Office Routine.	
"	25/5		Visited M.V.S. Conference of N.C.O.'s in the afternoon Inspected remounts.	
"	26/5		Col Fielding inspected M.V.S. 3 inspected 490th Field Coy R.E.	
"	27/5		Office Routine	

A.D.S.S./Forms/C. 2118.

Army Form C. 2118.

WAR DIARY
or
INTELLIGENCE SUMMARY.
(Erase heading not required.)

D.A.D.V.S. 8th Division

Instructions regarding War Diaries and Intelligence Summaries are contained in F.S. Regs., Part II. and the Staff Manual respectively. Title pages will be prepared in manuscript.

Place	Date	Hour	Summary of Events and Information	Remarks and references to Appendices
HEILLY	1/6/17	—	Preparations for and move to new Divisional area near MERRIS	
MERRIS	2/6/17		Eighth & D.A.C. and Artillery Bde. in Rest area at CLAIRMARIS	
" "	3/6/17		Office routine. Arranged for site for new Vet. Section	
" "	4/6/17		Inspected 24th Bde. Headquarters and Machine Gun Coy, 15th Field Coy R.E., 8th Divl Signals and Divisional Headquarters horses	
" "	5/6/17		Interviewed D.D.V.S. Second Army. Office Routine	
" "	6/6/17		Office routine. Visited 6 Horse Dept at ST JEAN CAPPEL for new arrangements etc for clothing horses.	
" "	7/6/17		Inspected 2/8 M.G.Cy on detachment at LOCRE, and the Rifle Bde. Transport for use arrangements etc	
" "	8/6/17		" 1st Wimereux Transport and 24th Field Ambulance	
" "	9/6/17		" 33rd and 45th Bde. R.F.A.	
" "	10/6/17		" 26th Field Amb., No 2 Coy A.S.C., 2nd Field Coy R.E, 20th M.G.Cy & Headquarters	
" "	11/6/17		Divisions moved to CAESTRE	
CAESTRE	12/6/17		Inspected No 1 Cy. A.S.C. M.V.S. Office Routine	
" "	13/6/17		Division moved to WINNIPEG CAMP.	
WINNIPEG (C)	14/6/17		Inspected 45th Bde R.F.A. and C.R.E. Horses.	
" "	15/6/17		" 33rd " " " and M.V.S.	
" "	16/6/17		" 24th " and 26th Inf. Bde.	
" "	17/6/17		" 22nd " D.L.9. and visited M.V.S.	
" "	18/6/17		" 45th Bde. R.F.A. and visited M.V.S.	

Army Form C. 2118.

WAR DIARY
or
INTELLIGENCE SUMMARY.
(Erase heading not required.)

Place	Date	Hour	Summary of Events and Information	Remarks and references to Appendices
WINNIPEG CAMP	19/6/17		Moved to Scottish Lines	
SCOTTISH LINES	20/6/17		Office routine. Visited 232 A.F.A. Bde attached to the Division	
"	21/6/17		Attended a Veterinary Conference at 23 Vet Hospital ST OMER.	
"	22/6/17		Inspected 8th Div. Squad. & Headquarters horses, B.W. Cable Section, 490th Field Cy R.E. Northants, & Divisional Train Transport.	
"	23/6/17		Inspected 2nd Field Cy R.E., No 2 Cy R.E., and 23rd Inf Bde Transport	
"	24/6/17		1 & 3 Cy A.S.C. and 24th Inf Bde.	
"	25/6/17		15th Field Cy R.E., 24th Field Amb, & Headquarters horses	
"	26/6/17		No 9/12 Field Cy R.E attached to 2nd Corps from 18th Division & 2nd Section D.A.C.	
"	27/6/17		Field horses of M.V.S. and No 2 Section D.A.C.	
"	28/6/17		Office Routine and visited M.V.S.	
"	29/6/17		Inspected remounts for the Division at Headquarters A.S.C.	
"	29/6/17		218 M.G.Cy, Conference of V.O.s	
"	30/6/17		Office Routine	

J Rowe Morgan
P.A.D.V.S. 8th Division

WAR DIARY
or
INTELLIGENCE SUMMARY

(Erase heading not required.)

Army Form C. 2118.

WA 32 D.A.D.V.S. 8th Division

Place	Date	Hour	Summary of Events and Information	Remarks and references to Appendices
BUSSEBOOM (SCOTTISH LINES)	1/7/17		Proceeded to TOURNEHEM area in order to arrange veterinary attendance of the 25th Inf. Bde. which was in rest. Reported to Bde. Headqrt. en route.	
" "	2/7/17		Inspected M.V.S. and 232 Bde A.F.A.	
" "	3/7/17		Inspected 24 M.G.Coy, 490 Field Coy R.E. and 2nd Rifle Bde. Transport.	
" "	4/7/17		" 2/8 M.G.Coy. 2nd M.V.S. Offrs Rodline	
" "	5/7/17		Visited units of 25th Bde. attended Euthanasing of 6 & 8th Divisions for veterinary attendance. The Cavh. Vet. Offrs. being away with the Cavh. Cavelry in training areas.	
" "	6/7/17		Conference of Divisional Vet. Offrs. Visited 46th Bde and 232 A.F.A.Bde.	
" "	7/7/17		Visited M.V.S. and 2nd Cav. Rebuilt no case of Mange & A.D.V.S. in 57th Battery.	
" "	8/7/17		Visited D.A.D.V.S. of 18th Div. informed him of his units attached belonging to 8th Div. arranged for M.V.S. to move to Pont Remy BOMY and for 1 bellow Sec. move with the M.V.S. of the 25th Division to await orders and remounts.	
" "	9/7/17		Visited 57th Battery arranged with D.A.D.V.S. 25th Division the bthny over of unit of 8th Division remaining in forward areas.	
" "	10/7/17		Division moved to BOMY, artilly remaining in the area.	
BOMY	11/7/17		Offrs visited. Inspected all Handyards charges and transport	
" "	12/7/17		Conference of Divisional V.O.'s Inspected No 3 Coy A.S.C. Offrs Rodline	
" "	13/7/17		Inspected 1st Sherwood Foresters Transport and the 24th M.G.Coy.	

Army Form C. 2118.

WAR DIARY
or
INTELLIGENCE SUMMARY.
(Erase heading not required.)

D.A.D.V.S. 8th Division

Instructions regarding War Diaries and Intelligence Summaries are contained in F.S. Regs., Part II. and the Staff Manual respectively. Title pages will be prepared in manuscript.

Place	Date	Hour	Summary of Events and Information	Remarks and references to Appendices
BOMY	14/7/17		Inspected 24th Bde. Headquarters and two horses that had been left in the sick by the 25th Division. Officer Realized. Arranged returning ambulance in unit of 28th Div.	Left at FRUGES Barn
"	15/7/17		Visited M.V.S. and inspected transport of his battalion.	Left with 74th # R.B. Bde.
"	16/7/17		Inspected No. 2 Coy A.S.C. and transport of one battalion 23rd Bde.	
"	17/7/17		Officer Realized. Inspected Bde. units.	
"	18/7/17		"	
"	19/7/17		Visited M.V.S. and arranged for their return to forward area.	
"	20/7/17		Visited No. 9 Coy A.S.C. Officer Realized.	
"	21/7/17		Division moved to BUSSEBOOM area. Visited D.A.D.V.S. 26th Division referenced units to take over.	
BUSSEBOOM	22/7/17		Arranged for establishment of an Advance Post of M.V.S. Officer Realized.	
"	23/7/17		Visited A.D.V.S. 2nd Cont. also inspected & area of thereafter in its relation etc and made arrangement.	64th A.F.A. Bde
"	24/7/17		Inspected 33rd and 45th Bdes. R.F.A., 42nd Army Troops R.E. and 22nd D.L.I.	
"	25/7/17		Officer Realized. Inspected 292 Bde. R.F.A.	
"	26/7/17		Visited M.V.S. and inspected all areas for evacuation. Inspected 277 A.F.A. Bde. 2nd Fuel Coy. R.E. Probably remount for the Division at PROVEN.	
"	27/7/17		Conference of S.O.S. Officer Realized. Visited M.V.S. and 33rd Bde. R.F.A.	

Army Form C. 2118.

WAR DIARY
or
INTELLIGENCE SUMMARY
(Erase heading not required.)

D.A.D.V.S. 8th Division

Place	Date	Hour	Summary of Events and Information	Remarks and references to Appendices
BUSSEBOOM	28/7/17		Inspected A.D.V.S. 2nd Corps. Inspected 33rd Bde. R.F.A. and 490th F. wd. by R.E. also visited 64th A.F.A. Bde.	
"	29/7/17		Inspected 277 Bde A.F.A.	
"	30/7/17		Inspected M.V.S. and instructed owner for inoculation. Also arranged for a site for M.V.S. further forward. Inspected 45th Bde. R.F.A	
"	31/7/17		Visited M.V.S, D.29, and Troop of Cavalry temporarily attached to the Division. Office Routine.	

D. R. McMurry.
D.A.D.V.S. 8th Division

Army Form C. 2118.

WAR DIARY
or
INTELLIGENCE SUMMARY.
(Erase heading not required.)

D.A.D.V.S. 8th Division

Vol 33

Instructions regarding War Diaries and Intelligence Summaries are contained in F. S. Regs., Part II. and the Staff Manual respectively. Title pages will be prepared in manuscript.

Place	Date	Hour	Summary of Events and Information	Remarks and references to Appendices
BUSSEBOOM	1/8/17	-	Office Routine. Visited and inspected sick horses for evacuation.	
"	2/8/17	-	Inspected horses of the 33rd and 45th Artillery Bdes.	
"	3/8/17	-	Office Routine. Conference of D.O.s of the Division.	
"	4/8/17	-	Attended Conference at Corps H.Q. Arranged for change in time of the M.V.S. Arranged for veterinary attendance of the 25th Inf. Bde. proceeding to Rest area at STEENVOORDE.	
"	5/8/17	-	Office Routine. Inspected 1 & 2 Coy. A.S.C. and No 2 Section D.A.C.	
"	6/8/17	-	Inspected horses of units which were received orders on mobilization of establishment with a view to steps re-issue to other units. Visited M.V.S. Inspected 23rd Inf Bde. transport	
"	7/8/17	-	Visited M.V.S. Inspected No 1 Section D.A.C. and Div. Headquarters Horses.	
"	8/8/17	-	Visited M.V.S. and inspected a number of sling arrivals with a view to their distribution. Inspected 292 A.F.A. Bde.	
"	9/8/17	-	Inspected 64th A.F.A. Bde. and M.V.S.	
"	10/8/17	-	Office Routine. Conference of D.O.s of the Division.	
"	11/8/17	-	Inspected 232 A.F.A. Bde. in conjunction with A.D.V.S. 2nd Corps. Attended Conference at Corps.	
"	12/8/17	-	Inspected all Headquarters horses, 1 & 2 Section D.A.C.	
"	13/8/17	-	Visited area for Advanced Collecting Post M.V.S. & selected situation, which will be carried down by R.E. Inspected Remount Reserve at PROVEN Buildings.	

Army Form C. 2118.

WAR DIARY
or
INTELLIGENCE SUMMARY.
(Erase heading not required.)

D.A.D.V.S. 8th Div.

Instructions regarding War Diaries and Intelligence Summaries are contained in F.S. Regs., Part II. and the Staff Manual respectively. Title pages will be prepared in manuscript.

Place	Date	Hour	Summary of Events and Information	Remarks and references to Appendices
BUSSEBOOM	14/8/17		Inspected 84th A.F.A. Bde. and 57th Bolton 45th Bde.	
"	15/8/17		Visited M.V.S. Office Routine	
"	16/8/17		Visited 57 Battery reference Strangles cases in that unit. Inspected 2nd Field Coy. R.E. and 15th M.V.S.	
"	17/8/17		Office Routine. Conference of D.O.S of the Division. Visited M.V.S. re cases for evacuation.	
"	18/8/17		Attended Conference of 2nd Corps H.Q. Visited M.V.S. & arrange for their move to next area.	
"	19/8/17		Division moved to CAESTRE. On arrival, 9 R.E. units arranged for D.A.D.V.S. inspecting Divisional & administering those whilst in this area.	
CAESTRE	20/8/17		Visited M.V.S. Office Routine	
"	21/8/17		Office Routine. Inspected re transport of the 22nd Inf. Bde.	
"	22/8/17		Inspected transport of the 25th Inf. Bde. and A.S.C. company attached.	
"	23/8/17		Inspected transport of the 24th Inf. Bde. and 15th Field Coy R.E. which had just arrived from BUSSEBOOM area.	
"	24/8/17		Visited M.V.S. re evacuations. Inspected no 2 Coy, A.S.C., 8th Div. Signal Coy, and Headquarters changes of Division	
"	25/8/17		Attended Conference at 2nd Anzac Corps. Office Routine.	
"	26/8/17		Visited M.V.S. Office Routine	
"	27/8/17		Divisional Units move to STEENWERCK area.	
STEENWERCK	28/8/17		Visited M.V.S. and inspected 22nd D.L.9 (Pioneer Regt.)	

Army Form C. 2118.

WAR DIARY
or
INTELLIGENCE SUMMARY.
(Erase heading not required.)

D.A.D.V.S. 8th Div.

Place	Date	Hour	Summary of Events and Information	Remarks and references to Appendices
STEENWERCK	29/7/17		Visited M.V.S. Inspected removals at 2a & Coy. A.V.C. before their move to unit of the Division	
"	30/7/17		Inspected 25th Field Ambulance. Divisional Squad horses Interviewed the O.C. of the Signal Coy. Ref. the availability of his horses. Wrote Railine	
"	31/7/17		Conference of D.O.S. the Division. Equipment appointed 15th Field Coy. and M.V.S. arrangements for assembling of horses, by Bridge from BAC. ST. MAUR	

D Mac Murry. O.C.C.
D.A.D.V.S. 8th Division

WAR DIARY
or
INTELLIGENCE SUMMARY.

D.A.D.V.S. 34th Division

Army Form C. 2118.

Place	Date	Hour	Summary of Events and Information	Remarks and references to Appendices
STEENWERCK	1/9/17		Attended conference at 2nd Anzac Corps. Inspected Mob. Vet. Section.	
"	2/9/17		Inspected 119th F.A. Artillery.	
"	3/9/17		Attended a conference at 8th Corps and Mobile Veterinary Section.	
"	4/9/17		Office Routine and arranged with O.C. M.V.S. for the evacuation of the sick by Barge from Bac St Maur.	
"	5/9/17		Attended exchange of Mules at Bac St Maur with the A.D.V.S. 8th Corps. Inspected all Mules of the Train, and 25th Field Ambulance.	
"	6/9/17		Inspected 2″ 15th & 490th Field Coy. R.E., 26th Field Ambulance & Mob. Veterinary Section. Inspected 1st & 5th D. attns. 45th Bde. R.F.A.	
"	7/9/17		Conference of D.O.s of the Division.	
"	8/9/17		Attended conference at 8th Corps. Inspected Ammn. Column of 1/1st Sth. Midland Heavy Battery, and 33rd Bde. R.F.A.	
"	9/9/17		Office Routine and visited Mob. Vet. Section.	
"	10/9/17		Inspected 6th Siege Battery and Mob. Vet. Section.	
"	11/9/17		Attended exchange of Mules at Bac St Maur. Inspected 8th Div. Signal Coy. and visited the O.C. government mobility stable management in that unit.	
"	12/9/17		Returned the A.A. & Q.M.G. on S. re clothing of Men. Inspected 24th Field Amb. and Mob. Vet. Section.	
"	13/9/17		Visited M.V.S., 6th Siege Battery, 5 Y Coy. and 3rd Battery and exhibits remounts for Division on Train arriving at STEEN WERCK.	

Army Form C. 2118.

WAR DIARY
or
INTELLIGENCE SUMMARY.   D.A.D.V.S. 8th Division

(Erase heading not required.)

Instructions regarding War Diaries and Intelligence Summaries are contained in F.S. Regs., Part II. and the Staff Manual respectively. Title pages will be prepared in manuscript.

Place	Date	Hour	Summary of Events and Information	Remarks and references to Appendices
STEENWERCK	14/9/17		Conference of 8.O.3 Division. Inspected 1/1 North Midland Heavy Battery, 22nd D.A.C. and 2nd Lt. Art.	
"	15/9/17		Conference at Corps. Inspected 2nd Field Coy R.E. and 2nd Bat. Scott.	
"	16/9/17		Buried M.V.S., No 2 Section D.A.C., 2, 3, 4 Coys Div. Train and 22nd D.A.C. accompanied by D.A.A.G. Division.	
"	17/9/17		Office Routine. Visited Mob. Vet. Section.	
"	18/9/17		Inspected A.S.C. Coys, 1/1 North Midland Heavy Battery, & the 6th Heavy Battery, also site for a Divisional Clothing Shed. accompanied by A.D.V.S. Corps.	
"	19/9/17		Inspected 32nd Battery, 33rd & 36th Batteries and 24th Field Ambulance	
"	20/9/17		Inspected 24th and 25th M.G. Coys and 2nd Field Coy R.E. Office Routine.	
"	21/9/17		Conference of 20 Division. Arranged with Staff Captain R.A. the clothing of all animals of the 33rd Div. R.F.A. Interviewed AA Q.M.G. with a view to obtaining the erection of a Clothing Shed. Also inspected 9th Battery R.F.A.	
"	22/9/17		Conference at Corps. Visited M.V.S.	
"	23/9/17		Visited Mob. Vet. Sect. Section. Inspected 8th Div. L.g. Coy. Office Routine.	
"	24/9/17		Office Routine. Inspect Horse Dir. Inspected memorials for the Division in New arrival.	
"	25/9/17		Office Routine	

Army Form C. 2118.

WAR DIARY
or
INTELLIGENCE SUMMARY.   DADVS 8 Division
(Erase heading not required.)

Instructions regarding War Diaries and Intelligence Summaries are contained in F.S. Regs., Part II. and the Staff Manual respectively. Title pages will be prepared in manuscript.

Place	Date	Hour	Summary of Events and Information	Remarks and references to Appendices
STEENWERCK	Sept 26		Office routine. Inspected 8th Div Train.	
	27		Inspected horse lines to evacuation. Visited horse std.	
	28		VO's conference. Visited CRE about clipping. Arranged clipping for ensuing week.	
	29		Attended conference at Corps. Inspected 8th Corps Cyclist Batt. Visited site of clipping std, found a party 1 50 RE at work on it. Inspected 8th DAC. Called out overnight to attend 12 animals of 8 Div Sig Coy RE wounded by shock during night - muzzle him.	
	30.		Office routine. Inspected 94th M.G. Coy, M.M.P. - Div All Div.	

for DADVS 8 Div

WAR DIARY or INTELLIGENCE SUMMARY

Army Form C. 2118.

D.A.D.V.S. 8th Division

Place	Date	Hour	Summary of Events and Information	Remarks and references to Appendices
STEENWERCK	1/10/17		Office routine.	
"	2/10/17		Office routine. Inspected all animals of the Division. Office routine. Inspected all animals of mounted personnel in precincts of A.D.V.S. Also attended ambulances of troops in bivouac at BAC ST MAHR.	
"	3/10/17		Inspected 119th Bde A.F.A. Office routine. Interviewed O/C A.D.V.S. 8th Corps re frames, clothing, shed and clipping of horses.	
"	4/10/17		Attended Conference at H.Q. 8th Division. Inspected C.R.E. horses, 8th Div. Engrs. and Headquarter horses of Division.	
"	5/10/17		Office routine. Attended ambulance of horses at BAC ST MAHR.	
"	6/10/17		" " attended ambulances at Corps H.Q.	
"	7/10/17		" "	
"	8/10/17		Occurrences A.D.V.S. Corps to Clothing Shed.	
"	9/10/17		Inspected 22nd D.L.9. Transport attended ambulances of sick horses.	
"	10/10/17		Inspected 15 M.V.S. Visited Clothing Shed. Inspected arrangements for the Division re sick animals.	
"	11/10/17		Visited M.V.S. Interviewed A.D.V.S. Corps re clipping of horses and visited Clothing Shed.	
"	12/10/17		Inspected all horses of the 33rd Bde R.F.A. 8th Div. Inspected and visited Conference of B.O. Artillery at Corps H.Q. Office routine.	
"	13/10/17		Attended Conference at Corps H.Q. Office routine.	
"	14/10/17		Inspected D.A.C. and Trench Mort. Bat. Section.	

Army Form C. 2118.

WAR DIARY
or
INTELLIGENCE SUMMARY.
(Erase heading not required.)

D.A.D.V.S. 8th Division

Instructions regarding War Diaries and Intelligence Summaries are contained in F. S. Regs., Part II. and the Staff Manual respectively. Title pages will be prepared in manuscript.

Place	Date	Hour	Summary of Events and Information	Remarks and references to Appendices
STEENWERCK	15/10/17		Visited a Clothing Shed at WESTHOUTRE with R.E. Officer to see working of Pit machinery. Visited M.V.S. and essential and Horse food to essentials.	
"	16/10/17		Inspected 33rd and 45th Bde. RFA with the A.D.V.S. Cork.	
"	17/10/17		Inspected 18th Regi. B. Artillery, Headquarters Coy. of the 8th Division, 9.24th Bde H.Q. horses.	
"	18/10/17		Visited clothing Shed. and all units of the 24th Infantry Bde.	
"	19/10/17		Conference of S.O.'s Division Office meeting. Inspected H.Q. 8 M D.A.C.	
"	20/10/17		Attended conference at Corps H.Q. Inspected 218 M.G.Coy. Visited Clothing Shed.	
"	22/10/17		Inspected 490th Field Coy., 24th Field Ambulance and M.V.S.	
"	23/10/17		Inspected 32nd Battery, 25th M.G.Coy, M.V.S. & Cobbled horses at Clothing Shed.	
"	24/10/17		Office routine. Visited M.V.S.	
"	24/10/17		Inspected 8th Div. Train. and M.V.S. Office routine	
"	25/10/17		Visited Clothing Shed with A.D.V.S. Corks, M.V.S. Inspection sick horses and Office routine	
"	26/10/17		Int. Office conference, Inspected 8th Div. Supply Col. and M.V.S.	
"	27/10/17		Attended conference at Corps H.Q. Veterinary S.O.C. Division on return all horses in general service horses of units of the Division.	
"	28/10/17		Received horses at Clothing Shed. Inspected units of 25th Bde.	
"	29/10/17		Inspected 32nd Bde. B Battery R.F.A. and sick horses at M.V.S. Horses to essentials	

Army Form C. 2118.

WAR DIARY
or
INTELLIGENCE SUMMARY.
(*Erase heading not required.*) D.A.D.V.S. 8th Division

Place	Date	Hour	Summary of Events and Information	Remarks and references to Appendices
STEENWERCK	30/10/17 — 31/10/17		Inspected 22nd D.A.C. 2nd Fuel Cy. R.E. and M.V.S. Inspected units of 23rd Inf Bde. Invited Clothing Nd. & M.V.S.	

D. Bruce Muir.
D.A.D.V.S. 8th Division

WAR DIARY or INTELLIGENCE SUMMARY

Army Form C. 2118.

(Erase heading not required.)

D.A.D.V.S. 8th Division

WM 36

Place	Date	Hour	Summary of Events and Information	Remarks and references to Appendices
STEENWERCK	1/11/17		Visited 15th Mob. Vet. Section. Inspected 25th Field Ambulance and the 15th Field Coy R.E. Inspected horses at Clipping Shed	
"	2/11/17		Inspected all horses of the 28th Bde R.F.A.	
"	3/11/17		Attended Conference of A.D.'s at Corps Headquarters. Visited Clipping Shed	
"	4/11/17		Inspected horses of Divisional Train. Also horses at Mob. Vet. Section.	
"	5/11/17		Inspected 45th Bde R.F.A. Visited horses and inspected all horses at the Clipping Shed	
"	6/11/17		Inspected 23rd Infy Bde horses. Visited veterinary officer re supply of blankets for cattle horses	
"	7/11/17		Visited Clipping Shed with A.D.V.S. Corps. Inspected sick horses at M.V.S.	
"	8/11/17		Inspected 22nd D.L.I. (Pioneer Bgt.) and Mob. Vet. Section	
"	9/11/17		Office routine. Conference of A.D.'s Division	
"	10/11/17		Attended weekly conference at Corps HQrs. Visited Canadian Corps HQrs with the A.D.V.S. reference the issuing out of flat army-vaccine if fit. Also visited Canadian Vet. Hospital & Mob. Vet. Section to be relieved by 8th Cdn.	
"	11/11/17		Inspected a number of wounded 8th Div. horses and Mob. Vet. Section.	
"	12/11/17		Office routine.	
"	13/11/17		Division moved from STEENWERCK to WATOU	
WATOU	14/11/17		Office routine. Inspected Headquarters horses.	
"	15/11/17		Visited Canadian M.V.S. which we are to be relieved by 15th M.V.S. Also button of 33rd and 45th Bde R.F.A.	

Army Form C. 2118.

WAR DIARY
or
INTELLIGENCE SUMMARY.
(Erase heading not required.)

D.A.D.V.S. 8th Division

Instructions regarding War Diaries and Intelligence Summaries are contained in F.S. Regs., Part II. and the Staff Manual respectively. Title pages will be prepared in manuscript.

Place	Date	Hour	Summary of Events and Information	Remarks and references to Appendices
WATOU	17/11/17		Office routine.	
"	18/11/17		Division moved to MERSEY CAMP – journeyed over.	
MERSEY CAMP	19/11/17		Inspected No 1 Coy A.S.C. Inspected M.V.S. and individual animals arranged refence further accommodation for sick horses and men sent from lines to assist in inspection.	
"	20/11/17		Inspected 8th Divl Signals and M.V.S.	
"	21/11/17		Inspected 5th Batty R.F.A. at YPRES. Office routine.	
"	22/11/17		" Field Coy. R.E. at VLAMERTINGHE and 232nd Inf. Bde near POPPERINGHE " Field Coy. R.E. at " and 33rd Bde R.F.A. and	
"	23/11/17		Conference of A.D's Division. Office Routine.	
"	24/11/17		Attended conference at Corps. Inspd M.V.S. a Canadian Railway Rail way Coy	
"	25/11/17		Visited M.V.S. to inspect sick horses. Office routine	
"	26/11/17		Inspected 45th Bde R.F.A. and M.V.S.	
"	27/11/17		Inspected fodder standings for R.F.A. Bdes. Office routine.	
"	28/11/17		Inspected R.F.A. Bdes of 49th Division.	
"	29/11/17		Attended entrainment of pack horses at Brielen. Inspected 26th Field Ambulance and Headquarts Transport.	
"	30/11/17		Office routine. Weather. A cool ground conditions throughout the month has been on the whole favourable to horses and attendant improvement in condition has been noticeable. All horses of the Division were shipped by A.V. & M. Res.	

N. Bone Maj. D.A.D.V.S. 8 Div.

Army Form C. 2118.

WAR DIARY
or
INTELLIGENCE SUMMARY
(Erase heading not required.)

D.A.D.V.S. 8th Division

Vol 3

Instructions regarding War Diaries and Intelligence Summaries are contained in F. S. Regs., Part II. and the Staff Manual respectively. Title pages will be prepared in manuscript.

Place	Date	Hour	Summary of Events and Information	Remarks and references to Appendices
MERSEY CAMP VLAMERTINGHE	1/12/17		Attended conference of D.D's Division. Handed over to D.A.D.V.S. 14th Division instructions regarding evacuation of units in Divisional area.	
—	2/12/17		Visited M.V.S. and inspected sick for evacuation. Office routine.	
—	3/12/17		Division moved its rest camp. Ran Artillery units and R.E.	
WIZERNES	4/12/17		Office routine.	
—	5/12/17		Inspected all Headquarters transport. Visited M.V.S. and road instructions to O.C.s that went no evacuation.	
—	6/12/17		Inspected transport of Hd 23rd Inf Bde.	
—	7/12/17		Office routine. Conference B.D.O.'s Division at my office. Inspected transport of Div. Pioneers.	
—	8/12/17		Attended conference at office D.A.D.V.S. 8th Corps.	
—	9/12/17		Inspected remount for the Division in stew covered at No 309 A.S.C. LONGUENESSE. Also inspected 15th Wounds. I went out at some Horse.	
—	10/12/17		Inspected command for evacuation at M.V.S. Office routine.	
—	11/12/17		Office routine.	
—	12/12/17		Inspected all transport of Divisional machine gun Corps.	
—	13/12/17		Inspected M.V.S. Office Routine.	
—	14/12/17		Conference B.D.O. Division. Inspected Headquarters and 25th Inf Bde.	
—	15/12/17		Inspected transport of 25th Inf Bde.	

Army Form C. 2118.

WAR DIARY
or
INTELLIGENCE SUMMARY.
(Erase heading not required.)

D.A.D.V.S. 8th Division

Instructions regarding War Diaries and Intelligence Summaries are contained in F. S. Regs., Part II. and the Staff Manual respectively. Title pages will be prepared in manuscript.

Place	Date	Hour	Summary of Events and Information	Remarks and references to Appendices
WAERNES	16/12/17		Office routine	
"	17/12/17		Inspected 24th Inf. Bde. Transport.	
"	18/12/17		Office routine	
"	19/12/17		Inspected M.V.S. Office routine.	
"	20/12/17		Visited 23rd Fd. Hospital. Office routine.	
"	21/12/17		Inspected truck at M.V.S. prior to their evacuation. Conference 8 D.O.S	
"	22/12/17		Attended conference at Corps H.Q.	
"	23/12/17		Office routine	
"	24/12/17		" "	
"	25/12/17		Divisional units moving to forward area	
"	26/12/17		" "	
"	27/12/17		Office routine	
MERSEY CAMP	28/12/17		Divisional moved to forward area→PRES and VLAMERTINGHE Conference of D.O.S. Division. Inspected R.E. units and Headquarters Transport	
"	29/12/17		Attended conference at Corps H.Q.	
"	30/12/17		Inspected remounts for the Division	
"	31/12/17		C.O. of the Divisional Train Inspected M.V.S. Office routine. on arrival also inspected all	

D. Dn Murry. D.A.D.V.S. 8th Div.

WAR DIARY
or
INTELLIGENCE SUMMARY.

(Erase heading not required.) D.A.D.V.S. 8th Division

Army Form C. 2118.

Vol 38

Place	Date	Hour	Summary of Events and Information	Remarks and references to Appendices
MERSEY CAMP WINCHESTER	1/1/18		Conducted Inspection of 24th and 25th Field Btns.	
"	2/1/18		Routine work	
"	3/1/18		Conducted Inspection of the 23rd Fd Btn.	
"	4/1/18		Inspected B.O. Division. Inspected all Mounted & Gun Gp and Reserve Battalion Lines & visited units Vet. Section and inspected all field animals	
"	5/1/18		Attended conference at A.D.V.S. Office 8th Corps. Visited D.H.Q. (Colonies)	
"	6/1/18		Visited 4th & 7th Fd. Section. Office routine	
"	7/1/18		Inspected stables with a view of their disinfection before being used by 45th Battery. Also inspected 5th Battery stables	
"	8/1/18		Visited 15th M.V.S. and inspected 5th Div. hospital & 26th Field Ambulance	
"	9/1/18		Inspected all units at M.V.S. forms & formation. Inspected 8th D.A.C.	
"	10/1/18		Took over duties of A.D.V.S. 8th Corps on Rest. Handing over by Capt. Edwards a.v.c. Handed over duties of D.A.D.V.S. 8th Div. to Capt.	

H. Price Manny
D.A.D.V.S. 8th Div.

Army Form C. 2118.

WAR DIARY
or
INTELLIGENCE SUMMARY.
(Erase heading not required.)

Instructions regarding War Diaries and Intelligence Summaries are contained in F.S. Regs., Part II. and the Staff Manual respectively. Title pages will be prepared in manuscript.

Place	Date	Hour	Summary of Events and Information	Remarks and references to Appendices
MERSEY CAMP VLAMERTINGHE	10-1-16	—	Took over duties of D.A.D.V.S. 8th Div.	
"	11-1-16		Conference of V.O's Div. Visited M.V.S. and inspected animals prior to evacuation	
"	12-1-16		Attended conference of A.D.V.S. & Office 8th Div. Arranged with ADMS 8th Div. for medical examination of AVC personnel. Inspected Mer 8th Corps Transport.	
"	13-1-16		Office routine. Inspected #0 animals also 8th Div Signals. Visited M.V.S and inspected animals prior to evacuation.	
"	14-1-16		Inspected transport of 25th Infantry Bde.	
"	15-1-16		Inspected transport of 23rd Infantry Bde. Office routine.	
"	16-1-16		Conference of V.O's Div. Inspected 24th Infantry Bde Transport.	
"	17-1-16		Moved with M.V.S. to WATOU area. Inspected remounts for 8th Div at STEENVOORDE	
"	18-1-16		Attended conference at A.D.V.S. Office 8th Corps. Moved to STEENVOORDE with 8th Div.	
"	19-1-16		Inspected 8th Div Signals Transport with A.D.V.S 8th Corps. Officer routine.	
STEENVOORDE	20-1-16		Inspected animals at M.V.S prior to evacuation and attended ditoing	
"	21-1-16		Inspected animals at M.V.S.	
"	22-1-16		at PESELHOEK. Handed over duties of D.A.D.V.S. 8th Div. to Capt Taylor A.V.C.	

Hamilton Capt
A/D.A.D.V.S. 8th Div.

Army Form C. 2118.

WAR DIARY
or
INTELLIGENCE SUMMARY.
(Erase heading not required.)

Instructions regarding War Diaries and Intelligence Summaries are contained in F. S. Regs., Part II. and the Staff Manual respectively. Title pages will be prepared in manuscript.

Place	Date	Hour	Summary of Events and Information	Remarks and references to Appendices
STEENVOORDE	January 1918 23		Delivered G.O.C.'s lectures on Horsemanagement by V.O's. Inspected MVS. Inspected 1 HQ horses	
"	24		8th Div Sig RE	
"	25		Conference of V.O's division. Inspected no 4 Coy 8th Div Train	
"	26		Attended conference at ADVS Corps Office Poperinghe	
"	27		Inspected two platoons of 24th Inf Bde. Examined horse presented at MVS	
"	28		Took measures of prevention in connection with cases of mange & swollen knees. Attended 15MVS with DDR. to note at animals for eating	
"	29		Inspected 3rd East Lancs transport & 24 Bde HQ.	
"	30		Inspected no 3 Coy 8th Div Train Inspected HQ horses + 8th Div Sig Coy RE	
"	31		Office routine. Visited MVS examined all sick animals	

... [signature]
c/DADVS. 8th Div

Army Form C. 2118.

WAR DIARY
or
INTELLIGENCE SUMMARY.
(Erase heading not required.)

DADVS 8th D.

VL 39

Place	Date	Hour	Summary of Events and Information	Remarks and references to Appendices
STEENVOORDE	February 1 1918		VO's conference. Inspected 8th D. HQ & Signals RE.	
	2		Conference at Corps HQ. Office Routine.	
	3		Inspected animals of MVS prior to evacuation. Issued 4 Coy 2nd Signals	
	4		Office Routine. Inspected several horses at & for wall dugout shell	
	5		Inspected 34 & 35 Field Ambulances	
	6		Held P.M. on horse at 4 Coy Train. Inspected 33rd Bde RFA	
	7		Inspected 45th B.C. RFA. attended at WIPPENHOEK.	
	8		Conference with VO's of Divisions. Visited MVS	
	9		Conference I Corps HQ.	
	10		Inspected remounts. Interviewed 10th KRR who found Owner 9th inst	
	11		Office routine. Inspected aerial line to evacuation of MVS	
MERSEY CAMP	12		Division moved to forward area.	
	13		Office routine. Handed over duties. 1 DADVS to Maj H BOME AVC.	

[signature]
a/DADVS 8th [Div]

Army Form C. 2118.

WAR DIARY
or
INTELLIGENCE SUMMARY.

(Erase heading not required.)

DADVS 8th Div

Instructions regarding War Diaries and Intelligence Summaries are contained in F. S. Regs., Part II. and the Staff Manual respectively. Title pages will be prepared in manuscript.

Place	Date	Hour	Summary of Events and Information	Remarks and references to Appendices
HERSEY CAMP	14/2/18		Took over duties of DADVS from Colonel Taylor O.V.S. on return from 8th Inch	
"	15/2/18		Inspected machine gun & Holcus Officers Riding School 45th Field R.F.A. also Bn.	
"			Battalion of 23rd Inf. Bde. Interviewed G.O.C. Division re arrival of horses in the	
"			Division.	
"	16/2/18		Conference at Corps Headquarters. SVPs were not a.c.s.	
"	17/2/18		Took over duties of DADVS from Maj. H. Bone who proceeded on 14 days leave to England	
"	18/2/18		Inspected annual of MVS. hrs to evacuation	
"	19/2/18		Inspected 8th DAC	
"	20/2/18		Inspected No. 1 Coy 8th Div. Train supply column	MVS
"	21/2/18		Inspected Nos 2, 3 + 4 Coy 8th Div. Train	
"	22/2/18		Conference with No. 1 Div. Supply 8th Div Sup Co + Div HQ	
"	23/2/18		Conference + Capt. MQ re Inspected remounts	
"	24/2/18		Inspected animal for feed at at No MVS Horse ambulance advanced 2 DADNS 8th Corp	
"	25/2/18		Conference with DAQMG 8th Div re proposal for evacuation	
"	26/2/18		Conference with DAQMG 8th Div re proposal for MVS. Inspected 491 (Kent) Field Coy RE	
"	27/2/18		Inspected 8th Machine Gun Battalion + 2nd DLI	
"	28/2/18		Inspected horse lines to evacuation + 36th Bde R.F.A. also 2nd + 3rd Rifle	

Geo C. Macroft
Cap l DADVS 8 D

WAR DIARY or INTELLIGENCE SUMMARY

Army Form C. 2118.

D.A.D.V.S. 8th Division

Place	Date	Hour	Summary of Events and Information	Remarks and references to Appendices
MERSEY CAMP VLAMERTINGHE	1/3/18		Office routine. Veterinary Officers conference.	
"	2/3/18		Attended conference at Corps H.Q.	
"	3/3/18		Inspected 23rd & 24th Bde.	
"	4/3/18		Office routine. Inspected 25th Inf. Bde.	
"	5/3/18		Horse show at M.V.S. Lectured to officers how to evacuate	
"	6/8/18		Returned to 8th Division from Course, and took over duties of D.A.D.V.S. from Capt. Taylor. O.C. 15th M.V.S.	
"	7/3/18		Conference of Veterinary Officers of the Division. Office routine	
"	8/3/18		Divn. Headquarters moved to ABEELE.	
ABEELE	9/3/18		Inspected all horses of Headquarters, 9 & 8th D.A.C. Headquarters	
"	10/3/18		Visited 8th D.A.C. Headquarters.	
"	11/3/18		Inspected 24th Infantry Bde. transport.	
"	12/3/18		" 8th Divisional Train transport	
"	13/3/18		Divisional Headquarters moved to WIZERNES (G.H.Q. Reserve). Inspected transport of Machine Gun Battalion.	
WIZERNES	14/3/18			
"	15/3/18		Conference of D.O.s of the Division. Office routine.	
"	16/3/18		Attended conference at Corps Headquarters. Inspected 33rd & 45th Bde. R.F.A.	
"	17/3/18		Office routine. Inspected 15th M.V.S.	
"	18/3/18		Inspected 23rd Infantry Bde. transport & 26th Field Ambulance. Visited M.V.S.	
"	19/3/18		Office routine	
"	20/3/18		Inspected 2nd Bn. Headquarters & transport of 10th K.R.R. Lectured attended to the Divnl.	

Army Form C. 2118.

WAR DIARY
or
INTELLIGENCE SUMMARY.
(Erase heading not required.)

Instructions regarding War Diaries and Intelligence Summaries are contained in F. S. Regs., Part II. and the Staff Manual respectively. Title pages will be prepared in manuscript.

Place	Date	Hour	Summary of Events and Information	Remarks and references to Appendices
WIZERNES	21/3/18		Attended conference of D.V.S. at ABEELE. Officers mentin Divisional Headquarters left WIZERNES for SOMME FRONT and detrained at CHAULNES.	
"	22/3/18		Divisional Headquarters moved by road to VILLERS-CARBONNEL. Same day.	
CHAULNES	23/3/18			
FOUCAUCOURT	24/3/18		Moved to HARBONNIERES with Rear Headquarters but returned to Advanced Headquarters the same day as Rear Headquarters were ordered back to DOMART. Set office and clerk to DOMART.	
"	25/3/18		Ordered M.V.S. to proceed to FRAMENCOURT and visited A.D.V.S. XIX Corps position to the Larger number posted at FOUCAUCOURT. Walering for horses was very unsatisfactory owing to water supplied from well by means of Motor Pump. Arranged with Div Veterinary Officer for the supply of Petrol for engine. The man in charge of same being informed me he was running short.	
"	26/3/18		Ordered M.V.S. to MARCELCAVE and proceeded there with Divisional Headquarters. Proceeded to DOMART with M.V.S. same evening. Arranged with AA & QMG for M.V.S. to proceed also in future with the Headquarters of the Divisional Train. Attended myself to Headquarters of the Train on the most convenient place to halt in touch with the veterinary officers and transport of the Division during movement. Arranged for the evacuation of sick from BOVES.	
DOMART	27/3/18		Paid visit to Headquarters Base & D.A.C. & informed veterinary officers of visits of M.V.S. etc. to A.D.V.S. 19th Corps.	

Army Form C. 2118.

WAR DIARY
or
INTELLIGENCE SUMMARY.
(Erase heading not required.)

Place	Date	Hour	Summary of Events and Information	Remarks and references to Appendices
DOMART.	28/3/18		Moved to NORISEL thence to front between JUMEL and ESSERTAUX about a mile out of JUMEL. Weather very unfavourable. Found it necessary to destroy three horses unable to march with M.V.S.	
JUMEL	29/3/18		Assisted by returning officers of Artillery & Infantry Dets. guards both of whom knew few amulin, to repatch. battalions & remnants of Divisions found all round.	
JUMEL	30/3/18		Moved to SAINS-EN-AMIENOIS and moved position to A.D.V.S. 19th Divn.	
SAINS-EN-AMIENOIS	31/3/18		No move. M.V.S. evacuated all sick from SALEUX to FORGES-LES-AUX.	

RBMc May.
D.A.D.V.S. 8th Division

Army Form C. 2118.

WAR DIARY
or
INTELLIGENCE SUMMARY.
(Erase heading not required.)

Instructions regarding War Diaries and Intelligence Summaries are contained in F.S. Regs., Part II. and the Staff Manual respectively. Title pages will be prepared in manuscript.

D.A.D.V.S. 8th Division

Vol 41

Place	Date	Hour	Summary of Events and Information	Remarks and references to Appendices
SAINS-EN-AMIENOIS	1/4/18	—	Visited and inspected Artillery Pack Transport.	
"	2/4/18		Inspected D.A.C.	
"	3/4/18		Division moved to CAVILLON.	
CAVILLON	4/4/18		Office routine. Visited FOUDRINOY with O.C. 15th M.V.S. for billets to billet all Headquarters Horses & Supply Transport. Inspected M.V.S. at FOUDRINOY.	
"	5/4/18		Visited M.V.S. at RIENCOURT. The section having received water & new place on Pte 5/4/18	
"	6/4/18		Inspected office of A.D.V.S. 19th Division also M.V.S. and No 3 Coy. A.S.C.	
"	7/4/18		Inspected Pk Transport of 2nd 16th and 49th Field Coy. R.E. & 22nd D.L.I. (Pioneer Regt)	
"	8/4/18		Inspected 8th M.G. Battalion Transport and 2nd A.A. Batter R.A.C.	
"	9/4/18		Inspected Transport of Pk 24th Infantry Bde	
"	10/4/18		Visited and Inspected reference near to SALEUX &c.	
"	11/4/18		Divisional HQ moved to BERTANGLE. Inspected V.B.S. at PICQUIGNY in relation of horses affected	
BERTANGLE	13/4/18		at LE FERRIER. A.D.V.S. Australian Corps at VIGNACOURT.	
"	14/4/18		Inspected 2.3rd Infantry Bde Transport	
"	15/4/18		8th M.G. Battalion and No 3 Coy. A.S.C.	
"	16/4/18		Transport of 25th Infantry Bde. 25th Fuel Ambulance and No 15 Coy R.E.	
"	17/4/18		Office routine. Headquarters Horses.	
"	18/4/18		Visited M.V.S. and inspected No 2 Coy. A.S.C.	
"	19/4/18		Arranged with BAVS in S. for move of M.V.S. to RIVERY. Visited A.D.V.S. Australian Corps	
"	20/4/18		Office moved to CAMON (Rear Headquarters 8 Division)	
CAMON	21/4/18		Visited Office of A.D.V.S. 3rd Cav Bde. and Divisional Columns Headquarters. Office routine.	

Army Form C. 2118.

WAR DIARY
or
INTELLIGENCE SUMMARY.
(Erase heading not required.)

D.A.D.V.S. 8th Division

Instructions regarding War Diaries and Intelligence Summaries are contained in F. S. Regs., Part II. and the Staff Manual respectively. Title pages will be prepared in manuscript.

Place	Date	Hour	Summary of Events and Information	Remarks and references to Appendices
CAMON	22/4/18		Inspected 25th Infantry Bde. S.A.A. Section D.A.C, & R.L.9. (Rear)	
"	23/4/18		" 2nd & 490th Field Cy. R.E. (Rear) Officer on leave	
"	24/4/18		Inspected all transport & armoured wagon line.	
"	25/4/18		" 24th & 23rd Field Ambulance. Horselines & horse and uninfected cars inspected, personnel examined by trained subs newly arrived, rifles fit to use and V. inspected. All by all ranks.	
"	26/4/18		Inspected officer of A.D.V.S. 3rd Bath at DOVELLES.	
"	27/4/18		Inspected Sub. at M.V.S. gave over to Francette. S.A.A Section D.A.C, 24th & 25th Field Ambulance,	
"	28/4/18		the extra work condusted by D.D.V.S. & A.D.V.S. 23rd R.F. to Transport and M.V.S.	
"	29/4/18		Inspected 15th Field Cy. R.E. Officer on leave. Attended P.M. on horse of 2nd Devon	
"	30/4/18		visited M.V.S. and attended P.M. on horse of 490th Field Cy R.E.	

JJ Bruce Murray
D.A.D.V.S. 8th Division

WAR DIARY
INTELLIGENCE SUMMARY

Army Form C. 2118.

D.A.D.V.S. 8th Division Vol 4

Place	Date	Hour	Summary of Events and Information	Remarks and references to Appendices
CAMON	1/5/18		Visited M.V.S. and S.A.C. Section.	
"	2/5/18		Visited R.A.H.Q. D.H.Q. Inspected Infantry Bde. Transport of 15th & 24th Inf Bde RE chaving march.	
"	3/5/18		Moved to SALOUEL. Visited M.V.S. Entrained for FISMES. 9th Cav Corps Area.	
CHERY-CHART-REUVE	4/5/18		Detrained. Reported to A.D.V.S. IX Corps at FERE-EN-TARDENOIS.	
"	5/5/18		Visited and inspected site for M.V.S. at DOLE. Inspected 24th Inf Bde. Transport and arranged for inoculation of Stable in the area. Inspected Reinforced Cav Transport.	
"	6/5/18		Visited M.V.S. at DOLE. Office routine.	
"	7/5/18		Office routine. Inspected M.G. Coys at Mount ST MARTIN.	
"	8/5/18		Inspected 23rd Inf Bde Transport at DRAVEGNY.	
"	9/5/18		" 25th " " " MAREUIL-EN-DOLE. R.V.I. Coy A.S.C. and	
"			45th Bde RFA Adv. D.A.C.	
"	10/5/18		Inspected 15th Field, W 3 Cav Train (A.S.C.) & 24th Field Ambulance.	
"	11/5/18		Visited A.D.V.S. 9th Corps with Return. Inspected Sick at M.V.S.	
"	12/5/18		Office routine.	
"	13/5/18		Moved to ROUCY.	
ROUCY	14/5/18		Visited M.V.S. at BOUVANCOURT. Inspected 29.4 Cav Train.	

Army Form C. 2118.

WAR DIARY
or
INTELLIGENCE SUMMARY.
(Erase heading not required.)

D.A.D.V.S. 5th Division

Instructions regarding War Diaries and Intelligence Summaries are contained in F. S. Regs., Part II. and the Staff Manual respectively. Title pages will be prepared in manuscript.

Place	Date	Hour	Summary of Events and Information	Remarks and references to Appendices
ROUCY	15/5/18		Inspected M.V.S. Inspected D.A.C.	
"	16/5/18		Office routine. Attended sick at M.V.S.	
"	17/5/18		Attended Enquiry Cy. H.Q. horses. Inspected M.V.S.	
"	18/5/18		Proceeded on duties to Bdes T.T. Taylor on history from deep Central Pown, was admitted to Art V.E.S. at COURLANDON.	
"	19/5/18 at 4.20 pm		Office routine. Sick evacuated to Art V.E.S. at COURLANDON.	
"	22/5/18		Inspected M.V.S. Office routine	
"	23/5/18		Inspected 33rd and 45th Bdes R.F.A.	
"	24/5/18		Inspected 15th & 490th Field Cos. R.E. Office routine	
"	25/5/18		Attended conference at Art. Headquarters.	
"	26/5/18		Division retiring. Moved to VENTELAY. Received message from Staff Sgt of M.V.S. returning O.C. wounded. Sent instructions to the N.C.O. to move B.M.V.S. JONCHERY and arranged for the evacuation there. Proceeded to MONTIGNY and met B.O. i/c D.A.C. Instructed the Officer to meet the M.V.S. at JONCHERY and take it along with him with D.A.C. Headquarters. Moved to SERZY.	
"	27/5/18		Returned to A.D.V.S. Carts at RUMIGNY. Moved to CHATILLON.	
CHATILLON	28/5/18		Moved to OEILLY. Inspected M.V.S. of MAREUIL-LE-PORT.	

Army Form C. 2118.

WAR DIARY
or
INTELLIGENCE SUMMARY.

(Erase heading not required.)   D.A.D.V.S. 8th Division

Instructions regarding War Diaries and Intelligence Summaries are contained in F. S. Regs., Part II. and the Staff Manual respectively. Title pages will be prepared in manuscript.

Place	Date	Hour	Summary of Events and Information	Remarks and references to Appendices
OEUILLY	29/5/18		Moved to St Martin D'Ablois	
ST MARTIN D'A	30/5/18		Moved to Villers-aux-Bois	
VILLERS	31/5/18		Office routine	

D. Bruce Mury
D.A.D.V.S. 8th Division

Army Form C. 2118.

WAR DIARY
or
INTELLIGENCE SUMMARY.
(Erase heading not required.)

D.A.D.V.S. & 5th Division

Instructions regarding War Diaries and Intelligence Summaries are contained in F.S. Regs., Part II. and the Staff Manual respectively. Title pages will be prepared in manuscript.

Place	Date	Hour	Summary of Events and Information	Remarks and references to Appendices
VILLERS-AUX-BOIS	1/6/18		Inspected A.D.V.S. 9th Corps with weekly returns, also Prob. Vet. Section	
— " —	2/6/18		Inspected D.A.C. and sick at M.V.S.	
— " —	3/6/18		Division HQrs moved to BERGERES-LES-VERTUS	
BERGERES	4/6/18		Inspected M.V.S. Office Routine	
— " —	5/6/18		Inspected Squad Coy horses. Office routine. Inspected A.D.V.S. IX Corps	
— " —	6/6/18		Inspected 33rd & 46th Bdes R.F.A. Inspected M.V.S.	
— " —	7/6/18		Inspected Machine Gun Battalion and 24th Inf. Bde Transport	
— " —	8/6/18		Inspected A.D.V.S. Corps with weekly return	
— " —	9/6/18		Inspected sick at M.V.S. Office routine	
— " —	10/6/18		Division HQrs moved to PLEURS	
PLEURS	11/6/18		Inspected M.V.S. at CONNANTRE. Inspected Infantry Bde. Transport	
— " —	12/6/18		Rode out to NOTTRELAN. Inspected Transport on the line	
— " —	13/6/18		Inspected A.D.V.S. IX Corps. D.H.Q. moved to HUPPY — now XIX Corps area. Office routine	
HUPPY	14/6/18			
— " —	15/6/18		Inspected A.D.V.S. XIX Corps at FONTREMY. Office routine	

Army Form C. 2118.

WAR DIARY
or
INTELLIGENCE SUMMARY.

(Erase heading not required.)

D.A.D.V.S. & Division

Instructions regarding War Diaries and Intelligence Summaries are contained in F. S. Regs., Part II. and the Staff Manual respectively. Title pages will be prepared in manuscript.

Place	Date	Hour	Summary of Events and Information	Remarks and references to Appendices
HUPPY	16/5/18		Held M.V.S. at LE HAMEL and for 1 Cav Divisional Train. Also inspected 93rd Bde RFA.	
HUPPY	17/5/18		Inspected 25th & B of Dlo. 7 Res. 89th Coy. Del. Train	
"	18/5/18		Inspected 29th & B. Plo. and Signal Coy	
"	19/5/18		Inspected 15th Field Coy. R.E. and Princess & Stables	
"	20/5/18		Inspected 33rd and 45th Bdes. RFA.	
"	21/5/18		Inspected 2nd and 490th Field Coy. R.E. and No 3 Coy Train issue	
"	22/5/18		Visited ADVS XIX with whom also inspected hundred of new Prince Ref. gained the Division but whose where on 2nd & 490 Field Cor RE & DHQ	
"	23/5/18		D.H.Q. moved to FRIVILLE	
"	24/5/18		Visited M.V.S. at VISSE-FRIVILLE. Also inspected and visited E MAISINIERES	
FRIVILLE	25/5/18		Inspected all artillery units of the Division with D.D.V.S. & D.D.R. Fourth Army	

Army Form C. 2118.

WAR DIARY
or
INTELLIGENCE SUMMARY.

(Erase heading not required.)   D.A.D.V.S. 8th Division

Instructions regarding War Diaries and Intelligence Summaries are contained in F. S. Regs., Part II. and the Staff Manual respectively. Title pages will be prepared in manuscript.

Place	Date	Hour	Summary of Events and Information	Remarks and references to Appendices
FRIVILLE	26/5/18		Inspected 8th M.G.C.	
—	27/5/18		Inspected 22nd D.L.S. and Mob. Vet. Sectn.	
—	28/5/18		Inspected 2nd, 15th and 490th Fd Coys R.E. and inspected M.V.S.	
—	29/5/18		Office routine	
—	30/5/18		Inspected M.V.S. & inspect sick for evacuation	

D. McMay
D.A.D.V.S. 8th Division

Army Form C. 2118.

WAR DIARY
or
INTELLIGENCE SUMMARY.
(Erase heading not required.)

8 D A D K S 8 Division   Vol 44

Place	Date	Hour	Summary of Events and Information	Remarks and references to Appendices
FRIVILLE	1/7/16		Inspected 32, 33 & 55 Batteries RFA & 24 & 7 old Bde Amb.	
"	2 "		Inspected sick at MVS & 1st & 3rd R. Mounds RFA	
"	3 "		Office routine. Inspected 2 & 5 Div Supply Coy.	
"	4 "		Insp. 67, 27 & 15 & 9 490 Field Cos RE. Alterns in arrangements at Ration and	
"	5 "		Remount A.D.V.S. 22 nr Evalu under inspection of orderly room	
"	6 "		Office Routine	
"	7 "		" "	
"	8 "		Insp MVS to inspect sick	
"	9 "		Inspected 28 & 46 Bde Transport	
"	10 "		Insp 67 RE units	
"	11 "		Insp 20 Headquarters Horses	
"	12 "		Insp XI 24 & 90/ Bde Transport all 1/4th Div (Francis)	
"	13 "		Office routine	
"	14 "		"	
"	15 "		Insp MVS	
"	16 "		Inspected 28 ? and 8 R. Msk (horse transport to establishment) Inspected VOs unit	
"	17 "		Office routine	
"	18 "		" "	
"	19 "		" "	
"	20 "		Divisional Headqrs to moved & joined near VILLERS-AU-BOIS Visited & ADVS VIII Corps.	
VILLERS-AU-BOIS	21/7/16		Conference DADVS, 46 & 2 Div (who were in suspension 8 H & V 46) & unusual hungus Divn. Insp of MVS and Bde VES & 05 DAC	
"	22 "		Insp MVS as & formal horses 205 DAC	

Army Form C. 2118.

WAR DIARY
or
INTELLIGENCE SUMMARY.

(Erase heading not required.)

D.A.D.V.S. 5th Division

Instructions regarding War Diaries and Intelligence Summaries are contained in F. S. Regs., Part II. and the Staff Manual respectively. Title pages will be prepared in manuscript.

Place	Date	Hour	Summary of Events and Information	Remarks and references to Appendices
VILLERS-AU-BOIS	23/4/18		Office work. D.H.Q & ADVS. Chateau D'Acq on ... Horse Arrangements A.D.V.S & D.A.Q.	
CHATEAU D'ACQ	24th		Inspected M.V.S., 1st Butn R.F.A and R.E. units, M.G. Battalion & visited A.D.V.S. Corps Office work.	
	25th		" " " A.D.V.S	
	26th		Accompanied A.D.V.S Corps on his inspection of Cavalry Division	
	27th		Insp. R.A Headquarters, 1 Butn R.E units and Lt. R. Dutton A/V.M & S. Reg	
	28th		Accompanied A.D.V.S Corps on his inspection of R.E units and 1st & 7th D.A.C	
	29th		Office work.	
	30th		Inspected H.Q. M.G. 28th Bn & D.H.Q. Inspected 1 & 5 q.v.c.	
	31st		Visited M.V.S. Office work.	

B___ Maj 7th Division
D.A.D.V.S

WAR DIARY
or
INTELLIGENCE SUMMARY. D.A.D.V.S. 8th Division   Vol 46

Army Form C. 2118.

(Erase heading not required.)

Instructions regarding War Diaries and Intelligence Summaries are contained in F.S. Regs., Part II. and the Staff Manual respectively. Title pages will be prepared in manuscript.

Place	Date	Hour	Summary of Events and Information	Remarks and references to Appendices
CHATEAU D'ACQ	1/8/18		Office routine. Inspected biurcloset of 8th Div Sup. Coy. and sick horse for evacuation at Mob Vet Section	
"	2 "		Inspected biuvouac of the 24th, 25th & 23rd Infantry Bdes. also Sussex Battalion and 8th Div Train Coy.	
"	3 "		Office routine	
"	4 "		Inspected Remounts for the Division and M.M.P.	
"	5 "		Visited M.V.S. Inspected 1st & 32nd Battery R.F.A.	
"	6 "		Inspected 24th Field Ambulance, A.S.C. Coy.	
"	7 "		Inspected 1st Battery R.F.A. and Mobile Veterinary Section	
"	8 "		Inspected 33rd, 36th and 1st Battery R.F.A. also 490th Field Coy R.E.	
"	9 "		Office routine	
"	10 "		Inspected all Infantry Transport of the Division	
"	11 "		Visited M.V.S. Inspected 57th Battery, R.F.A. and 25th Infantry Bde. 2nd Field Cy, R.E.	
"	12 "		Visited F.A.V.S. Inspected 5th & 3rd Battery. R.F.A.	
"	13 "		Office routine	
"	14 "		Inspected 8th D.A.C. 24th, 26th & 26th Field Ambulance	

Army Form C. 2118.

WAR DIARY
or
INTELLIGENCE SUMMARY.

(Erase heading not required.)

D.A.D.V.S. & Division

Instructions regarding War Diaries and Intelligence Summaries are contained in F. S. Regs., Part II. and the Staff Manual respectively. Title pages will be prepared in manuscript.

Place	Date	Hour	Summary of Events and Information	Remarks and references to Appendices
CHATEAU D'ACQ	15th		Attended conference at A.D.V.S. Office 8th Corps. Inspected 2nd Infantry Bde Transport	
"	16th		Inspected 8th Div Train Coy & D.A.C.	
"	17th		Inspected 1st and 33rd Brittren R.F.A. and Mobile Veterinary Section	
"	18th		Inspected 5th, 7th & 36th Brittren R.F.A.	
"	19th		Inspected 28th Infantry Bde Transport. Visited M.V.S.	
"	20th		Office routine	
"	21st		Visited M.V.S. Inspected 8th Div Am. Coln and D.A.C.	
"	22nd		Inspected 24th Infantry Bde & 55th Battery R.F.A.	
"	23rd		Office routine	
"	24th		" "	
"	25th		Visited M.V.S. Inspected 45th Bde R.F.A.	
"	26th		Overlooked 8th Corps S.O.C. in whole of week on Div Horses	
"	27th		Visited M.V.S. Inspected 15th & 2nd Field Coys R.E.	
"	28th		Inspected 490 T.F. Fiel Coy R.E. Office routine	

Army Form C. 2118.

WAR DIARY
or
INTELLIGENCE SUMMARY.

(Erase heading not required.) D.A.D.V.S. 8th Division

Place	Date	Hour	Summary of Events and Information	Remarks and references to Appendices
CHATEAU D'ACQ	29th		Inspected 33rd Bde R.F.A. and M.V.S.	
"	30th		" 45th " " "	Also 8th Div Sig Coy
"	31st		Inspected 8th Divl Train Corps	

J. More Maj.
D.A.D.V.S. 8th Div

Instructions regarding War Diaries and Intelligence Summaries are contained in F. S. Regs., Part II. and the Staff Manual respectively. Title pages will be prepared in manuscript.

Army Form C. 2118.

WAR DIARY
or
INTELLIGENCE SUMMARY.
(Erase heading not required)

D.A.V.S. 8th Division

WR 46

Place	Date	Hour	Summary of Events and Information	Remarks and references to Appendices
CHATEAU D'ACQ	1/9/18	—	Inspected 55th and 32nd Batteries. Nucleus Gun Battalion and D.A.C.	
"	2/9/18	—	Inspected Infantry Transport of the Division	
"	3/9/18	—	" "	
"	4/9/18	—	Inspected R.E. Field Coy of the Division	
"	5/9/18	—	Office routine. Handed over my duties to O.C. 15th M.V.S. on proceeding on leave to U.K.	
"	6/9/18	—	Inspected Signals and Divisional Headquarters	
"	7/9/18	—	Inspected 45th Brigade all Batteries. No.1 Coy 3rd Div. Train. Inspected horses at M.V.S. prior to evacuation.	
"	8/9/18	—	Inspected remounts at Train H.Q. Also animals for evacuation at M.V.S.	
"	9/9/18	—	Office routine. Inspected 32nd and 33rd Batteries. (L) 490th field G.R.E.	
"	10/9/18	—	Inspected 87th and 3rd Batteries	
"	11/9/18	—	Inspected 1st and 5th Batteries and 45th Bde Headquarters	
"	12/9/18	—	Office Routine. V.O.s conference in the afternoon.	
"	13/9/18	—	Inspected 25th, 36th Batteries and 33rd Bde H.Q. Inspected animals prior to evacuation at M.V.S.	
"	14/9/18	—	Inspected 2nd and 15th Field Coys R.E. and 8th Battalion M.G.C.	
"	15/9/18	—	Inspected 464 Coy Train. Inspected horses prior to evacuation at M.V.S.	
"	16/9/18	—	Inspected 23rd Inf Bde and 25th Field Ambulance	
"	17/9/18	—	Inspected No.2 and 3 Coy and Train H.Q. Inspected animals prior to evacuation at M.V.S.	
"	18/9/18	—	Inspected 24th Inf Bde and 1/4 D.L.I.	

Army Form C. 2118.

WAR DIARY
INTELLIGENCE SUMMARY.
(Erase heading not required.)

D.A.D.V.S. 8th Division

Instructions regarding War Diaries and Intelligence Summaries are contained in F.S. Regs., Part II. and the Staff Manual respectively. Title pages will be prepared in manuscript.

Place	Date	Hour	Summary of Events and Information	Remarks and references to Appendices
CHATEAU DACA R/9/18				
"	20/9/18		Inspected 26th Inf. Bde.	
"	21/9/18		Inspected 24th and 28th Field Ambulances and 26th Battery. Major Bone returned from leave and handed over to him	
			Signed Capt. A.V.S.	
"	22/9/18		Office routine. Inspected all transport of Div. H.Q.	
"	23/9/18		Inspected transport of 23rd and 24th Infantry Bdes.	
"	24/9/18		Inspected 33rd Bde. R.F.A. and sick animals at the mob. vet. section	
"	25/9/18		Attended conference at 8th Bde. headquarters. Inspected 2nd & 3rd bays of the 8th Div. Train	
"	26/9/18		Inspected 45th Bde. R.F.A.	
"	27/9/18		Inspected all Field Cops R.E. & Divnl. also no. 1 Coy Div. Train and D.L.9.	
"	28/9/18		Inspected 25th Infantry Bde. & machine gun battalion	
"	29/9/18		Office routine	
"	30/9/18		Inspected remount for the Division on their arrival. Visited D.A.C. H.Q.	

J.J. Done Major
D.A.D.V.S. 8th Division

Army Form C. 2118.

WAR DIARY
or
INTELLIGENCE SUMMARY.
(Erase heading not required.)

D.A.D.V.S. 8th Division Vol 48

Place	Date	Hour	Summary of Events and Information	Remarks and references to Appendices
CHATEAU D'ACQ	1/10/18		Inspected 33rd and 55th Batteries R.F.A., and 33rd Div. Headquarters. Inspected sick of M.V.S.	
"	2/10/18		Inspected 8th Divisional Train and Supply Coy.	
"	3/10/18		Division moved forward to ECURIE. Inspected 1st and 5th Batteries R.F.A. also 24th F.A. Bde Transport	
ECURIE	4/10/18		Inspected units found in new area of Division. Officers Routine and reported on same	
			to Division H.Q.F.	
"	5/10/18		Inspected sick animals at the Mobile Veterinary Section	
"	6/10/18		Inspected 8th Divisional Ammunition Column	
"	7/10/18		Inspected 33rd Div. R.F.A. and 2nd Field Coy R.E.	
"	8/10/18		Inspected 15th & V490 F.T. & R.E. Coys R.E., Inspected M.V.S.	
"	9/10/18		Inspected all transport of the 23rd & 25th Inf. Bdes., also 1st and 5th Battery R.F.A.	
"	10/10/18		Officers routine Conference of 8th Division	
"	11/10/18		Selected Site for the M.V.S. for the forward move. Divisional area Inspected Field Ambulances	
"	12/10/18		Inspected M.V.S. Office work.	
"	13/10/18		The transport of our work having returned some mules, if was found necessary to collect	
"			animals awaiting post A.M.V.S. in vicinity of N.C.O. and Horse area	
"	14/10/18		D.H.Q. moved to to Stirling Camp near ATHIES.. Inspected artillery Horse on	
"			forward move & inspect watering arrangements etc.	
ATHIES	15/10/18		Inspected 33rd Bde. R.F.A., S.A.A. Park, 23rd Inf. Bde., Pioneer Bgt., D.Coy., M.G., Battalion and	
"			examined returning post	
"	16/10/18		Inspected 2, 3rd & V. 25th Inf. Bde Transport	
"	17/10/18		Inspected Divisional Train Transport.	

Army Form C. 2118.

WAR DIARY
or
INTELLIGENCE SUMMARY.

(Erase heading not required.)   D.A.D.V.S. & 17th Division

Instructions regarding War Diaries and Intelligence Summaries are contained in F. S. Regs., Part II. and the Staff Manual respectively. Title pages will be prepared in manuscript.

Place	Date	Hour	Summary of Events and Information	Remarks and references to Appendices
ATHIES	18/10/18		DHQ³ moved to FLERS. Inspected MVS & went to FRESNES via to BUISSIERE	
FLERS	19/10/18		Inspected 26th DAC. and all units in forward area. Submitted to MVS to bury	
			MVS to PLANQUE as ours as he had mounted sich Command. with ADVS & RVA	
			as further of 18th VFE.	
	20/10/18		DHQ moved to CATTELET. Insp 9 Wiltshire further ground. Inspected DAC. Indented	
			MVS & form casus part of TACHES	
CATTELET	21/10/18		Found balance pat of MVS at TACHES. Called on ADVS VIII Corps re horses	
			of VSS and camels. Got relief MVS to move to TACHES in Tuesday/s	
	22/10/18		moved to MARCHIENNES. Inspected Divn Battle transport and 26 Field Amb—	
MARCHIENNES	23/10/18		Inspected ERC. RFA and Infantry of 4th Dvision. Arranged with Divison to arrived	
"			AD vist oys and estry drawn parks in the area vacated	
"	24/10/18		Insp. MVS. Offrs members Conference of 3.0th Division	
"	25/10/18		Inspected 25 FA and D.V.C. Inspected Wheeled Ech. and MVS at RUE DU ROSIER	
"	26/10/18		Insp HT Field Coy and Cav Coy of Divison. Insp'd all ATM VS	
"	27/10/18		Inspected DAC.	
"	28/10/18		Insp'd ADVS. at VIII Corps HQ. Office routine	
"	29/10/18		Inspected 45 th RHA RTA	
"	30/10/18		Inspected personnel for 17 Division or Rear arrived	N. Price A_____
"	31/10/18		Insp'd 33 ___ Bde. R.F.A.	D.A.D.V.S & 17 D___

Army Form C. 2118.

WAR DIARY
or
INTELLIGENCE SUMMARY.
(Erase heading not required.)

D.A.D.V.S. 8th Division

Instructions regarding War Diaries and Intelligence Summaries are contained in F. S. Regs., Part II. and the Staff Manual respectively. Title pages will be prepared in manuscript.

Place	Date	Hour	Summary of Events and Information	Remarks and references to Appendices
MARCHIENNES	1/11/18		Inspected and took command of the Mobile Veterinary Section. Visited A.D.V.S. 8th Div.	
"	2/11/18		Inspected all Montagnes Surgeons and Travelled. Visited M.V.S.	
"	3/11/18		Inspected Lieutenant of the 23rd Infantry Bde. Officers mules.	
"	4/11/18		Inspected Sick at M.V.S. Visited advanced Horses which militia of 8th Div had been posted by the Germans. Visited the A.D.V.S. 8th and ordered Division on Cavalry and Horses not if Horses & all lack.	
"	5/11/18		Office routine.	
"	6/11/18		Inspected Sick at M.V.S. also 2nd & 15th F.& 10th C.G.T. R.E.	
"	7/11/18		Visited D.A.C. Stables. Confirm. 0.03 at D.H.Q.	
"	8/11/18		Inspected Lieutenant of the 25th Infantry Bde. and Machine Gun Battalion.	
"	9/11/18		Inspected Divisional Stables Lieutenant. Office routine.	
"	10/11/18		Visited M.V.S. D.H.Q. moved to ST AMAND. Visited M.V.S. & new to ST AMAND	
ST AMAND	11/11/18		Office routine. Division standing by.	
"	12/11/18		D.H.Q. moved to TERTRE. Visited M.V.S. & new to MARCHIES	
TERTRE	13/11/18		Visited M.V.S. no Lieutenant of any sort on case of a future move. Inspected 33rd R.L. FFA & 9 & 15 Bde.	
"	14/11/18		Proceeded to MARCHIENNES and arranged with the O.C. 15 V.E.S. there to send party to ST AMAND when to take over such horses including part of the M.V.S. at mobile. It is when it was in case of further advance.	
"	15/11/18		Proceeded to GALEN Remount Depot.	
"	16/11/18		D.H.Q. moved to TOURNAI. Visited M.V.S. L STAMAND. Arranged B/H Asst O/G A.S.S 8th Battery. Officers mules to be put into 18th V.E.S., cut this to meet the Lt by arrangement with A.D.V.S. 8th Div. and to proceed to LESDAINS on the following day. Sec. D.D.O. Division no bus suffer.	
TOURNAI	17/11/18		Office	

Army Form C. 2118.

WAR DIARY
or
INTELLIGENCE SUMMARY.

(Erase heading not required.) D.A.D.V.S. 8th Division

Place	Date	Hour	Summary of Events and Information	Remarks and references to Appendices
TOURNAI	18/11/18		Inspected M.V.S., Cyclists, 45th Bde R.F.A.	
"	19/11/18		Inspected 33rd C.L., R.F.A. and 4 Batteries of 117 Bde A.F.A.	
"	20/11/18		Inspected transport of the 24th & the 9th Div. Gunner Battns.	
"	21/11/18		Inspection of B.O.s Divison. Inspected 8th Div. Pigeon Coy	
"	22/11/18		Inspected 18th & 7th Fd Coy R.E. Inspected A.D.V.S. 8th Div horses	
"	23/11/18		Inspected 24th & 7th C.L. Inspected also 8th Div Pigeon Coy	
"	24/11/18		Held D.A.C. and Bde A.D.V.S. re a number of cases reink.	
"	25/11/18		Inspected the M.V.S. and 2nd & 7th Fd Coy R.E.	
"	26/11/18		Visited M.G.C. Battalion and M.V.S. I noted transport very weak	
"	27/11/18		Inspected around for visiting to Reinforcements of 8th Div. Train H.Q. Offices mobile	
"	28/11/18		Officers mobile Conference of V.O.'s Divison.	
"	29/11/18		Inspected 87th Bde R.F.A. also cattle in two farms at WILLEMEAU noted to be not much disease	
"	30/11/18		Inspected 117 Bde R.F.A. to make arrangement regarding the veterinary transport for veterinary H.Q.Q. so dispatch transport	

D.N.B. in away 8th Division

D.A.D.V.S. 8th Div.

WAR DIARY or INTELLIGENCE SUMMARY

Army Form C. 2118.

Vol 50

D.A.D.V.S. 8th Division

(Erase heading not required.)

Place	Date	Hour	Summary of Events and Information	Remarks and references to Appendices
TOURNAI	1-12-18		In conjunction with Artillery Bde officer made preliminary selection of brood Mares of the Division.	
"	2-12-18		Attended final selection of brood Mares.	
"	3-12-18		Routine work.	
"	4-12-18		" "	
"	5-12-18		" "	
"	6-12-18		" "	
"	7-12-18		" "	
"	8-12-18		" "	
"	9-12-18		Attended conference at III Corps H.Q.	
"	10-12-18		Attended bathing Parade by D.D.R. 5th Army.	
"	11-12-18		Routine work.	
"	12-12-18		Weekly conference of Veterinary Officers. Discussed suppression of foot and Mouth disease in the area.	
"	13-12-18		Routine work.	
"	14-12-18		" "	
"	15-12-18		" "	
"	16-12-18		" "	

Army Form C. 2118.

WAR DIARY
or
INTELLIGENCE SUMMARY.
(Erase heading not required.)

D.A.D.V.S. 8th Division

Place	Date	Hour	Summary of Events and Information	Remarks and references to Appendices
TOURNAI	17-12-18		Divisional Headquarters moved to ENGHIEN.	
ENGHIEN	18-12-18		Routine work.	
"	19-12-18		"	
"	20-12-18		Attended conference at III Corps H.Q.	
"	21-12-18		Routine work.	
"	22-12-18		"	
"	23-12-18		"	
"	24-12-18		Handed over to Capt. M.F.O'SULLIVAN. R.A.V.C. and proceeded to III Corps H.Q. to perform duties of A.D.V.S. during his absence on leave to U.K.	
"	25-12-18		Orders received to start immediately the classification of animals for demobilisation.	
"	26-12-18		Routine work.	
"	27-12-18		Conference at III Corps H.Q.	
"	28-12-18		Routine work.	
"	29-12-18		"	
"	30-12-18		"	
"	31-12-18		"	

M.F. O'Sullivan Capt.
R.A.V.C.
act.g D.A.D.V.S. 8 Div

Jan – April 1919

Vol 57

Army Form C. 2118.

WAR DIARY
or
INTELLIGENCE SUMMARY.
(Erase heading not required.)

D.A.D.V.S. 8th Division

Instructions regarding War Diaries and Intelligence Summaries are contained in F.S. Regs., Part II. and the Staff Manual respectively. Title pages will be prepared in manuscript.

Place	Date	Hour	Summary of Events and Information	Remarks and references to Appendices
ENGHIEN	1-1-19		Routine work and classification of animals in connection with demobilisation	
"	2-1-19		Weekly conference of veterinary officers and routine work	
"	3-1-19		Routine work and classification of animals in connection with demobilisation	
"	4-1-19		"	
"	5-1-19		"	
"	6-1-19		"	
"	7-1-19		"	
"	8-1-19		Major S. Bone took over duties on his return from 3rd Corps H.Q. from T. Sullivan Capt.	
"	9-1-19		Routine work & Classification of animals for demobilisation	
"	10-1-19		"	
"	11-1-19		"	
"	12-1-19		"	
"	13-1-19		Received word from 3rd Corps to HQ redirect to all animals of the Division	
"	14-1-19		Routine work	
"	15-1-19		"	
"	16-1-19		"	

Army Form C. 2118.

WAR DIARY
or
INTELLIGENCE SUMMARY.
(Erase heading not required.) D.A.D.V.S, 5th Division

Instructions regarding War Diaries and Intelligence Summaries are contained in F. S. Regs., Part II. and the Staff Manual respectively. Title pages will be prepared in manuscript.

Place	Date	Hour	Summary of Events and Information	Remarks and references to Appendices
ENGHIEN	27/1/19		Routine work. Received intimation that 3rd Echn from O.V.S. that in no account were animals to be passed fit to proceed to England & the event of their being led there for distribution	
"	28/1/19		Routine work connected with classification of animals etc	
"	29/1/19		"	
"	30/1/19		"	
"	31/1/19		"	
"	1/1/19		"	
"	22/1/19		"	
"	23/1/19		"	
"	24/1/19		"	
"	25/1/19		"	
"	26/1/19		"	
"	27/1/19		Arranged for animals to be returned before their despatch on demobilisation in accordance with instructions from 3rd Echn	
"	28/1/19		Routine work	
"	29/1/19		Left Divison to act- for A.D.V.S 3rd Echn	
"	30-1-19		Lost O.C. & instn of D.A.D.V.S from May 13 to Nov. 1918 inclsv work	
"	31-1-19			Rannells Capt

Army Form C. 2118.

WAR DIARY
or
INTELLIGENCE SUMMARY

(Erase heading not required.)

D.A.D.V.S. 8th Divn

Place	Date	Hour	Summary of Events and Information	Remarks and references to Appendices
ENGHIEN	1-2-19		Classified remaining animals of Divn HQ for demobilization	
"	2-2-19		Malleinated animals of 25th Infantry Brigade	
"	3-2-19		Attended Conference at Divn HQ	
"	4-2-19		Routine work	
"	5-2-19		Examined and reclassified "Y" animals rejected by O.C. 10 Mobile Vet Section. Attended	
"	6-2-19		Conference at III Corps H.Q.	
"	7-2-19		Welsh Engineers of Veterinary Officers and routine work	
"	8-2-19		Malleinated animals of 24th Field Ambulance	
"	9-2-19		Malleinated Divn HQ units	
"	10-2-19		Inspected and Mallein tested animals of 25 Field Ambulance	
"	11-2-19		Routine work	
"	12-2-19		"	
"	13-2-19		Mensch conference of Veterinary Officers and routine work	
"	14-2-19		Routine work	
"	15-2-19		"	
"	16-2-19		"	
"	17-2-19		Examined "Z" animals for butchery at 2 V.E.S. and "Y" animals for	
"			registration at 15 M.V.S.	
"	18-2-19		Mallein tested remainder of animals of 8th Divn HQ units and 25 by Bde	

Army Form C. 2118.

WAR DIARY
or
INTELLIGENCE SUMMARY.

(Erase heading not required.)

D.A.D.V.S. 8th Divn

Instructions regarding War Diaries and Intelligence Summaries are contained in F. S. Regs., Part II. and the Staff Manual respectively. Title pages will be prepared in manuscript.

Place	Date	Hour	Summary of Events and Information	Remarks and references to Appendices
ENGHIEN	19-2-19		Mallein test reported complete by all Veterinary officers of Divn 119 & 108 Pm	
"	20-2-19		Inspected 16th Mobile Veterinary Section. Weekly Conference of V.Os	
"	21-2-19		Routine work	
"	22-2-19		"	
"	23-2-19		Inspected animals of 25th Infantry Bde.	
"	24-2-19		Routine work	
"	25-2-19		"	
"	26-2-19		Examined Y animals for repatriation at 16th M.V.S. Weekly Conference of V.Os	
"	27-2-19		Routine work.	
"	28-2-19			

D.A.D.V.S.
8TH DIVISION.
No:
Date 3 · 3 · 19

B Plummer
Capt R.A.V.C
A/D.A.D.V.S. 8th Divn

Army Form C. 2118.

WAR DIARY
or
INTELLIGENCE SUMMARY.

(Erase heading not required.)

DADVS 8th Division

March 1919

Place	Date	Hour	Summary of Events and Information	Remarks and references to Appendices
ENGHIEN	1-3-19		Routine work	
"	2-3-19		Inspected Y horses proceeding to Base	
"	3-3-19		Moved Office to ATH	
ATH	4-3-19		Routine work	
"	5-3-19		Weekly conference of Veterinary Officers	
"	6-3-19		Routine work	
"	7-3-19		Inspected 2 animals proceeding to TOURNAI for slaughter	
"	8-3-19		Routine work	
"	9-3-19		" "	
"	10-3-19		Inspected 15 Mob Vet Section	
"	11-3-19		Routine work	
"	12-3-19		Weekly conference of Veterinary Officers	
"	13-3-19		Inspected 2 animals proceeding for sale in France	
"	14-3-19		Routine work	
"	15-3-19		" "	
"	16-3-19		" "	
"	17-3-19		" "	
"	18-3-19		" "	
"	19-3-19		Inspected Y animals proceeding to Base	
"	20-3-19		Weekly conference of Veterinary Officers	
"	21-3-19		Inspected 2 animals proceeding for sale in France	
"	22-3-19		Routine work	
"	23-3-19		" "	

Army Form C. 2118.

WAR DIARY
or
INTELLIGENCE SUMMARY.

(Erase heading not required.)

DADVS 8th Division

Place	Date	Hour	Summary of Events and Information	Remarks and references to Appendices
ATH	24-3-19		Routine work	
"	25-3-19		Inspected SS and RP horses proceeding to Base	
"	26-3-19		Inspected X. H.D. horses proceeding to Base	
"	27-3-19		Weekly conference of Veterinary Officers	
"	28-3-19		Routine work	
"	29-3-19		"	
"	30-3-19		"	
"	31-3-19		"	

P Hamilton Capt. RAVC
A/DADVS 8th Division

Army Form C. 2118.

WAR DIARY
or
INTELLIGENCE SUMMARY.
(Erase heading not required.)

April 1919

D.A.D.V.S. 8th Division

Place	Date	Hour	Summary of Events and Information	Remarks and references to Appendices
ATH. BELGIUM	1-4-19		Routine work.	
"	2-4-19		" "	
"	3-4-19		Weekly conference of Veterinary Officers	
"	4-4-19		Routine work	
"	5-4-19		" "	
"	6-4-19		" "	
"	7-4-19		" "	
"	8-4-19		Capt J Donaldson. R.A.V.C. 119 Bde R.F.A proceeded U.K. for demobilization	
"	9-4-19		Routine work	
"	10-4-19		Weekly conference of Veterinary Officers	
"	11-4-19		Routine Work.	
"	12-4-19		" "	
"	13-4-19		" "	
"	14-4-19		Inspected × mules proceeding to Corps 1.O	
"	15-4-19		Routine work.	
"	16-4-19		" "	
"	17-4-19		Weekly conference of Veterinary Officers	
"	18-4-19		Routine work	
"	19-4-19		" "	
"	20-4-19		" "	
"	21-4-19		Inspected and recharged × mules of 119 Bde R.F.A). Z	
"	22-4-19		Routine work	
"	23-4-19		Inspected and marked 2 animals for sale on 24th inst at 15th Mob Vet Section	

Army Form C. 2118.

WAR DIARY
or
INTELLIGENCE SUMMARY.

(Erase heading not required.)

April 1919

Instructions regarding War Diaries and Intelligence Summaries are contained in F. S. Regs., Part II. and the Staff Manual respectively. Title pages will be prepared in manuscript.

D.A.D.V.S. 8th Division

Place	Date	Hour	Summary of Events and Information	Remarks and references to Appendices
ATH BELGIUM	24-4-19		Inspected and marked animals for Sale on 26th inst, at 15th M.T.Vet. Section. Weekly Conference of Veterinary Officers. Routine work	
"	25-4-19		"	
"	26-4-19		"	
"	27-4-19		"	
"	28-4-19		"	
"	29-4-19		"	
"	30-4-19		"	

P. Rainie
Capt R.A.V.C.
A/D.A.D.V.S. 8th Division.

D.A.D.V.S.
8TH DIVISION.
No. ....
Date 3-5-19